THE GOOD FIGHT

THE GOOD FIGHT

FROM BULLETS TO BYLINES –
45 YEARS FACE-TO-FACE WITH TERROR

JIM MCDOWELL

Gill Books

Gill Books
Hume Avenue
Park West
Dublin 12
www.gillbooks.ie
Gill Books is an imprint of M.H. Gill and Co.

© Jim McDowell 2017
978 07171 7572 7
Print origination by O'K Graphic Design, Dublin
Edited by Rachel Pierce

Printed by Clays Ltd, Suffolk
This book is typeset in 11/17 pt Frutiger.

All photographs reproduced in this book have been supplied by the author and from *Sunday World* archives.

The paper used in this book comes from the wood pulp of managed forests. For every tree felled, at least one tree is planted, thereby renewing natural resources.

5 4 3 2 1

To Lindy

ABOUT THE AUTHOR

Jim McDowell is a retired journalist. For twenty-five years he served as the northern editor of the *Sunday World*. He lives in Belfast with his wife, Lindy.

CONTENTS

PROLOGUE

I couldn't sleep.

I was down from Belfast for the Ireland v. Wales rugby game at Lansdowne Road, the first clash of the Celts in the then Five Nations Championship on 18 January, 1992. I'd only arrived in the Dublin hotel after three in the morning. Now, as I switched on the bedside radio in the dark, the luminous clock with its red digits was telling me it was 5.59 a.m. One minute to RTÉ's first news bulletin of the day.

I wanted to know if anything terrible – or even more terrible – had happened in the killing fields of Northern Ireland the previous night.

At six on the dot, there was the ringing of bells on the radio; before the news, the Angelus. The daily morning prayer call for Catholics. It is a thing of beauty, meant to convey goodwill to all, and it offers a warm and welcoming embrace of belonging – not just to members of the Catholic faith, but to all. I fall into that 'all' category. A Protestant from 'the Black North'.

Normally, I would bend an ear and listen – the chimes of the bells can be gently calming in themselves. But in this pre-dawn, they sounded like the very bells from Hell. After what I'd witnessed, and reported on, from the Teebane crossroads in County Tyrone the previous night, with no disrespect to anyone, this to me was more like Hell's Angelus. The sound of those bells awoke in me again memories I'd tried to ward off in sleep, but couldn't: images of the terror, the trauma, the savagery and the searing sadness of the night before in the quiet country townland of Teebane.

A massive IRA landmine, planted at the side of the road, had been detonated at the end of a wire by a cowardly bastard sitting a smug half-mile away. The bomb blew to pieces a company van, which had been ferrying fourteen decent men home from their week's work. Eight of those men were killed instantly, the rest horrifically injured. Their crime? Carrying out construction work on a UDR base in Omagh, County Tyrone. But because this was what the Provos deemed working for the crown forces, it was, in their depraved eyes, 'collaboration with the forces of occupation' and as such deserved the death penalty.

I was working with the Ulster Press Agency (UPA) that Friday night. We were covering shifts for three different newspapers, two in Ireland, one in the UK. But I'd already made plans to travel to Dublin later in the evening. I'd booked a hotel, hoping nothing big news-wise would happen, and that I'd get to the rugby international the next day. But then the first calls started to reach me in Belfast about the atrocity in Teebane, and those plans were instantly put on hold.

I got in the car and headed for Teebane crossroads, which was on the road from Dungannon to Omagh, a good 45 miles from Belfast. By the time I got there, the area was already crowded with police, soldiers, doctors, nurses, firefighters and rescue personnel – the whole spectrum of the emergency services. And, not least, the first stunned and grieving relatives of the victims. Hugging, weeping in huddles, they had been alerted by the first breaking news bulletins, and knowing that their menfolk would have been on that road and being all too aware of the danger they were in by doing the work they were doing, they had intuitively realised that the very worst had happened.

One side of the van had been blown out and it had careered for a distance along the road before shuddering to a halt in a hulk of tangled metal and mangled bodies. The roadway was strewn with debris from the van and with human bodies. A short time before, these had been living, breathing, joking workmates, looking forward to a Friday night out, with their brown envelope pay packets still in their pockets.

Of course, reporting the Troubles, the pitiful sight of the bloodied remains of human beings was not new to me. But the horror always engulfed me. And it has remained with me. It wasn't only the clichéd 'stuff of nightmares'. It haunted my waking hours as well. I know I was not alone in this. That horror stalked all those who ever witnessed it – and especially the security and emergency services, who were almost always first on the shocking scenes of such atrocities.

Those heroes had to do their job. And hacks like me, we had to do ours: to open the window to the wider world about this kind of senseless slaughter. To open people's eyes to the sheer savagery and horror of terrorism – a terrorism that back then was mostly confined to our small corner of Europe but sadly today is rampant throughout the continent and indeed the world.

So that night I set to work gathering as much information as I could. Then I headed to a nearby farmhouse. This was in the days before mobile phones. Back then, we had to rely on the generosity of local people to allow us to use their home telephones so we could file copy. I got a landline, made reverse charge calls, filed copy off the top of my head to the newspapers for which the UPA was on duty that night. (I didn't take notes. I didn't have to. I simply reported what I saw with my own eyes, and whatever information I could pick up from people on the ground.)

Having done as much as I could, I headed back for Belfast, monitoring the breaking news radio bulletins on the way. My wife, Lindy, also a journalist, was waiting for me to go to Dublin that night. We eventually left around midnight. We were in two minds about going at all, since it was now so very late, but we headed south anyway. Once over the border, we switched the car radio to RTÉ. And on a news bulletin I heard something that both stunned and sickened me, even though I would have thought it impossible I could be any more stunned or sickened on that infamous night.

Peter Brooke, then Secretary of State for Northern Ireland – dubbed 'Babbling Brooke' by the Belfast press for his seismic failure to grasp the essence and nuances of his job – had gone ahead that Friday night with a live guest appearance on *The Late Late Show* on RTÉ television, hosted by Gay Byrne. In the very shadow of the valley of death that had been Teebane crossroads just a few hours earlier, the senior British Cabinet Minister with responsibility for Northern Ireland hadn't only gone ahead with the chat show appearance, he'd even given them a song. The rendition? 'My Darling Clementine.'

How bloody cruel. How bloody crass. How utterly, utterly insensitive.

Later Brooke, who was in Dublin because he was due to be a VIP guest at the rugby international at Lansdowne Road, did apologise. He said he'd been taken unawares at the request for a song and felt he couldn't get out of it.

We all make mistakes, yes. But listening to news reports that morning about the Northern Ireland Secretary of State singing on a television entertainment show against the backdrop of the horror I'd just witnessed was stomach-churning. What message did that send to the ordinary people of Northern Ireland about how seriously their plight was being taken at government level? More than that, what did it say to the bereaved families of the victims of terror, all those many, many bereaved families?

'You are lost and gone forever, dreadful sorry, Clementine ...'

The mantra of journalism is that reporters are always meant to be 'objective and impartial', but anyone with a heart, a soul, a conscience, and who actually came from – was born, bred, brought up in – the cauldron of conflict that was Ulster would know there is only one word to describe that supposed code of conduct.

Impossible.

It is impossible to witness such horror and then dispassionately distance yourself from it. I felt rage and despair at the savagery I'd seen that night. But also disgust at the government minister who'd blithely sing as reports of that atrocity unfolded.

Meantime, Lindy and I had dragged ourselves into the Dublin hotel lobby about 3.30 a.m. on the Saturday morning. Ireland were playing Wales that day. The bar was still open. The men from the Valleys – and everywhere else in the principality – were in full song. But even their rendering of 'Bread of Heaven' tasted stale, and it stuck in my throat. We went straight to our room.

The next morning, we trudged around Dublin. The evolving story from the Teebane massacre was still headlining on the bulletins, and was all over the front pages of the newspapers. The pubs in Dublin were throbbing with excellent banter and rising expectation – from both the home and visiting fans. I knew all our lads, a tens of thousands-strong scrum of Irish rugby supporters, would be in the usual watering holes: Scruffy Murphy's, The Palace, the old hacks' bars of The Oval and Mulligan's in Poolbeg Street would all be bunged. Instead of joining them, Lindy and I trudged – not walked, trudged – round to Trinity College. Far from the madding crowd. I'm not particularly religious, Lindy is atheist. But we time-warped, poring over the ancient Christian *Book of Kells* buried deep in the bowels of that revered citadel of learning.

On the way back we bumped into two Welsh fans, who were asking did we know anybody with spare tickets for the game. Their lucky day. Rugby is a bit of a religion to me. But that day my heart just wasn't in it. We gave the lads our tickets. Refused to take their money. They must have wondered, but we didn't explain.

I walked away, my head bowed, thinking of those men murdered the previous evening, their by now deep-in-grief families and friends, and the bombers who blew them up probably now sitting in a bar, gloating. I didn't know those murdered men personally. But I knew men like them. I grew up among them. Decent, hard-working men doing their best for their families, their parents, their wives, their children. Men who'd never done anyone a bad turn in their lives, singled out because of their religion and their job. And I thought of Peter 'Babbling' Brooke and his performance on *The Late Late Show* as the bodies of those good men lay on a dark and cold country road in County Tyrone.

Teebane is just one of the very, very many horror stories I covered in the course of the Troubles. My journalistic career – I prefer the word hack to journalist – began just as the first rumblings of what was to become a full-blown sectarian war were being felt. I covered many stories of massacre and mayhem down all those long, dark years, and also during the murky years that followed the signing of the Belfast Agreement in 1998. Visiting newsmen and women used to seek out local hacks like myself for help with background information on a story, or on how to contact so and so. Or for a brief rundown on who was who amid Northern Ireland's complicated array of paramilitary groupings. We'd sit in the bar and chat, and inevitably these visiting reporters, whether from elsewhere in the UK, America, France, Germany, whatever, would get round to the questions that most intrigued them.

What was it like living amid a terror war where, unlike visiting newsmen and women such as themselves, you couldn't just get up and leave after a few days – where you (and your family) could face the wrath of those terror chiefs who didn't like what you wrote about them?

And second … why?

Always that word … why?

They just couldn't get their heads around the Northern Ireland Troubles. 'Fighting over religion!' they'd laugh. That was medieval, wasn't it? Reliving old battles. 1690. 1798. 1916. The rest of the world had moved on. Nobody fought over religion anymore except us. What the hell was wrong with us?

Why?

Needless to say, the Troubles were a bit more complex than just a battle over religion. But sadly, as we all now know, Northern Ireland's conflict is no longer unique on even that score. Many of the countries those reporters came from have in the years since also been touched by terror waged by those who claim to be fighting their own holy war. And throughout the wider world the media is having to adapt to reporting on the horror of home-grown terror – of having to speak and write openly and fearlessly about the warlords and the gangsters in their own midst, knowing of the risks that entails not just to their own lives but sometimes to their families as well.

But the journalist's job is to tell the story, whatever the cost.

Of the stories I have covered, some made me laugh, but very, very many have made me cry. I covered heart-wrenching stories that highlighted the very best of human nature. And I covered stories that plumbed the depravity to which others stooped.

My colleagues and I were always aware of the dangers of some of the stories we worked on. In the most horrific instance of all, my colleague at the *Sunday World*, Martin O'Hagan, was brutally murdered one September evening. My own life was threatened many times. When the security forces used to arrive with a report about another threat to my life, they'd bring with them a form – called a PM1 – which I then had to sign to confirm I'd been made aware of the relevant intelligence. I have enough of those forms to paper a room. Twenty-one, I think, at the last count. The threats came from paramilitary groups on all sides, from drug dealers and other gangsters.

I have been beaten up in the street, abused and spat at. I've received bullets in the post. At one point terrorists attempted to murder my son to get at me. Our home, with its bullet-resistant windows, security cameras, monitors, hand-held 'Hawkeye' panic button with its direct link to the nearest police station, sometimes resembled a bullet- and bomb-proof bunker.

But those stories – even the ones that put my life in danger – had to be told. That was my job. That was what I did. It is what I do.

And this, now, is my story.

1

THEY TRIED TO KICK ME TO DEATH ...

'Cover up! Cover up and curl up!' my brain was screaming at me.

I wanted to get up and fight. I'd been decked, down on the ground, once. Tried to get up. I thought I'd connected with one punch. But the brutal barrage of the bare-knuckle blows to my head beat me back down again.

'Cover up! Cover up!' was the tattoo drumming inside my head.

So I did. I covered up and curled up on the ground. Then the boots started drumming. And my baldy head was the drum. It was like the red-hot rivets from the shipyard caulker's glove being sledged into the hull of the *Titanic*: time and time again.

The impact was stunning. And just like the *Titanic*, I went down. But I wasn't out. I didn't black out.

The big, bulky, brown overcoat I'd bought in a pawnshop many years before – my friends said that when I wore it, from the back I looked like a garden shed – acted a bit like a flak jacket. It cushioned my torso, and saved my ribs from being kicked in.

Finally, finally, the assault stopped.

I tried to struggle up. I couldn't. There were people all around me. They had stood and watched what one man, a renowned writer, later described as the 'most savage thing' he had ever seen. It certainly must have been a surreal scene. Fairy lights twinkling in the half light in the background. Festive music blasting out. Shoppers, revellers and excited children bustling through Belfast's Christmas continental market. The smells from the various hot food stalls wafting through the crisp late November air. The cinnamon scent of mulled wine … And suddenly, the sight of me being jumped on from behind and savagely hammered by the boots of a team of gangsters.

The crowd – and the market that day was absolutely jam-packed – had parted into a circle. People stared down at me in open-mouthed shock as I struggled to get up. A few came to help me. I was bleeding, from my mouth, from my head, and from an ear. Those good people helped me up.

I staggered over to the wall of Belfast City Hall, just a few feet from me, leaning against it, trying to get my bearings. Someone called for an ambulance.

What the hell had just happened to me?

I hazily recalled what I thought were the words one of my four attackers had said before the battering began: 'You're trying to get my brother killed.' Later, from my own sources, I was to find out that what the ringleader actually said was: 'You're trying to get my boss killed.'

His boss was Stephen Matthews, the so-called commander of the East Belfast battalion of the Ulster Volunteer Force (UVF), a lethal loyalist paramilitary gang. The main man fronting the attack on me, and who had stuck the boot, again and again, into my head was one of Matthews's henchmen, a gangster, drug dealer and convicted armed robber called Jamsey Reid. Both myself and my colleagues in the *Sunday World* had written about Matthews and about Reid many times before. We were to do so again afterwards.

But that weekend, on the front page of the paper, we published a picture of my battered and bloodied head and face. The headline summed up what I had felt was a real possibility as I lay there on the ground with those boots blattering in on my head. It read:

THEY TRIED TO KICK ME TO DEATH

They'd come up on me from behind. I'd had a few pints on me. I'd been at a very special celebration that day with my friends in the *Irish News*, the Belfast morning paper, for the great James Kelly (now sadly deceased), who'd first started as a cub reporter in the *Irish News* way back, some eighty years before. That morning there'd been a reception for Jimmy and a formal presentation in the offices of the *Irish News*. Afterwards, a busload of us headed for a much less formal lunch in the Billiard Room of the Ulster Reform Club in the city's Royal Avenue.

At the formal presentation, various folk from the many strands of life who'd known Jimmy – he was in his late nineties at the time – had been asked to say a few words. The Fitzpatrick family, who own the *Irish News*, had asked me to pay homage to him on behalf of the press. I was last on my feet after a phalanx of tributes.

Now, Jimmy was still writing a Saturday column for the *Irish News*. And he was no friend of the Orange Order, who, in his eyes, were distinctly out of order on many occasions, especially with regard to their insistence on marching through nationalist areas. So, for a joke with a wee bit of a jag, I had an Orange sash, a collarette, especially made for him. It was embroidered with the words 'Kelly's Heroes Loyal Orange Lodge', with the number of the supposed lodge being the date he started in the *Irish News*.

When I got to my feet, I paid due and colourful tribute to the legendary scribe. And at the end, I began taking the sash out of the plastic bag it was in behind my back, so Jimmy wouldn't see it as I walked towards him. A ripple of laughter ignited behind me as folk sitting at the lunch tables realised what it was.

James was sitting in his wheelchair, so it made it easier to whip it out and stick it over his shock of white hair and onto his shoulders before he could react. And react he did: in typical, sharp – and this time, sweet – Kelly style. Taking the microphone, he said: 'McDowell, I'll wear this in bed at nights from now on – just in case, when I get to the Pearly Gates, St Peter turns out to be a Prod!'

After the lunch a posse of us went out into the late afternoon for a final pint, or two, at a beer tent in the grounds of Belfast City Hall. The annual pre-Christmas continental market was in full swing. There were hundreds of people thronging the stalls packed with goods, and food, from throughout Europe. We were having a great time. Until, that is, I left the beer tent to head to the toilets.

OK, I'd played rugby for some 37 years. Represented Ulster Schools, captained the Ulster Junior XV to a couple of Inter-Provincial titles, and was proud to turn out, even just once, for an Ulster President's XV at Ravenhill captained by the great Willie John McBride. I was still turning out for the club known euphemistically in Belfast as the 'Cregagh Red Sox', otherwise the legendary Malone Rugby Football Club, when I was 48 years of age (it was their 'golden oldies' Tankards team). Plus, I'd got round eleven marathons in my time. Ran under three hours in the Belfast Marathon. And I'd done a bit of boxing: both inside and outside the ring.

But I was no Jack Reacher. I was 62 years of age. Still fit, yes. Still jogging – or, to use a good oul' Ulster Scots word, still hirplin'. But I was no match for that UVF 'team' who simply walked up to me in the dark and, without warning, got stuck in.

With my *Irish News* friends, I'd been sinking a few pints in one of the big marquee bars at the City Hall market to finish off the day. The only WCs were portaloos away at the other side of the grounds. That's where I'd headed.

Reid and his gangster mob had been drinking in the big beer tent, too. I hadn't spotted them, although I should have. But they'd seen me. They followed me. And as I dandered back from the toilets, they attacked me, the only warning being that single sentence: 'You're trying to get my boss killed.'

That night, and the next morning, the daily newspapers and the broadcast bulletins carried reports of the assault. Within hours, our own reporters, through their sources, had sifted out who was responsible. We even discovered that Reid had phoned his boss, 'Ugly Doris' Matthews, when he'd spotted me in the beer tent. He'd asked Matthews for permission to attack me. 'Ugly Doris' gave the go-ahead.

When you are raised in the brilliant city of Belfast, there is an old saying that you were 'born, bred and buttered' in that great town. Or as I referred to myself in subsequent interviews, 'born, bred, buttered and recently battered in Belfast'.

I love this city so well – and its magnificent, ordinary, decent, spirited people. Some of my friends later expressed shock that none of the many onlookers had waded in to help me during the attack. I don't blame them. The attack upon me was sudden and savage. So sudden, I couldn't identify my attackers. They came from behind so I didn't get a full view, or any view, of their faces. And, of course, at that time on a dank November night, it was dark.

No one in that milling crowd at the Christmas market came forward to say they could ID the culprits either, or even to offer a description. I didn't blame those people then. And I still don't. Most had absolutely no idea what was going on. Many of them didn't know, or realise, who I was in the panic of the moment. Some of them did, they told me afterwards, especially the people who helped me up and phoned an ambulance.

But this is Northern Ireland. Often to act, to speak out, to help the police can have consequences – especially if the bogeymen, the paramilitaries, are involved. And anyway, many of those people had young kids with them. How were they to know that in acting the Good Samaritan to help me, they, or more particularly their children, wouldn't be dragged into the violence and hurt? Reid and his hoods may have been 'carrying': perhaps knives, possibly a gun. I'm convinced, though, that if the gang had been armed, I'd have been more seriously injured. Or even dead. But I still believe those folk who were witnessing what was happening before their very eyes were right not to interfere. What could they have done anyway? It had happened so suddenly. Nobody could have envisaged it.

The element of surprise is always one of the terrorists' best weapons. And they know that well. The attack on me at that Christmas market in Belfast was a bloody reminder of that.

Initially I had no idea of the identity of the men who'd attacked me. When our *Sunday World* sources got the names, I tried to get evidence to put these UVF gangsters behind bars. In the paper we had already dubbed the East Belfast mob, who were dealing both death and drugs and were up to their necks in protection rackets, the ParaMafia. I scoured whatever CCTV footage I thought could turn up clues. There had been a huge sightseeing wheel in the City Hall grounds – a smaller version of the London Eye – during the continental market. I got CCTV footage from that, but it didn't cover the location of the attack. CCTV footage from anti-vandalism cameras on buses parked nearby were also examined. Nothing there.

I went down into the control room, buried deep in City Hall, which monitors the security in and around the city's beautiful centrepiece building. There was footage from one security camera that had captured the assault, but it was so grainy as to be useless in ID'ing my assailants. Thankfully, there was enough in one clip we lifted from the security disk the City Council kindly gave me to show a certain member of the gang sticking the boot into me.

Again, we quickly learned from our sources that the boot boy was Reid. But that was the only evidence the police had to work on. They did their best. They passed what they had on to the Public Prosecution Service (PPS), as is the norm. But eventually, inevitably, I got a letter from the PPS saying there was insufficient evidence to prosecute Reid, or any of his UVF cohorts.

That letter arrived at my home on a Saturday morning. The next day, we splashed Reid's picture on the front page of the paper, naming him as my main attacker. He never sued. And we hammered him, in print, many times afterwards – not least over a botched armed robbery he and his team carried out ... after being spotted scouting out their target by a good ex-cop who later filled me in on the whole cartoon-style cock-up.

Reid was banged up behind bars. And not before time.

While he and his mob may have gotten away with hammering me, our extensive and saturation coverage of him, his boss Stephen Matthews and the sordid East

Belfast UVF battalion proved that the pen is not only mightier than the sword. It is also mightier than the boot.

We dubbed UVF godfather Matthews 'Ugly Doris' because of his bleach-blond hairstyle and off-the-wall wardrobe. An earlier gangster from East Belfast, Jim Gray, who had been 'brigadier' of another loyalist paramilitary outfit, the Ulster Defence Association (UDA), had a similar hairstyle and swanky mode of dress: what people in Belfast used to call the 'Miami Sammy' look, day-glo tans and all. Gray was the first in a series of what we dubbed the loyalist 'Brigadiers of Bling', gangsters with a taste for expensive jewellery, designer labels and garish wardrobes. That definitely applied to Jim Gray, who was later shot dead by his own, a UDA assassin, after he was 'court-martialled' and expelled from the organisation for treason. We had nicknamed Gray 'Doris Day' – with his bouffant blond hairdo, his flowery shirts, his fake tan and his lavish gold chains, the UDA boss was known as a bit of a preening diva.

While Stephen Matthews was cut from the same garish cloth as Gray, he was, in contrast, just brute ugly. Hence the nickname we gave him – 'Ugly Doris'. I don't think he appreciated it. Maybe that was another reason he gave the go-ahead for me to get the kicking at City Hall.

For years I'd been on my guard against just such an attack. And not just from the UVF. I had many enemies I'd exposed in print. I'd got used to looking over my shoulder. Keeping an eye on who was coming in the door. Being careful about where I was drinking. That day I'd let my guard down a little. But then, I was in company, in a crowded public place, with literally hundreds of people milling around. The atmosphere was happy and festive. And there was no warning.

But I shouldn't have needed a warning. For years I'd been in no doubt that I was a target for paramilitaries and drug pushers and other lowlife whom I'd offended by having the temerity to highlight their violence and gangsterism. I held these people in utter contempt. Not just the savagery and misery they inflicted, but because they were parasites – all of them – living off, wrecking and bringing fear to their own working-class communities. The same working-class community I come from – am proud to come from.

When I first started off in journalism, it was a different world. Such a different world that I was even told back then that coming as I did from a poor background, I was thinking above my station in life to even consider journalism as a career. I didn't listen. I always knew what I wanted to be. From my earliest days I'd wanted to be a reporter. I never wanted to be anything else. And no bullyboy thugs with their heavy boots, their threats and their hatred were going to change that. Ever.

2

INK IN THE BLOOD

I never dreamed I'd captain an Ulster grammar school rugby team First XV.

I never thought I'd play for an Ulster Schools XV that would win an Inter-Provincial title, unbeaten against the other three provinces – Leinster, Munster and Connacht.

I never had an inkling that I would skipper the Ulster Junior XV side when we made a clean sweep of the other provinces.

And I never imagined I would lineout at the Holy Grail of Ulster rugby, Ravenhill, with the likes of Ulster, Ireland and Lions legend Willie John McBride, wearing the Red Hand of a full Ulster XV above my heart.

I did that. Only once. It was a President's XV.

But I was so proud.

And why not? If the dour-as-dough Presbyterian clergyman who ran his Old Testament writ over where I was born and brought up in the inner-city community of

Donegall Pass, close to the gasworks wall in Belfast, had had his way, I'd never have gone to a grammar school at all – and a brilliant one at that – or played the oval ball game as a consequence. Because that bumptious Bible-thumper told my mother, Cherry – who was holding down two jobs to help my Da, 'Big Jimmy' McDowell, feed us and keep a roof over our heads – that as a boy from a working-class community, I had 'no right' to go to a grammar school.

I'll not tell you what my Ma told him.

And he seldom crossed our door at 17 Howard Street South again: except when my grandparents, who lived with us – as was the custom in such communities those days – were ill and needed pastoral care. That pest of a pastor had tried to intervene just after I had passed the then Qualifying Examination, later to become the controversial 11-Plus exam, which dictated whether kids, at eleven years of age, went to grammar or secondary school.

The year before, I had lain for four months in an isolated hospital-cum-convalescence home eight miles from Belfast as I recovered from a bout of rheumatic fever. The clergyman – our so-called family clergyman, who had baptised me in Donegall Pass Presbyterian church – never came to visit me once. That spell in the Lissue House convalescence facility had also cost me vital months away from my desk at Porter's Public Elementary Primary School on the run-in to the vital Qualifying Exam tests. As was the norm in such schools in areas like ours, not many pupils were expected to pass that test. Unfortunately, that is still the case in similar 'areas of social deprivation' across Belfast and elsewhere. However, two of us from Porter's did pass: myself and Davy Fitzsimmons, who also went on to become a half-decent rugby player, a clever scrum-half at both Grosvenor High School and Cooke RFC. And we succeeded in spite of the then principal, a sadistic child-beater called Mr Todd. His nickname, both among teachers and on the street, was 'Bazzler'. I never did find out why. I didn't want to. School for us kids was, simply, a reign of terror under him.

They talk about the sins of the Christian Brothers in their maltreatment of pupils in their schools in the old days. 'Bazzler' Todd would have fitted neatly into the habits they wore – and their cruel child punishment habits as well. Todd even used to split the end of his cane with a Stanley knife and Sellotape up the strands, so that when he caned you on your open hands, the palms and fingers would blister, and then go down after a short time and not bleed. Imagine that kind of vile corporal punishment being meted out to six-, seven- and eight-year-olds now.

Today, 'Bazzler' would be behind bars. And rightly so.

Indeed, after he died, I encountered someone close to him in Barney O'Neill's pub, beside the City Hall. He informed me that Todd was deceased. I asked him where the grave was. He told me. He asked was that because I wanted to visit it and pay my respects? I told him straight.

'No,' I said. 'I want to go and piss on it.'

He didn't offer to buy me a pint.

However, in spite of that clergyman, and in spite of the sadist called Bazzler, I did go to a grammar school, and an excellent educational establishment at that. Annadale Grammar School sat on the banks of the River Lagan. It was named after the one-time family home of the Duke of Wellington when they lived in Ulster. The school blazer's badge bore the cockatrice from the duke's family crest.

Annadale was spearheaded by a pioneering headmaster, Douglas Paulin. The idea was to give boys from a background that might not endear itself to the established 'big' Belfast grammar schools – the Royal Belfast Academic Institution, Methodist College, Belfast Royal Academy – a chance to shine in a new school, with a markedly more relaxed or liberal regime and outlook. It worked. Spectacularly well. Even though I was almost expelled three times. But I still insist that it was a school where the masters, as they were termed then – and there were a galaxy of stars in the staffroom, among them 'Jap' Humphreys, 'Chuck' Evans, David Coffey, Ronnie McNamee and, of course, 'The Doug' himself – never taught us. Instead, we learned from them, and as much about life as the subjects on the syllabus.

And as for those near-misses on expulsion: well, let's just say there were a couple of fighting matches with boys from other schools at school dances who fancied themselves as ballroom boxers, rather than dancers. (Incidentally, the signal for the scraps to start was when someone nodded to the DJ and he played the Long John Baldry hit 'Let the Heartaches Begin' and they certainly did for some of our foes.)

There were a couple of carpetings in front of 'The Doug' as a corollary. But there was one incident where I and a trio of other sixth formers narrowly escaped being shown the school doors – and having the collars of our blazers felt by the cops. That happened on a hot Friday afternoon in June, after we'd sat our final end-of-term exams. We'd gone up to the big playground at the back of the gym, laid down our blazers as goalposts, stripped off our sweaty bri-nylon shirts – remember those? – and started a game of soccer with about twenty a side.

When it finished, Stuarty Dougal – who was to succeed me as first XV skipper the following year – Michael 'Mickey' Murdoch, Garth Morrow and I were strolling out the main gate on to the Annadale Embankment, to dander past the Annadale Flats complex flanking the banks of the River Lagan. Now, there was a bit of history between us four and some of the boys who lived in the Flats. Particularly the sons of a well-known gentleman in the area at that time. He was a member of the Travelling community whose family had settled, for a spell anyway, in the brown-brick, Weetabix box-like edifices. The old boy hadn't maybe settled quite so well. He still preferred the open air.

This gentleman's sons had been picking off first-formers getting off buses to come into school on Monday mornings, and literally mugging them for their school dinner money. A couple of the kids we knew from our own districts came to us. The next Monday morning, we got off the bus with the 'Firsties'. Well, let's just say the boys who'd been bullying them came off second best. The first-formers were left alone after that.

Unfortunately, and completely accidentally – I still swear! – the oul' boy himself wasn't so lucky. What happened was that as Mickey and Stuart and Garth and I dandered down towards the River Lagan, we noticed an old Ford Prefect car parked up partly on the pavement, beside the grass embankment that sloped down to the shallow edge of the river itself. There were no iron railings running along the embankment, as there are now. The battered oul' banger looked like it had been abandoned for scrap, so we decided to do the Belfast City Council Cleansing Department a favour.

We were four strapping lads. So we put down our schoolbags, hunched down along one side of the rust-bucket jalopy, and rolled it over the embankment and into the Lagan. As it turned out, thank God, it landed on its wheels in the shallows, rather than on its roof.

On the Monday morning, I was late getting in to morning Assembly. As is the norm, the seating in school Assemblies was that first and second forms sat in the front, running through the rest of the school to the sixth forms at the back. As I went to take my seat at the back, the whole Assembly hushed. 'The Doug' spoke first.

'Mr McDowell, Mr Murdoch, will you come to the front of the hall, and join me on stage.'

Of course, that's where the headmaster and the teachers sat for Assemblies.

So I dumped my old army surplus shop haversack, which handily doubled as a school and rugby kit bag, at my feet, and started to walk towards the stage with Mickey, wondering what was going on. As we walked up the middle aisle towards Mr Paulin, who was sitting centre-stage at a desk, a rumble of cheering started to roll out, row upon row from the serried ranks of the pupils. A sharp order from 'The Doug' silenced that tsunami of noise.

And then, as I got closer to the steps at the side of the stage, I noticed an oul' codger sitting just behind the headmaster, beside the deputy head. He'd a face like a boxer's used leather punch bag. His flat cap was sitting askew on his silvery, white-haired bonce. There was a bandana tied around his neck, over a collarless, striped turfcutter's-style shirt. And he wore a black button-up waistcoat under a jacket with so much shine on the shoulders and elbows, it looked like it had been buffed with Brasso.

'Jay-sus,' I thought. The recognition was instant.

It was the 'Da' himself, whose sons we'd scrapped with over the mugging of the first formers.

'What the hell is he doing here?' I wondered. 'And what the hell are we doing here, too?'

I soon found out. In front of the whole school.

For you see, that rusty and, as we thought, 'scrap' Ford Prefect we'd rolled into the Lagan on the Friday afternoon wasn't scrap after all. In fact, it belonged to the oul' boy, who'd now got to his feet and was standing beside the headmaster. And worse still, the rust-bucket on wheels hadn't been empty when we'd tipped it into the river. Your man had been in it, full drunk from drinking a bottle, or maybe two, of that infamous monks' brew, Buckfast wine – otherwise known as 'Lurgan champagne', a County Armagh soubriquet for rocket fuel. And when he woke up he was, literally, in the drink … although only up to his knees. If the car had landed on its roof, well, that might have been a different matter. He might have drowned: happy, and drunk, the best way to go. But myself and the rest of the boys could have been facing a manslaughter charge.

As it was, the oul' fella didn't just look like Albert Steptoe, he had his fellow rag and bone man's love of hard dosh. He settled for reparation of a couple of hundred quid. Luckily, all four of us had been working full-time in pubs and clubs to save up for a summer holiday together in the then sixth-form haven of Jersey. We cobbled together the cash. And that, along with the compassion of 'The Doug' – who nevertheless gave us the tongue-lashing of our lives – kept us in class, just about, instead of being handed over to the long arm of the law.

Oh, and I must mention one other notable brush with the law – although my dear mother was the unsuspecting culprit this time.

Myself, my brother Tom and our mates were playing 'shootie-in' in the street, our goal marked in white out on the battery company gable wall. We were playing with a plastic Frido football – cost, back then, one shilling and three old pence. We were only kids. But in those days, the cops from nearby Donegall Pass police station took a dim view of kicking a ball in the street. And if they caught you, you'd get a kick up the arse from the cop, or a clip round the ear.

But there was one peeler in particular who liked to catch us at it. He was a motorbike cop, the only one, incidentally, in the local barracks. In Belfast at that time, motorbike officers were known by the moniker 'the Durango Kid', after a TV cowboy. On this day, the Durango Kid comes roaring round the corner of Charlotte Street straight into our street, Howard Street South, and catches us cold. We scarper in every direction – up alleyways, round corners, over backyard walls.

Now, in our 14 shillings a week rented house, with its outside toilet – like every other down 'the Pass' – there was no carpet on the floors. There was only oilcloth, the forerunner of modern-day vinyl. But those houses – with sculleries and big white Belfast jaw-box sinks and hot water having to be boiled in kettles or basins on the gas stoves – were kept like the proverbial 'Wee Palaces'.

That Saturday morning, my Ma was mopping the oilcloth in the front room. The front door was open. The Durango Kid had removed his black leather-covered helmet with the plastic peak, and was making a beeline for – who else? – me! I saw that our front door was open. My escape route, I thought, was through the house, through the scullery, into the back yard, up on to the metal bin (no wheelie bins in those days) and then all I'd have to do was shin over the yard wall and into the back entry.

Problem was, my mother, Cherry, was still mopping the living-room oilcloth just inside the front door. I startled her as I sprinted in and past her.

Normally, I'd have got a clip with the mop for tramping over the still wet floor. But bursting through the door after me was this cop. My Ma didn't know who he was, especially with his police helmet off. All she saw was this strange punter chasing her own son into *her* own house, her family citadel, her Wee Palace. So she whacked him with the wet mop, full frontal, right up the face.

All hell broke loose ...

Fortunately, my Da was able to get it all smoothed over and keep my Ma (and me) out of court and out of the clink. He was running a bookie's shop at the time, in Ventry Street, just off the Dublin Road. Situated up a flight of skinny wooden stairs the pitch was, ironically, called 'the Elbow' – because you had to stand elbow-to-elbow with other punters to pick your horses off the big chalk boards on the walls and then queue shoulder-to-shoulder to get to the counter to place a bet. The pitch was just a few hundred yards from Donegall Pass police station.

In those days, before the Troubles got a grip, a lot of police officers in the Pass barracks enjoyed a pint and a punt. And the Durango Kid was no exception. He owed my Da a few quid on beaten dockets that were still lying in the losers' drawer in the bookies. What resulted was, as they say in soccer circles, a scoreless draw. The peeler's bad bets, and debts, were wiped out.

And so was the notion of any charges being brought against my beloved Ma – who, after all, was just wiping the floors with a mop when she used it to whop the Durango Kid.

That wasn't the only time my Da steered me onto the right path and away from trouble. It was because of my Da, 'Big Jimmy' McDowell, that I fell in love with newspapers and, indeed, with the very scent and feel of newsprint and the fresh ink on its pages. In passing that on to me, he changed my life forever.

My father – raised in a wee street in the heart of the wistfully named Sandy Row – had actually served his time as a butcher, but he ran a bookie's and was fond of a punt himself, either on the horses or on the dogs. So he always kept two greyhounds in a big kennel in the back yard, squeezed in between the bin and the outside toilet.

Those dogs were treated as if they were heading for Crufts, rather than running at the then Dunmore or Celtic Park race tracks in Belfast (both now sadly bulldozed). Often, those dogs got the best of minced beef – the same as we got with our Ulster fry on a Saturday.

Often, too, when one of the dogs won – my Da had a knack of picking good greyhound pups and bringing them on, as they say in the game – a posse of my Da's mates would arrive back at the house in one of Tommy Dunne's black taxis, with parcels of chips and pigs' feet in brown paper bags. And with brown paper bags full of bottles of Morton's Red Hand stout and a couple of bottles of Bushmills whiskey, too.

They were a colourful crew, straight out of a Damon Runyon story: 'Pan Rice', 'Isaac the Jew' (who wasn't, actually), 'Wee Joe the Blow', and Joe 'Rob' Roy among them. And when a singsong started among that win-celebrating impromptu choir, it wasn't exactly a London West End musical: it was better.

We kids, sitting on the staircase that ran up the side of the living room, were encouraged to join in as we picked at our pigs' feet, chomped on our chips. If we couldn't sing, we had to 'say a recitation'. Real romance: they really were the good old days, cosseted in the fold of your family and their friends. A bygone world now, hijacked by iPhones, iPads, iPods, and monster TVs stuck to walls on which there seem to be no off switches – no matter who is in the house.

My romance with newspapers started with my Da, and the dogs. Because every morning, even before we were got up for school, my Da would have packed his pair of greyhounds into the back seat of the old Hillman Minx he drove and headed to walk them over the fields in the city parks, the Ormeau, Botanic and Barnett's civic parks which breathed fresh air, greenery and space into the heart of what was then a very heavily industrialised city. Out there, in season, he would have picked and brought back a big bag of giant mushrooms. And we'd come downstairs to the sweet scent of those being fried in the pan, with slices of brown Veda bread being toasted over a ring on the gas stove. A big fried mushroom between two toasted slices of Veda, with the butter melting and running down to your wrist … a right royal feast. It was far away from the fried kippers and braised kidneys of the breakfast menus at Buckingham Palace, but in our eyes – and on our tongues – a dawn feast fit for any king.

On his way home with the dogs, my Da always picked up a virtual rack of morning newspapers: the now defunct *Northern Whig*, the *Belfast News Letter*, the *Irish News*, the Ulster edition of the *Daily Mirror*. All of them, of course, carried the greyhound cards listing runners for that night's racing at the two city greyhound stadiums, as well as the winners from the previous night. They also carried the predictions of the dog race tipsters for that night's racing.

Those professional journalists who were paid full-time wages to exclusively cover greyhound racing in those days – men like 'Wee Matt' Rossbotham, Harry Duff, Jim Davey, Brendan Smyth – stoked my Da's ire when they nominated one of his dogs as 'favourite' or 'danger' (meaning that pick could pose a threat to the favourite). Because such a nomination would bring down the betting odds against one of his dogs: and he almost invariably bet on his own.

However, I loved that reel of newspapers coming into the house every morning. The fresh news blasting out in the headlines on the front page, the fresh ink that smudged the tips of your fingers as you flicked through them, the fascinating pictures – the window on the pages – that opened your eyes to a world oceans away from the back streets of Belfast, the wars, the love stories, the triumphs and tragedies of all the peoples of the earth – as well as those back on your own doorstep.

When we came home from school, even at a young age, I still went first for those newspapers, which by late afternoon were stuffed under the cushions of the settee. That was real romance: a romance that was sparked almost sixty years ago, and which still burns bright in my breast, and still beats strong in my fingertips as, after almost half a century as a pencil-pusher, hack, reporter, sometime broadcaster, and twice newspaper editor, I tap this out, alas not on a trusty old typewriter, but on a computer keyboard.

When my history master at school, David Coffey, approached me in the library one day and asked me, when I was just fourteen, what I wanted to be in life, he heard just two words: newspaper reporter. And even years before then, the newspapers my Da had brought into our humble 14 shillings a week home in the looming shadow of the gasworks wall every morning had injected ink into my blood.

And it has never left it since.

3

BANDS AND BALLS

The days of my childhood and teenagehood were hard times, but good days, down in Donegall Pass, in the Pale of the city. People looked after each other. Families, and their neighbours, were close-knit.

The McDowells – my mother Cherry, father Jimmy, brothers Tom and Billy and wee sister Anne – were part of that module. We were embraced with love. And we understood discipline, and respect for everyone: especially our hard-working parents. There is an old saying in most working-class districts of Britain and Ireland: 'Just wait until your father gets home …'

We never had to wait for our Da to get home. Our mother ruled the roost when it came to meting out – ahem – corrective measures. When she reached for the 'pot stick' – half a brush shaft that was used for swirling around the whites, the shirts, the bed sheets, that were boiling in the tin bath on the gas stove – there was no point in us brothers running for cover. When you felt the weight of that whacking across your shoulders, you knew you had done wrong. And would try to do right in the future.

Like everyone else around us, our family didn't have much. There is still much guff around these days about Protestant working-class boys just walking into jobs and apprenticeships in the shipyards, aircraft factories and foundries of Belfast at the time, but that didn't happen with myself and my two brothers, or anyone else we knew. There was as much chronic unemployment in many Protestant/unionist areas when I was growing up as there was in Catholic/nationalist districts in Belfast. There was every bit as much deprivation.

And as for us? Tom served his apprenticeship as a 'spark' – an electrician – with a commercial firm and eventually, in later years, ended up working for the US Army in Iraq and Afghanistan. And before that, he was the other half of our sporting brotherhood; he played soccer, rather than rugby. He excelled at that, too. He represented Northern Ireland at schoolboy level, had a chance as a teenager to trial for Chelsea FC in London, but stayed home and played Irish League soccer for Linfield, Portadown, and narrowly missed an Irish Cup Final appearance with Carrick Rangers: something for which he has only recently forgiven the then Carrick manager.

Not bad, the two of us, from that wee house in Howard Street South, from those hard-as-Mourne-granite streets, both representing our province and country while still at school, and in both soccer and rugby.

Coincidentally, Tom from Howard Street South in The Pass loved and married Marlene, from Charles Street

South in Sandy Row, and raised two fine children, Ryan and Cheryl, now of course adults. Sadly for them, and for all of us, Marlene passed away in June 2016

As for Billy, who is now married to Dawn, he too served his apprenticeship, again not in any of those established industries in which Protestant schoolboys were supposed to simply walk into and be clocked on. He served his time as a plumbing and heating engineer, and is still doing that job to this day.

Anne, who died at the tragically young age of forty-four, worked for a time as a dental nurse. She and my brother-in-law, Billy 'Bow' Bowman, whom she married young, had four great kids, Chelé, Marc, Kathy and Laura. Over the years she held down a number of jobs – often at the same time – to bring extra money into the household.

And then there was my surrogate sister, Joan Clark, whom I've known and loved all my life. She is a Glaswegian, but came to stay with us with her parents, 'Aunt' Cathie and 'Uncle' John, and they became family every summer. And our Joan and husband Neil, and their daughter and son, Gillian and Stuart, with their families, remain part of our family to this day.

There was no privileged upbringing, no silver spoons, no special advantages, no gilded path. Being a working class Protestant didn't open doors for us or give us a leg-up in life – we had to graft, prove ourselves, work our way up and everything we got was hard-earned.

Tom and I also did another double: we are proud to have both played in the Donegall Pass Defenders Flute Band.

Belfast back in the 1960s was gradually becoming a more 'mixed' city. New estates were being built where Protestants and Catholics were living side by side, but it was still essentially a divided place where the two tribes – particularly in working-class areas – lived separate lives. I'm not going to pretend we were any different. Like so many people who grew up back then in this great city, I was a product of my background. I make no apology for that. I am proud of the area I came from and the decent people I grew up among.

For us, parading with our band or walking on the Twelfth was about taking part in a tradition handed down through the generations. It was about music and getting together with friends and family for a day out. It wasn't about offending our Catholic neighbours, any more than them enjoying a GAA game or supporting their own bands was about rubbing our noses in it.

Some Protestant flute bands these days have earned the dubious soubriquet of 'blood and thunder' or 'kick the Pope' outfits. The Pass Defenders, who met to practise three nights a week in a tiny hall on the Wee Street, a dead-end little cul-de-sac whose full title was Little Charlotte Street, weren't blood and thunder. No, we were one of the best bands in the country.

We were taught tunes on the flute – and intricate tunes, too, like the military marching song 'Officers of the Day' – by the likes of Band Captain Sammy Taylor. He used a classroom pointer, or stick, to teach us by literally pointing at letters of the alphabet chalked up on a blackboard in the band hall. Few, if any, of us could read music. So the notes to be fingered on the flute were

A, B, C and so on instead. There was iron discipline, and tailored uniforms: none of the sometimes clownish outfits you see so-called marching bands strutting about in now. We *had* to be in that band hall three nights a week to earn the right to parade with the band.

There were absolutely no 'dummy fluters': boys and men who could only play a tune or two, and had to fake playing the rest when on parade to boost band numbers. And as for that discipline, well, the Wee Street Band was the pride of the whole district. Mothers and fathers and brothers and sisters would line the street on the morning of the annual Orange parade on the Twelfth of July – the anniversary of King William (of Orange) beating his father-in-law, the Catholic King James, at the Battle of the Boyne in 1690 – to hear the band play the hymn 'Abide With Me' before marching off to collect their banner and heading for the rallying point at 'the Field'.

And did I say discipline?

These may have been the heydays of mop-head haircuts, like those sported by the Beatles or the rebellious and rockin' Rolling Stones. But Donegall Pass Flute Band members wore obligatory short-back-and-sides haircuts under their peaked caps. And no sideburns were permitted to grow more than halfway down the ear.

The leader – the iron-rod-backed bandsman who carried the ornate pole at the front of the band (it was crowned, literally, with a replica of the Queen's coronation crown) – carried a cut-throat razor in the inside pocket of his uniform. When the band was lined up in the Wee Street before moving off on parade, the leader, 'Big John' Strahan, would stalk through the ranks, and if he saw anyone whose sideburns were even a millimetre below the permitted level, he would pull out his razor and shave those sideburns off. There was no shaving foam or gel used in this very public operation, often carried out in front of family and friends. It was dry shaving. And, as such, it could hurt. And draw blood.

Yes, I did say it was deemed to be a privilege in our Donegall Pass community to play for the Wee Street flute band, but, at times, that could be a painful privilege.

One Twelfth weekend we had to march, and play, three days in a row. That's not only hard on the legs, it's murder on a fluter's lower lip.

We took the boat over and back on the Saturday for the Scottish Orange pre-Twelfth procession in Glasgow. Next day, after the overnight boat back from the old Broomielaw berth, it was a Sunday morning and then a Sunday afternoon church parade, with a Lodge in tow. Then Monday was the real Twelfth, the fourteen-mile walk to the Field in Belfast and back. From all the playing, we fluters had blisters on our lower lips.

So on the way up the Lisburn Road in Belfast on Monday, we were ordered to put our flutes in our music pouches for a while, to give us a break – and to start singing. There we were, a fully uniformed and kitted out band, dandering up the Lisburn Road, letting rip with 'It's a Long Way to Tipperary' and 'Pack Up Your Troubles in Your Old Kit Bag' and a string of other marching songs ... of the music hall, rather than band hall, variety. Not only did the Lodge members behind us join in, but the spectators standing ten deep on either side of the packed road started giving it a go, too. It was a unique sort of singsong.

We were all starving by the time we were eventually parading past the King's Hall in Belfast. The Field, in those days, wasn't very far away: in Finaghy Road North. There was a wee woman standing at the side of the road with a handcart. She was selling cockles and mussels and potted herrings. The band captain – I forget who it was – shoved a fiver into my hand and said: 'Away and get a couple of buckets of potted herrings off her, and we'll eat them at the Field when we get to the Lodge's stopping point.'

I duly did as requested. We devoured the potted herrings at the Field, and washed them down with bottles of stout: Guinness.

That feast went down fast at the time. And it came out even faster on the seven-mile walk back to 'drop the banner' at the Sandy Row home of the Worshipful Master of the Orange Lodge.

We'd started out on the road home with eight side drummers, two big drummers, the leader of the band, a cymbal and triangle player, and about twenty-eight fluters. By the time we were back in Bradbury Place, nearing the end of the procession, we'd three drummers and a dozen fluters left in the ranks. The rest were scattered in every pub or club that was open on the four-mile stretch of the Lisburn Road. They hadn't gone into those emporiums for a pint. They'd literally 'gone to pot' – ducking, dashing and diving into the pubs and clubs to get on to the pot … the toilet pot, that is.

You've no doubt heard of a drum roll in a band: the band of the Coldstream Guards, for instance, are particularly good at those when fronting ceremonial parades for the Queen of England. Well, in the Pass

Defenders, we witnessed one with a difference. One of our band members was a tiny, bubbly wee lad called Jimbo. He was the triangle player. He liked to compensate for his lack of height by always carrying the big bass drum when we were travelling or when the band dispersed after playing and parading. One Saturday night, we were coming home from the Glasgow Twelfth parade. We were taking the boat home from the old Ardrossan ferry terminal, where the train from Glasgow ran right up a pier and stopped just short of the ship. The boat was always packed on those occasions, with other bands and Orange lodges from Ulster who had been over for the Glasgow parade, and also hundreds of 'Scotchies' heading for Belfast to see, or participate in, the Twelfth there, usually within the next few days. So when the train shuddered to a halt at the end of the line, there was a wild scramble of people opening the old compartment doors and sprinting for the gang-plank, eager to get either a smelly old (unreserved in those days) berth in third class, or just a chair to get a night's kip on the overnight sailing.

As we all jumped out, wee Jimbo, as usual, grabbed the big drum. But in the stampede for the boat, he slipped … and so did the bass drum, breaking loose from his grip. It started rolling along the dock, and towards the tide. Jimbo was frantically running after it on his short legs, trying to grab it. He didn't make it. The drum barrelled over the edge of the pier, and into the sea.

Jimbo was going at full pelt. His wee legs were whirring like a Catherine wheel at Hallowe'en. He couldn't stop. The last we saw of him before he did a Jacques Cousteau and plummeted into the Forth of Clyde was his band hat billowing up into the air.

But, before a couple of us could sprint back, slither down the sloping boulders at the side of the pier and haul a very drooked Jimbo out of the drink, it was the big drum that saved his life. Full of air, watertight and roped around its wooden rims, and sealed with goatskin, it floated. Jimbo caught it and clung on, using it as a makeshift life-raft. He floated, too, until we got both him and the drum out.

And, to be fair, the boul Jimbo shook himself down, dried himself off on the boat, downed a wee short or two, and walked with the band at the Belfast Twelfth two days later.

On that occasion, we all marched to a different drumbeat, because the skin on the big drum sagged after its salt-water ducking and dousing. As for Jimbo, he related the experience of his very own unique drum roll for years later – and downed, rather than drowned, many's the pint on the back of it.

Alongside my band exploits, my rugby career was progressing well. On the pitch anyway. Off it was a whole different ball game. While skippering the Ulster Junior XV, I had a couple of experiences with a horse, and an arm, that caused me more than a little consternation. The first involved a mummified arm. It had once been the prized limb of Ireland's best-known boxer, way back in the late 1830s. His name was Dan Donnelly. He came from the Curragh, that famous beautiful plain, resting right in the bosom of Ireland and most famous for breeding and training the blue-blooded royalty of horse racing.

The folk down there commemorated the exploits of bare-knuckled digger Dan by building a statue of him. It sits in the centre of the Curragh to this day, in what is known as Dan Donnelly's Hollow. No one has ever tried to pinch that heavy stone statue.

But Dan's mummified arm – or maybe it was a replica – was a different matter.

One Sunday the Ulster Junior rugby team were in a bus travelling home from playing, and beating, Munster in Limerick on the previous Saturday afternoon. We stopped for a lunch and a few sherbets – well, we'd clean-swept the Inter Pro-Championship, again – in a pub on the Curragh. This bar boasted a glass case, screwed up on a wall, with Dan Donnelly's mummified arm as a treasured trophy inside. More than a few pints of stout had washed down the steak'n'spuds dinner. It was time to head home, and get back on the bus.

A few of the boys came to the table where I was sitting and told me: 'Take your time, skipper, and finish your pint. We'll round up the rest and get them on the bus, and you come and join us when you're finished.'

There was no resisting that kind invitation.

There was also no resisting, 20 miles up the road from the pub, a request from a Garda sergeant using a loud-hailer from the passenger seat of a police car, instructing the bus driver to pull over to the side of the road and stop.

I wondered what was happening. I didn't have long to wait.

The Garda sergeant climbs up the steps into the bus. 'I'm here in search of an arm,' he loudly declares.

I'm sitting in a seat halfway down the single-decker bus. The alickadoos, the badged and blazered Ulster Branch rugby officials who were with us and were sitting at the front, hadn't a clue what the sergeant was talking about.

Neither had I.

Especially when the rest of the players starting pointing down to me and telling the sergeant: 'He's the skipper, talk to him.'

So I got up, went to the front of the bus, breathing still-fresh fumes of Guinness on the sergeant, and told him: 'Sir, there are no arms on this bus. We are the Ulster Juniors rugby XV. We are not terrorists, sir. We are not smuggling arms across the border.'

'Oh,' says the sarge, taking off his peaked cap, 'I'm not looking for arms. I'm looking for *an* arm. I need to search the bus.'

So he started moving down the aisle, bending down to peer under the seats as he went. As he moved down, the boys started cheering. And as he got closer to my seat – number 24, if I recall correctly – the cheering rose to a crescendo.

And it almost ripped the roof off when the sergeant put his arm under my seat and started sliding out a glass case with – you've guessed it – Dan Donnelly's arm inside!

'Talk your way out of that one, McDowell,' says the player sitting next to me.

I did. But to this day, I don't know how I did.

I only found out much later that the big sergeant himself played rugby for the Garda Síochána representative rugby XV. But that's another story …

As for the other incident: well, that happened the night we played Connacht in a howling gale of slicing sleet and sticky muck way over in the west. We won that game, too. By three points, in an open-running, spectacular game where the score ended three points to six, to us – with a penalty goal in the last minute settling the result.

You can guess from the scoreline that the 'spectacular' tag didn't really apply that bitter winter's day. And that night, the wind and sleet didn't ease off – as I found out after I went to bed.

Our bivouac that night was a really swish converted castle hotel. Again, after the teams' dinner and speeches, more than a few refreshments were imbibed. And after the usual marathon singsong, it was time to head for bed: in the very wee small hours.

When we had arrived on the morning of the match, I'd been allocated a big ground-floor room to myself – as skipper – with French windows looking out on to a vast meadow. I hadn't noticed a rank of stables adjoining the back of the hotel and the meadow, and quite close to my room. But about half-five in the morning, after about an hour's kip, I woke up. And even though I had a lasagne layer of blankets over me, I was foundered – absolutely freezing.

I glanced up in the dark, and noticed that the French doors had blown wide open – or so I thought – and the wind and sleet were howling into the room. And then I smelt a strong scent of something like aniseed. I flicked on the bedside lamp. And there, right beside my bed, was a steaming pyramid of … fresh horse shit, sitting prime on the plush carpet, whose pile was about savannah-grass high in this five-star hotel.

Then I heard a whinnying noise.

I swivelled round, startled. And at the other side of the bed stood a pony. Suddenly there was a rap at the door.

I asked: 'Who is it?'

'It's the night porter, sir,' came the reply. 'Someone has just rung me at reception to say you've got a horse in your room.'

The b*****ds. They'd waited until I was well into a stout-induced slumber, sneaked out, got a horse out of the stables, and smuggled it in through the French doors.

And when I opened the bedroom door, the night porter was, sure enough, standing there. So were half the team of the Ulster Juniors XV – with knowing smiles the width of the bloody River Shannon on their faces.

Again a lone voice piped up. And again it said: 'Talk your way out of that one, McDowell.'

I couldn't. And thanks to the team's horseplay, I was now saddled with a bill for the hotel carpet.

Those were days of innocence in many ways. Days on the cusp of the Troubles that were to stalk our youth, and our future and our country.

We couldn't have imagined back then what lay ahead.

4

BELFAST IS BURNING

The biggest privilege, in terms of realising my dream to be a newspaper reporter, was an almost freakish marriage of my involvement in flute bands and running out on the rugby pitch at Ravenhill to represent Ulster Schools.

In those days, in the mid- to late 1960s, the editor of the *Belfast News Letter* – founded in 1737 and still bearing the mantle of the longest continuously published newspaper in the English-speaking world – was a big bear of a man with a swept-back mane of white hair that would have done a hippy-style polar bear proud. And to say he was a colourful character was like describing Picasso as a house painter.

The difference was that Cowan Watson painted pictures with words – with what the poet Dylan Thomas called 'the colour of saying'. He was a skilled sub-editor when designing pages, as well as a gifted writer. As I was to discover later, when he took me in, and took me on, as a cub reporter, he would write 'Beanos' every morning – self-penned circulars to all editorial staff, including hacks, photographers (known as 'monkeys' in those days, because of their penchant for climbing up trees to get pictures), and sub-editors – pointing out the plus points in that day's paper. But also pummelling any pen- or pencil-pusher he thought hadn't put in a full shift or hadn't hit the mark with the story they were covering, be it a court case or the cacophony of a riot on the streets.

The *News Letter* regularly topped 100,000 daily sales during the nadir of The Troubles: it's now lucky to top 20,000 on its ABCs (circulation figures verified by the Audit Bureau of Circulation), and plummeting sales of other regional newspapers reflect the same fact – back then, bad news certainly sold newspapers. But amid the mayhem of bombs, bullets, blood and political bloody-mindedness, sport and the spirit of sport survived, right across the spectrum: rugby, soccer, boxing – especially boxing – Gaelic football and hurling, a pantheon of playing games for fun. It was a way of forgetting about the pain and panic on the streets.

As a former pupil at Portora Royal School in the Ulster lakelands capital of Enniskillen, Cowan Watson had a deep passion for rugby. His penchant for the oval ball game included going to watch not only the Ulster senior team of its day – the Cecil Pedlows, the Willie John McBrides, the Syd Millars, the MCH Gibsons – but the Ulster schoolboys' team as well. As it turned out, he'd seen me play at number eight for the Schools XV at Ravenhill. I didn't know that, though, until the day he sent for me to go and see him in his office in the Peacock building in Donegall Street.

I'd appeared – somewhat reluctantly – in the pages of the *News Letter* the previous day.

I'd been out watching an Orange march with bands parading two nights before. Our own band, the Pass Defenders, weren't marching that night. We came from south Belfast, and this parade was the particular pride and joy of the east of the city, over the Queen's and Albert bridges which crossed to the other side of the River Lagan from the gasworks where we lived. It was, and still is, held every year on 1 July, or the next day to it if 1 July falls on a Sunday. It was, and still is, staged to commemorate the bravery and sacrifice of the 36th Ulster Division at the Battle of the Somme in 1916, whose ranks, excepting a corps of some experienced English officers, were made up almost exclusively of Ulstermen.

I was watching that parade when a wee lad, who was standing on the parapet of a bridge, fell into the river below. The child was from nearby Catholic Short Strand. In those days band parades weren't as divisive as they are now, and the boy, along with others from his street, was watching the spectacle when he slipped. As he fell, people screamed. I went in after him.

It wasn't a big deal. The Lagan is tidal. The tide was on the ebb. The water wasn't that deep. The nipper probably had more chance of suffocating in the thick, cloying quicksand-like mud than drowning. But I got him out of the water and onto a mudbank. Other people then hauled both of us out.

The next day, a reporter from the *News Letter* – Neil Johnston, a very talented journalist I was later to befriend, and who went on to put in an astounding decades-long shift with the *Belfast Telegraph* – came to our door. He wanted to interview me. I didn't want to know.

This wasn't false modesty. I was a big, strapping rugby forward. What other punter in my position wouldn't have done what I did? It really was no big deal. However, the dogged Mr Johnston got enough of the story from my mates, and managed to get a mugshot of me, too.

The story, and the headshot picture, appeared in the paper the next morning. Editor Mr Watson recognised the mugshot: it was hard for him not to. Someone once told me I'd a face like something sculpted by an artistic druid. I started to smile, until he added: 'McDowell, the druid was drunk at the time.'

Anyway, Cowan Watson, with his newspaper man's knack of forensic photographic memory, had copped that picture in the paper, and the report. He called in Neil and asked him for my address.

That afternoon, an emissary from the editor's office arrived at the door of 17 Howard Street South. I wasn't in. A note was left asking me to call to Mr Watson the next morning, at his office, at 10.00 a.m. I did just that. He asked me what I wanted to be. I told him the same as I'd told my history master Mr Coffey at Annadale four years previously, when I was only fourteen.

'A reporter.'

He enveloped my hand in his huge mitt, and took me on as a cub reporter.

When I was being interviewed by Neil Johnston I had happened to mention to him that I had always wanted to work for a newspaper myself. Unknown to me there were vacancies at the *News Letter* at that time for two trainee reporters. (The *News Letter* served the unionist community and, just as its nationalist counterpart the *Irish News* employed mainly Catholics, it recruited primarily from the Protestant side of the community.)

I assume that when Cowan Watson invited me in for a chat he already knew that I wanted to be a reporter although I wasn't aware that he did at the time. I'd already taken my A-level exams which would have qualified me for further education. Maybe in time, I would have landed a job on another newspaper or in another media role.

But landing this job – having come to the notice of Editor Watson through playing rugby and featuring in a story in his paper – was a lucky fluke. And people who came from my sort of background didn't often benefit from lucky flukes!

My mother had to pay for my first suit to start work with a Tower Cheque, a form of credit in those days which had to be paid back at twelve shillings and sixpence a week. I then paid her back out of my first few wage packets. And there's a resonance there with my earlier school life.

At the start of each term, my mother, Cherry, would take me to the nearest pawnshop – Harry Mitchell's on Donegall Pass – to buy me a new school blazer. The blazers sold by official school outfitters in those days cost about twenty quid and had bone buttons on the front and sleeves. My pawnshop blazers cost a quarter of that, around five pounds.

But they had brass buttons on them.

My enterprising mother bought a set of bone buttons. Every year she would cut the brass buttons off the pawnshop blazer and sew on the bone replacements and the school badge, the cockatrice. No one ever spotted the difference. Not that either I, or my dear Ma, would have cared.

I wore several pawnshop blazers during my time at the school. But only ever one set of buttons.

Now that I'd landed my first job, my years of study weren't entirely at an end. Mr Cowan informed me that the *News Letter* would send me to the College of Business Studies to learn the rudiments of the job, and to get a qualification then known as a Proficiency Certificate in Journalism.

I started full-time as a trainee journalist in 1969. That was the year the Troubles really started in earnest. The increasing tension between the two sides of the community in Northern Ireland had exploded into street violence, riots and attacks, which saw large numbers of people forced from their homes and the sectarian division of the population become ever more pronounced. Violence begat ever greater violence, hatred and fear. It was a terrible, seemingly unstoppable spiral of conflict. The local newspapers daily carried pages and pages of reports of the increasing carnage. We were working flat out to cover both the shocking violence in the streets and the seismic political events.

And there was plenty to cover. The British Army had been sent in. Initially welcomed by Catholic residents, they then became targets for republican attacks. In Protestant areas there were riots too, against the security forces.

The first RUC officer shot dead in Northern Ireland was gunned down on the loyalist Shankill Road. Meanwhile, there were riots in interface areas, with Protestants and Catholics involved in almost nightly street battles.

In my new job there were some scary moments – and even scarier half-hours and hours – out reporting riots until 6.00 a.m. In those days, the *News Letter* had a final city edition, which was printed in time for the Harland & Wolff shipyard workers, the Short's aircraft workers and the various foundry workers crossing the city to clock in for their jobs at 8.00 a.m. Given the tens of thousands of workers there were in manufacturing industries in those days, it was a prescient, and profitable, proposition to put out an edition that late: or that early.

Back then, everyone except kids too innocent and too young to worry were Troubles news bulletin junkies. The first thing folk did when they woke up every morning was to chase the breaking news of the latest atrocity on their bedside radio. The *Who, What, When, Where, Why?* mantra was never so acute as when the killings and murders were being committed virtually on our own doorstep. And always, lurking in your heart, never mind your head, was the haunting dread that the next person found dead, in the boot of a burning car, or in a hastily dug grave in a windswept bog, might be one of your own: your father, mother, a sister, a brother, another member of your family, or simply a friend.

In those days, when gangs of sectarian ghouls stalked the city streets and the country roads, you could not only feel fear: you could bite it. And I know it's a well-worn cliché, but there really were times when, especially when you were caught in the teeth of life-threatening trouble, if you didn't laugh, you'd cry.

Or die.

So it was one dark, dire night at the top of the Republican New Lodge Road in north Belfast. A riot was raging. Hijacked cars and a lorry had been turned into a burning barricade across the nape of the New Lodge, with riot squad soldiers coming under blistering bombardment from bricks, bottles and petrol bombs.

The core of the press pack took cover in the shelter of a pub doorway, from where we could view the action and nip into the pub to use its public phone to file running copy back to the copytakers, the girls with headphones knocking out our on-the-spot reports on typewriters; there were no mobile phones or laptops linking back into the office computers in those days.

But there was one very young and eager reporter – not me, but no names, no pack drill: he's still around – who didn't take the advice of the old hands just to act canny and report what he saw from the cover of the bar balustrade. He insisted on continually darting to and fro across the front of the burning barricade, notebook and pen in hand – as if you could make notes amid that mini-Armageddon – and popping his head up above the blazing parapet to get a better look.

Then, suddenly, he hit the deck … as predicted by the press veterans. He lay unmoving and prostrate on the petrol bomb-peppered tarmac.

I knew him. I ran to him. He was KO'd. Out for the count. An Army medic rushed to help me as I knelt by his side. The medic summoned a stretcher to get the out-cold casualty off the street and out of danger. And then both of us looked at each other. Beside the hack's bleeding head lay a big frozen cod. A frozen fish. We looked all round us. The road was littered with other species: Lough Neagh eels, mackerel, skate … you name it. All frozen hard.

And then it dawned on us.

One of the big trucks the rioters had hijacked hadn't been burned for the barricade. They were running out of bottles and bricks to throw. So they broke into the refrigerated lorry, discovered it was stacked full of frozen fish – and were firing that commandeered freight at the troops. Your man, the intrepid reporter, had been taken out cold by one of those: a big, foot-and-a-half-long frozen cod.

To this day, he has gone down in the annals of Belfast journalism as the only reporter during the Troubles to have been KO'd by that deadly assault weapon – a flying fish!

Talk about the scales of justice …

Such moments of levity were rare, though. Gradually the riots and the violence were becoming ever more barbaric. It is hard to convey the scale and the savagery of the conflict back then. Sometimes even to those of us who lived through it. I look back now at some of the statistics of horror and I think: 'My God, did that really happen in my lifetime?'

To give an idea of the enormity of what was happening nightly in a city with a population of around half a million people, I've lifted the following stark statistics from the CAIN[1] website on the chronology of the Troubles. And this is for just a few days in July 1972.

1   The CAIN (Conflict Archive on the Internet) website contains information and source material on the Troubles and politics in Northern Ireland from 1968 to the present. CAIN is located in the University of Ulster.

WEDNESDAY, 12 JULY 1972

A Protestant man was found shot dead in Portadown.

Two men, one Catholic and one Protestant, were shot dead in a public house in Portadown.

Two men were shot dead in separate incidents in Belfast.

THURSDAY, 13 JULY 1972

Seven people were shot and killed in separate incidents in Belfast.

FRIDAY, 14 JULY 1972

Six people were shot and killed in separate incidents in Belfast. Three were British Army soldiers, two were members of the Irish Republican Army (IRA) and one was a Protestant civilian.

SUNDAY, 16 JULY 1972

Two British soldiers were killed in an IRA landmine attack near Crossmaglen, County Armagh.

An RUC officer was shot dead by the IRA in Belfast.

A member of the youth wing of the IRA was killed by a rubber bullet in Strabane, County Tyrone.

TUESDAY, 18 JULY 1972

The 100th British soldier to die in the conflict was shot by a sniper in Belfast.

A Protestant man was found shot dead in Belfast.

And then, on Friday, 21 July 1972, came a day that will stay in my memory for ever. The day that is remembered in the history of the Northern Ireland Troubles as Bloody Friday.

5

BLOOD ON THE STREETS

The then Dublin-based Provisional IRA Chief of Staff, Seán Mac Stíofáin, said that the mostly car bomb blitz of Bloody Friday 'was a message to the British Government that the IRA could and would make a commercial desert of the city [Belfast] unless [its] demands were met.'

Those demands – the essence of which was that 'the British' should withdraw from Northern Ireland by 1975 – had been the subject of secret talks that had led to the IRA calling a ceasefire in late June of 1972. The talks floundered. The Provos announced they were pulling the plug on their ceasefire on 9 July.

Just a dozen days later, with Brendan 'Darkie' Hughes as their Belfast OC (Officer Commanding), over twenty

Provo Active Service Units (ASUs) delivered and detonated their payloads on the unsuspecting streets and citizens of Belfast. It was their payback to 'the Brits' for not acceding to their 'Bombs R Us' blackmail tactic. It was also the biggest blitz suffered by any region in the UK since the Nazis had bombed British cities, including Belfast, during the Second World War.

More than twenty bombs planted around the city exploded over a period of around an hour and twenty minutes. Many people fleeing from one blast were caught in another. The sickening fact was that the terrorists had planned it that way to maximise casualties.

The targets stretched from Smithfield bus station in the very heart of the city, where the first bomb exploded at just after 2 p.m., to three railway stations, the Queen Elizabeth Bridge, the city's gasworks, a ferry terminal, a bank and then, at around 3 p.m., the Oxford Street bus station. When the bombs detonated, nine people, including two soldiers and a fourteen-year-old schoolboy, were slaughtered. Over 130 others, including 77 women and children, were injured, many of them critically, amid an ear-splitting, head-spinning cacophony of calamity.

A war of words erupted afterwards, with the Provos claiming that they had given 'adequate' telephone warnings to the police, the press and other organisations that the bombs had been planted. As the blood of the dead and injured was still flowing into street gutters and congealing on the walls and floors of so-called strategic targets, Mac Stíofáin even had the gall to goad the police, saying 'it only required one man with a loud-hailer to clear each target in time'.

I know, more than most, what happened on that brutal, bestial Bloody Friday, because I was in the middle of it, reporting it. Indeed, I actually ran to the scene of the worst bomb blast, the then Ulsterbus depot in Oxford Street, right in the heart of the city. And the smell, the sounds, the screaming, the sheer terror of panic-stricken people fleeing, racing for their lives, will never leave me. Nor will the stunned wall of silence as the shock waves set in, before the screeching sirens of ambulances and fire engines split the air like the wailing of banshees. And nor will the sight of what remained of the people who actually lost their lives, or who were in the last throes of losing their lives.

Or what had to happen to their remains – or what was left of them – in the aftermath.

Suffice to say that in some instances, body parts had to be painstakingly collected in plastic bags.

What had just minutes before been decent human beings going about their daily routines were reduced to remnants, what remained of their clothes rendered ripped and shredded bloody rags hanging off, not on, their bodies.

The sights I saw that day really do haunt me still. That's not a cliché. Even as I sit writing about it all these years later, I feel churning revulsion and distress.

And never mind the impact it had on hardened hacks who had already reported, since 1969, a soaring catalogue of atrocities. Imagine how it impacted upon the members of the emergency services – firefighters, doctors, nurses, police officers, fellow soldiers of the pair of troops killed – who had to face that, too.

And all of this was happening while a gelignite-packed necklace of other bombs continued to explode around the city. Rivers of terrified people poured through the streets, trying to get out of the smoke-choked city centre, only to find that there were no trains or buses running. Because, of course, the main public transport hubs, like the Oxford Street Ulsterbus depot, were all part of the Provos' 'strategic target' bombing plot.

As for us hacks, once back in our Belfast bureaux, we had to relive, recount, report and put down on paper – laboriously, on typewriters: no computers or laptop keyboards in those days – every horrific and heartbreaking scene we had witnessed. And those reports, turning and kerning the massacre that occurred that day (and on many other days and nights) into a matter of record, were being replicated in every newsroom in Belfast, in many cases to be despatched beyond, to London, Dublin, New York, Sydney, wherever a global audience gaped at the pictures and gasped at the words.

Bloody Friday, by its very scale and vicious intent, summed up what the term 'terror on your doorstep' really meant: and what it means today. Now, a glance at any news bulletins from around the globe – in Paris, in Berlin, in Nice, in London, in the USA at the Boston Marathon, in Afghanistan, in Syria or almost anywhere in the Middle East – bears testimony to how many people around the world are living with the same spectre of terror that Northern Ireland endured for almost forty years.

The spectre of terrorism now exploding on their own doorsteps, too.

In the newspaper office where I worked back then, we knew all about terror on our own doorstep – literally. Just over three months before the Bloody Friday bombings, a massive car bomb, one of the very first to have been planted during the Troubles, exploded outside the offices of the *News Letter* in Donegall Street. Initial telephone warnings from the IRA had claimed that a bomb was planted in nearby Church Street, and shoppers, workers and a large group of schoolgirls were evacuated by police from that area into what was assumed to be the safety of Donegall Street. A bin lorry and its crew of workers were going about their business. Police officers were shepherding the crowd.

And then a new and final warning was telephoned through: the bomb was in Donegall Street.

I was out of the office that day on a story. But I could well imagine the panic as the word came through to my colleagues in that familiar old building, with its warren of offices and corridors. Staff were used to bomb scares and evacuation drills. But this time the warning came far too late.

The huge bomb ripped through the street and the hundreds of people unknowingly trapped in its path. Six people were killed outright (another elderly man was to die later in hospital). Two police officers were among the dead, as well as three of the then Belfast Corporation binmen. It was a scene of apocalyptic carnage. Dozens were horrifically maimed by the blast itself and by flying shards of glass. Emergency amputations were carried out at the scene. Among those badly injured were many of my fellow *News Letter* workers.

The next day, as so many times before and in the years afterwards, the pages of the paper would carry not just the words but, more graphically, photographs of the bloody aftermath and the bloodied victims of the bomb. Some scenes were, of course, just too ghastly to publish – on that day as on many others. But the pictures that did appear were a harrowing reflection of the barbarity that was now almost a daily occurrence. Atrocities were being carried out by both republican and loyalist gangs seemingly trying to outdo each other in their tit-for-tat sectarian savagery.

Among the many savage acts committed by the loyalists in those years was the bombing of McGurk's bar in Belfast in 1971, in which 15 people were murdered, two of them young children. In 1974, just before the loyalist strike of that year, five people were murdered in a bomb attack on the Rose and Crown bar. And the UVF also carried out the 1974 Dublin and Monaghan pub bombings in which 34 people were massacred – the greatest loss of life in a single day in the Troubles.

On and on and on it went.

Those of us whose role it was to report such carnage over the years may have got used to the call-outs. We never got used to the carnage.

6

'ULSTER ON THE BRINK'

Many headlines were written during the cataclysmic days of crises in Northern Ireland – the various agreements that fired the ire of the loyalists and sparked mammoth street protests and riots; IRA or loyalist terror gang atrocities and outrages; the murder of terrorist godfathers on, and by, both sides.

But perhaps the most prevalent, and the most used headline, by all sections of the media, was:

ULSTER ON THE BRINK

And no more was that so, and no closer did Northern Ireland come to civil war – or sectarian war – than in May 1974.

I am not going to give a history lesson here about the reasons for the so-calledl loyalist workers' strike that paralysed the province. The strike had been called by the Ulster Workers' Council and was backed by, among other unionist leaders, Rev. Ian Paisley. Suffice to say that the Rev. Ian Paisley and his Democratic Unionist Party (DUP) wanted to bring down the then power-sharing Executive at Stormont. The main loyalist paramilitaries rallied behind him (although later, they would reject him and wash their hands of him and his party). The working-class loyalist people, in particular, were tired of simply, as they saw it, being kicked around by the British and Irish governments, and felt they were being held to ransom over events over which they believed, rightly or wrongly, they had no direct control. Plus, they believed they were being shunted towards their worst political nightmare: a united Ireland.

Meanwhile, the loyalist paramilitaries – particularly the UDA – weren't only itching for a fight, they wanted to flex their massive muscle, of an estimated 20,000 men, and put them on the streets in a showdown show of strength.

And one other crazy ingredient was added to this explosive mix.

At one stage Harold Wilson, then Prime Minister of Great Britain and Northern Ireland, had warned that if the loyalist strike went ahead and electricity supplies were hit at the province's main power plants – one was on the banks of the River Lagan estuary in the docklands of Belfast, the other major facility was at Ballylumford in Larne Lough – he would send a nuclear submarine and use the power from it to keep the electricity grid, or at least an emergency element of it, going.

On the streets of Belfast, the PM was laughed at as a stooge. But then he came out with a caustic comment that proved to be the spark that lit the bonfire of rage. He pointed to how much the British Exchequer doled out in benefits to the people of Northern Ireland, describing the local population as 'spongers'. The so-called loyalist workers' strike was on in earnest after that, with protestors wearing bits of sponge in their lapels as a sneering riposte to Wilson.

In spite of the best efforts of the trade union movement – then TUC General Secretary Len Murray even came over to lead a march in protest at the strike – the Belfast shipyard and other major manufacturing plants were forced to close by wildcat strikes. Those workers who wanted no part of the paramilitary-powered protest were intimidated into compliance. And Northern Ireland was paralysed.

The UDA and UVF strung human barricades across roads and streets to stop traffic getting through. Only the emergency services were exempt. Rubbish was piled on the streets as bin collections stopped. Shops ran out of food. Even the grave-diggers went on strike.

It was a frightening time; there was a real fear that the situation would spiral entirely out of control. But as always, even in the direst times, there was a black humour about events.

I'm not in any way seeking to trivialise the mayhem and misery the terror gangs inflicted on the ordinary population. But one daft incident that occurred during this strike, and another I will relate with it, blows away the myth that the loyalist and republican paramilitaries were the sophisticated and intelligence-led (in both senses of that word) outfits they liked to style themselves.

The loyalist example first.

It was the first day of the UWC strike. I was a reporter on the news desk of the *Belfast News Letter*. One of the first actions of the leaders of the strike was to issue a decree to all newspaper head offices stating that reporters would only be allowed onto the streets and to photograph and report on the picket and protest lines, and any other action, if they were accredited by the strike organisers. Multilaterally, chapel (union) meetings were held in those editorial offices, and this demand was rejected outright. The strike leaders were bluntly told that the National Union of Journalists (NUJ) cards we all carried were recognised by state agencies throughout the UK and Ireland, and no other was needed: especially not to show to a bunch of bully boys in black balaclavas.

The UWC leaders relented.

So it was that I was despatched on the first day of the strike by my old news editor, David Kirk Sr, to cover a human barricade protest by the UDA. It was the first test of the NUJ press pass accord. It worked.

Lines of UDA men, many in Aussie-style bush ranger floppy hats, and wearing (of all things) German army surplus khaki combat jackets, stood in ranks across the main traffic artery. On one corner stood a great old traditional Belfast boozer. It was closed. All the pubs in loyalist areas were ordered to shut their doors for the duration of the strike – a kind of paramilitary prohibition, if that isn't too absurd a notion. (But, significantly, it wasn't long before the UDA's own shebeens opened for booze, and business, again.)

The human barricade had been in situ for some time. There was little or no traffic. What cars did appear were turned back, and the drivers warned not to be out on the roads again. Later in the strike, offending motorists had their cars summarily hijacked and burned at paramilitary checkpoints. However, commercial trucks and lorries – because they were trying to do business as usual – were not to be tolerated, even on the first day.

So the local UDA commander posted a scout, a lookout, to spot and report any trucks on the move. Suddenly, the scout saw a lorry coming towards them.

'Commander, commander,' he guldered. 'There's an artic..., there's an artic..., there's a f*****g big lorry coming towards us, sir!'

'Right,' ordered the CO to his serried ranks. 'Close ranks. This lorry is not getting through. But as it's the first day of the strike, no harm will come to the driver. We will let him go with a warning. But we're commandeering the lorry, turning it round across the road, and turning it into a burning barricade as a warning to other firms still defying us and doing business.'

There was a clearly audible staccato murmuring in the ranks that lasted almost a minute. Then the men delegated their sergeant, a well-known 'tea leaf' (thief) in south Belfast, to be their spokesman and approach the CO.

The sergeant explained that the men – and, not least, himself – thought that the strike might last for weeks. Therefore, they would not be able to draw what is known in 'Norn Iron' as the 'Broo', their dole money, unemployment and other benefits, from offices manned by civil servants, who had also been ordered to quit work. So the sergeant suggested that perhaps a peek could be taken inside the back of the big lorry to see what was inside, before it was overturned and torched. 'Just to see, sir, if there is any stuff that could be, like, taken and stored, just until the strike is over, sir, and then we can, like, move it on and get some of the money back that we'll have lost from the Broo. That lorry, sir,' insisted the persistent sergeant, 'could be full of fridges, or TVs, or microwave ovens, sir.'

The commander was having none of it.

'The UDA is a disciplined organisation,' I heard him chastise his sergeant. 'There will be no looting. This lorry will be turned on its side, the back doors forced open, and two molo... two molo... two petrol bombs will be flung inside.'

Just like his scout on the bridge, the CO had a bit of trouble with big words. He couldn't pronounce Molotov cocktails.

The sergeant went back to address the ranks. More animated murmuring. The sergeant went back to the commander.

'The men said, if you're going to petrol bomb inside that lorry without looking in first, sir, do it yourself.'

The CO, to his credit, took that as a challenge and not, as he might have, a declaration of mutiny over the bounty that might, or might not, be in the back of the big truck.

'All right then,' he snapped. 'I will lead by example.'

The lorry was turned round, to straddle the road, and turned over. The commander positioned himself at the rear.

'Right,' he ordered, 'hand me two of them petrol bombs.'

The doors were busted open as the soaked tapers on the petrol bombs were lit. The CO flung both bottles, right- and left-handed, at the same time into the packed belly of the truck.

And then ... *WHOOOOSHHHH!*

He was hit by a massive ball of flame, a fireball, full in the face and down the front of his body. He lost his eyebrows and much more. He would spend weeks in hospital, getting skin peeled off his posterior and grafted onto the burnt parts.

If only he had peeked into the back of that lorry before blindly hurling in the two petrol bombs, he would have discovered that it wasn't full of fridges, or TVs, or ovens as his sergeant had suggested.

It was packed with Sunny Jim firelighters!

As the TV ads say: 'Should have gone to Specsavers ...'

On the other hand, it wasn't fire, but freezing cold, that exposed the IQ – or lack of it – of an IRA second-in-command who worked down on the deep-sea dock in Belfast.

The story goes that he came down the dock one winter's day. It was 6.00 a.m. and the frost coated the quays white. It was about minus six degrees. Your man was wearing a big duffle coat, two jumpers, three T-shirts under those, two pairs of denims, and he doubled up on socks inside his steel-toe-capped docker's boots as well. One of the other boys asked him why he'd got so many clothes on. He lived with his family in a public authority rented house owned by the Northern Ireland Housing Executive, which was akin to a council owning and renting homes in Dublin or England.

He told his mate: 'It's that f*****g Executive. Of all the times of the year they decide to come in and re-lag the lining of the chimneys – the dead of winter, and the worst big freeze of the year. It means we can't light the fire in the house. So last night me and the wife and the children all lay in the same bed with every blanket and big coat in the house over us, and we were still bloody half-frozen. And I'm still freezin' this mornin', which is why I've got so much gear on.'

So his mates are having a tea break later on, and they're yarning about his icebox house dilemma.

One of them says: 'Listen, until you can light a fire again, why don't you get the Housing Executive to loan you one of them gas cylinder fires, a Superser. I've heard they've done that before.'

'Naaah,' says your man. 'I've already asked them about one of them. But they say they don't do that anymore.'

'Well,' says another docker, 'you're going to have to come up with something.'

However, the next morning – and the thermometer is still showing minus six – he comes bouncing down the dock. He's wearing just a tartan shirt underneath a leather jacket, one pair of jeans, and a single pair of socks.

'How was last night?' asks another docker.

'Warm as toast,' he says. 'I got a big, powerful three-bar electric fire, planked it in the middle of the room. Had it on all night.'

'Wait a minute,' says another savvy docker. 'If you kept that electric fire burnin' all night, it'll cost you a fortune in electricity.'

'No, it won't,' says your man. 'Sure it isn't mine – I borrowed it off the brother.'

They certainly weren't the brightest sparks, so many of the terrorists on both sides. And it is a matter of record that when one loyalist paramilitary was once asked what his rank in his organisation was, he replied: 'T.O.'

When asked what that stood for he replied: 'Telligence Officer'.

But the misery they routinely inflicted on the people of Northern Ireland was no laughing matter. It seemed we were all locked in endless conflict.

To paraphrase a later comment by President Bill Clinton during a peace process visit, the abnormal had become our normal. When darkness fell each evening, Belfast became a ghost town. During the day the city centre was protected by a 'ring of steel', which was a pretty literal description. To get into city-centre streets, you had to first pass through metal corrals in the middle of massive steel gates.

These corrals were not unlike a cattle crush. You stood, arms outstretched, to be frisked by civilian searchers. Women's handbags were gone through. You had to empty your pockets.

To enter a shop you were frisked again by the shop's security staff. In bars and what few eating houses there were, toilets were routinely locked and if you needed to 'go', you had to ask for the key.

With horrific atrocities being committed on a regular basis, entertainers and bands, not surprisingly, gave Northern Ireland a wide berth. But we did have one very high-profile visitor, I recall. And her tour landed me in a right royal row.

7

THE QUEEN AND I

Noel 'Chipper' Thompson was the skipper of the Annadale Grammar School first XV, which I helped coach to the St Patrick's Day final of the Ulster Schools' Cup in 1978. He was dubbed Chipper because his brother, Ian, had a somewhat similar soubriquet: he was known as Chopper. Chipper and Chopper. As boys, their parents had bought them both bikes. Noel got what was known as a Chipper bike in those days. Ian, another Annadale man, was gifted a Chopper.

Both of them went into the cops. As did a fair proportion of that Schools' Cup Final team. And this was at the height of the terror war in Northern Ireland. That's a fact of which I am still very proud. Maybe my attitude towards the bogeymen – of either hue, orange or green – murdering innocent people in some way influenced them. Both the Thompson brothers-in-arms made fine police officers. Unfortunately, and tragically, both died young. I had the heartbreaking task, asked both times by their lovely and loving mother, Bea, of delivering the eulogy at their funerals.

One of Chipper's favourite songs – and he was a master minstrel with a wide-ranging repertoire of songs, some reverent, some, because of the rugby musical idiom, absolutely irreverent – was a marathon ditty called 'The Ducks of Magheralin'. It had a phalanx of verses: many of them only ever so slightly irreverent to some historical figures, others fawning in their praise. But to give you a flavour, I'll record here, for posterity, the most appropriate verse and the chorus.

Before I do, however, it is pertinent to inform you that Magheralin is not a metropolis the size of Manhattan Island in New York. Rather, it is a humble hamlet nestling deep amid the rolling drumlins of County Down. Still, here's the verse relevant to my right royal experiences, and also the chorus, relevant to nothing except Magheralin: or the folk still residing therein.

It's just about a year ago, I went to see the Queen,
She decked me out with medals, the trimmings they were green.
She decked me out with medals, but they were made of tin.
'Oh go home,' says she, 'ye skitter ye, you're the Mayor of Magheralin'.
CHORUS: Oh it is a famous city in the fine old ancient style,
A credit to sweet County Down and the pride of Eireann's Isle,

It has the finest harbour for the bread carts to sail in.
And if ever you go to Ire-land you'll sail by Magheralin ...

Now, there are other verses concerning Antony and Cleopatra, 'the great Napoleon Bonaparte', King Billy and the Battle of the Boyne, and Winston Churchill, who, according to the song, knew he would win the war 'because he knew the Ulster Rifles were all born in Magheralin'.

I relate this part of the story primarily in fond memory of Chipper and Chopper, but also because of the first verse, and its relevance to royalty.

Because I met royalty twice.

Not by invitation, though, thanks mainly to a note left by Mo Mowlam indicating that I would never be on a shortlist for a knighthood: or words to that effect. But more of that later ...

I met Queen Elizabeth II and Prince Philip a couple of times, purely as part of the job. Once was on the royal yacht *Britannia*, during Queen Elizabeth's 1977 Silver Jubilee celebration tour, when the ship docked off the North Antrim coast, close to the Giant's Causeway and the seaside town of Portrush. The second time was at Windsor Castle in London, when a posse of newspaper editors from throughout the UK were invited to another celebration party at that august royal gaff.

On the first occasion, I nearly got the newspaper I then worked for, the *Belfast News Letter*, closed down by royal writ.

I'd been reporting Her Majesty's tour of Ulster all day. Another *News Letter* reporter was supposed to go on board the royal yacht that night, where the Queen was hosting a reception for politicians and the local hoi polloi. That reporter cried off at the last minute.

I was staying in a hotel in Portrush that night. I'd gone back there and changed out of suit, shirt and tie and tossed on a casual green tweed suit and an open-necked cheesecloth shirt. The top button had to be undone because the shirt collar was a size too small. I thought my royal 'marking' for the day was done, so I was heading out for a few pints with a big police sergeant who was stationed in Portrush at the time, and who'd been one of the platoon of cops chaperoning the monarch's visit to the north-west.

The sergeant was one Louis Craig, a former front-row forward with the 'Creggie Red Sox', aka Malone RFC, a famous Belfast club mentioned elsewhere on these pages (and for which Chipper Thompson and another of the Annadale Schools' Cup XV, Colin Morrison, also went on to play: Colin Morrison also became a police sergeant, and played in the second row for Ulster).

Louis had knocked off duty, too. He'd headed straight for the Harbour Bar, close to where the royal reception guests were gathered to be ferried over in officially supervised tenders to *Britannia*. I joined the big fella. But I'd only had a couple of swallows of my first pint when the hotel got a message to me. The editor of the paper had been on the phone to the hotel looking for me.

The message was that the other reporter, who was supposed to go on the *Britannia* and do the 'colour' social diary-style double-page spread, with a photographer, had cried off ill. The short and succinct message was that I had to get out there and do the business instead.

In a green tweed suit and open-neck cheesecloth shirt, *sans* tie, braces or bloody cufflinks.

Big Louis solved that problem. Except for the braces and cufflinks. He was still in uniform, his peaked cap with crest perched on the bar counter. The IRA was waging a pernicious campaign against the police then, of course. But that didn't bother boys like Louis Craig. They could handle themselves with the best on a rugby paddock. And, many times, they had proved themselves more than adept at handling themselves off the pitch: on duty, or off.

Anyway, Big Louis simply whipped off his black police-issue tie with its regulation, and very appropriate, triangular Windsor knot and said: 'Stick that on, McDowell – it'll do the job.'

So there I was, kind of half-suited – in green, just like the medal trimmings for the Mayor of Magheralin – and ready to set sail for the royal yacht *Britannia* to meet the Queen, just like that mayor of song and fable.

There was another slight problem, though. All the tenders taking visitors to the big boat berthed out in the bay had vamoosed: gone. I had no way of getting out there, unless I swam.

Sergeant Craig to the rescue once again. He knew a skipper having a pint down the end of the bar who owned what Louis called 'a small merchant vessel'. He went and talked to the skipper. The skipper said 'sure', he would get McDowell out of a hole: another one.

And thus it was that I must have been the only hack in the universe to be the last 'guest' to be piped aboard the *Britannia* – having unceremoniously arrived at the gangway steps up to the deck to alight ... from a black and sooty coal boat!

Plus, we could have been blown out of the water. Remember, this was at the height of what the Provos called their Long War. The Queen was a prime target, especially while visiting what the republicans called the Occupied Six Counties. But Louis had contacted his local police station and they had alerted the security detail on board the *Britannia*.

Still, it was always with a raw guffaw in the future that Big Louis would greet me with the clarion call of: 'Here comes King Coal McDowell!'

The big man has since passed on. But, to use the old word for a police officer, if ever there was a 'people's peeler', that title would have fit Sergeant Louis Craig perfectly. Just like his policeman's black tie fit the bill for getting me on that big boat.

But it was on board the *Britannia* that an incident occurred that almost sunk the old *News Letter* – ironically, the voice of unionism and the people loyal to the Queen in Northern Ireland.

There was a space shuttle-style lift-off of tension at the royal reception on the *Britannia*. It was the last engagement of the royal visit. Before she had arrived, the IRA had ominously promised the Queen 'a visit to remember'. In the run-up to the tour, there had been a spate of fire bombings of shops and businesses. And a week beforehand, in a limp attempt to gain worldwide publicity for the terrorists, a bomb had exploded at the University of Ulster campus at Coleraine, a visit to which was included on the royal agenda.

But neither the Provos nor any other terror gang had been able to penetrate either the covert or the in-your-face security cover protecting the Queen's entourage. That led to one high-ranking royal aide having, as we say in Ulster, 'a wee drop too many'. Which is a gross understatement. If the *Britannia* itself had had as much (albeit liquid) ballast in its bilges, it would have capsized. And, Brahms and Liszt, the aide came out with a potentially explosive statement within earshot of myself and just a few others that I thought would make one helluva headline for the next morning's loyal and true *Belfast News Letter* front page.

Buoyed by the whole two-day Silver Jubilee jaunt going off almost incident-free, he expostulated something along the lines of: 'We fecked the IRA!' (And yes, it was with an 'e' after the 'f', not a 'u', and pronounced the same way posh Brits, polite Dubliners and, indeed, the anything-but posh or polished Mrs Brown and her Boys say it.)

Now, when the Queen is giving an audience or reception for guests and it is being covered by the press, the protocol is that what she says to the folk gathered is off the record and cannot be quoted directly. But nobody had told me there was a ban on quoting a G&T-filled old fart from her legion of Buckingham Palace lackeys.

I got hold of one of the *Britannia*'s ship-to-shore telephones. I started dictating the 'Fecking the IRA' story off the top of my head to a copytaker back in the office in Belfast. But unfortunately, just like the Queen herself, I was being chaperoned – by another of her officials. He had set up the phone for me to use and was, unbeknownst to me, standing behind me, just feet away, but within easy ear-wigging distance.

All hell broke loose.

The official pulled the plug, almost physically, on the call. My then editor was phoned back in his office. Writs, of a legal, rather than a royal kind, were threatened. The editor pulled the story, under immense pressure.

But the *News Letter* readers would have loved that splash page one headline:

FECKING THE IRA

That would, literally, have been a right royal scoop.

But as I'm writing this in 2017, you, the folk who kindly bought this book, are reading it for the first time, even though it's forty years later. So, in a way, it's still a scoop.

As for my second assignment with royalty ... well, that word 'scoop' comes readily to mind again.

There's the old story told about a one-time professor of psychology at an Irish university. He had two young sons. One was the eternal optimist, the other the eternal pessimist. So late one Christmas Eve, he decides to conduct a personal, family-focused experiment. While the pessimist son is asleep, he creeps into the bedroom and silently sets up a top-of-the-range model electric train set. In the room of the other wee lad, the optimist, he brings in a bag and builds a pyramid of horse dung. Early Christmas morning, around six, there's movement in both rooms. The Da hears crying and cussing from the pessimist's room. He goes in. The train set is not working. Nothing is right in the world, even on Christmas morn.

He then heads for the other boy's room. The smiling kid has been down to the backyard. He's got the coal shovel in both hands. He's digging away, heartily singing 'Jingle Bells'. The professor of psychology asks him what he's at.

'Aah, Da,' says the boy, 'sure with all this horseshit, there must be a pony here somewhere.'

Ditto me and the Duke of Edinburgh.

Honest.

This was at the Windsor Palace gig for editors. So I'm standing in a long line with other guests from the press. Her Majesty is pressing the flesh along another line, directly facing and running parallel with us. On our line, we've got the royal court jester, the Duke of Edinburgh, renowned for his off-the-cuff, often quirky quips. And he's dandering down the line towards me. And we shake hands. Not a knuckle cruncher. Just a kind of Masonic squeeze. Although I wouldn't know definitely about that. I'm not in the Masons. They wouldn't let me in: not with all those secrets. Too tempting for an oul' hack like me to blow the gaffe.

However, my old friend Andy Kennedy is a Mason. He's also an ex-rugby referee. He once threatened to send me off in a match, not for doing anything improper. He blew me up and awarded a penalty against me at a line-out.

I said to him: 'I did nothing wrong, sir.'

As he marked the spot for the penalty kick to be taken, he retorted: 'Aye, do nothing again, Mr McDowell, and you're off.'

As for the Masons, Andy insists that it is not a secret society, but rather a society with secrets. The Duke of Edinburgh, after all his years as consort to the Queen, must have plenty of those. But whether or not he's in the Masonic Order, I couldn't say.

So, at the Windsor Castle event, he says to me something along the lines of: 'I take it with a face like that you have an equestrian background?'

Now I'm definitely not as pretty as Muhammad Ali. But I thought to myself, I do not have a face like a horse. Jaysus, even a horse would be insulted by that insinuation ...

No, what I speedily surmised was that, with the cauliflower lugs and busted snout, His Royal Highness must have thought I'd been kicked in the head a few times, by feisty ponies rather than prop forwards. So I replied to HRH that I did indeed have something of a family connection with equestrianism. He promptly and pleasantly inquired what that was.

Employing my best Belfast slang, I told him: 'My Da was a cream cookie. Ran a pitch in Ventry Street off the Dublin Road in Belfast for years.'

His Royal Highness had one more prescient query: 'What's a cream cookie?'

Says I: 'A bookie ... a bookmaker, Your Royal Highness.'

I thought he'd have been chuffed with that, given his merry wife of Windsor's love of horse racing.

He evidently wasn't.

He abruptly burled round on his well-heeled and shiny Savile Row brogues, and shuffled off, shaking his head.

So that was the second occasion when the royal prerogative of mercy was not extended to McDowell. And if ever Her or His Royal Highness reads this, it is highly unlikely it ever will be. Nor, unlike that 'skitter' of a Mayor of Magheralin, am I likely ever to have medals pinned on me by the Queen – whether made of tin or not, and whether the trimmings are green ... the same colour, may I remind you, as that casual tweed suit I wore getting a lift on a coal boat out to the Royal Yacht *Britannia*.

8

ACE IN THE HOLE

Amid the madness and sectarian strife of those troubled times in Northern Ireland, there was still one great uniting force.

Sport.

There is a myth that reporting and writing about sport is a dream job. To an extent, it is. Sport, I've always maintained, is about one word: romance. But reporting it daily – and nightly, as the job requires – can sometimes be a nightmare. Especially when a sportsman/woman takes umbrage at what you've written about his/her performance. Or a furious parent uses you as the anvil to hammer out the ire when their offspring is not selected for a club or county team. They think you've got the ear of the selectors, or have an inkling or inner sanctum angle on why they acted the way they did. Sometimes, you had. Often, you hadn't. But that didn't stop you getting an earful of admonishment that, sometimes, could go on for a l-o-n-g time.

Until you put the phone down.

And then you were the worst in the world, of course, in the eyes and mind of the aggrieved party, anyway.

And some of them could have outdone Donald Trump in terms of demonising the press – especially the sports press – and accusing us of writing 'fake news'. Which is why, sometimes, you had to tell them to fake off ... or words to that effect.

But then there are the upsides.

The international travel, for example, if you reach the plateau of reporting sport – soccer, rugby, athletics, boxing – at that highest level. I got there. And on the whole, in spite of the fleas in my cauliflower ears from time to time, I had a ball.

That's when I switched from news reporting in the daily *News Letter* to sports reporting, in the late 1970s and early 1980s. The then *News Letter* sports editor, George Ace, knew I had played rugby to at least a half-decent standard. He was on the lookout for a new Rugby Correspondent, as the rather grandiose job title went back then. He came head-hunting. I moved nextdoor from the news reporters' room to the sports room.

But George being George, he hadn't told me mine was to be a quadruple brief. It was only when I arrived on my first day in the new job that he informed me, as he took a slow drag on his fag, that I was covering boxing, athletics and cricket as well. In doing so, the inimitable Mr Ace dealt me an ace card. But he handed a new editor of the paper a bum deal on another occasion.

The world-famous sporting spectacular, the Oxford and Cambridge Boat Race, almost sank the *News Letter*: just like that yarn from another boat, the *Britannia*, that was spiked. It was late on a Sunday afternoon. I was the *News Letter*'s rugby and boxing correspondent in the winter, doubling up with cricket and athletics in the summer. It was springtime, coming to the end of the oval ball game season.

Now, remember that old saying: rugby is a game played by big men with odd-shaped balls. Well, my sports editor at the time, George Ace, certainly had balls – but his were pure steel. They had to be. He was a betting man. The horses were his forte. And he bet – *big*. But he also played the bookies off one against another. When he owed one establishment, say, five grand, he'd go to another, and bet with them – on tick, or what is now known as 'on account', until he had enough money to pay off the first bookie, and so it went, right down the racing line.

But this Sunday evening, a new editor was starting in the *News Letter*. He was a bit of a toff: old school tie and all that crap, chaps. I was just finishing my rugby round-up of Saturday's then Ulster Senior League games, and was beginning to write a preview of the old Boston Cup floodlit tournament game. Sponsored by the Bass Ireland brewery, it was to be played on the Tuesday night. It was about 6.30 p.m. Herbie Cooper, our horse-racing tipster, was writing his copy for the next day, pencilling in his naps and doubles. Eoin McQuillan was subbing the sports pages as he sat sipping a glass or two of Mateus Rosé in his wheelchair – a brave man, he gamely fought motor neurone disease, even though he had to be brought up to the sports department floor in the goods lift every evening to start his shift. Golf writer Denis 'Deano' O'Hara, who also covered boxing, and the soccer writer Jimmy 'Dubious' Dubois were probably hovering around the sports room, too.

It was then that your man, the new editor, waltzed in.

The sports editor was sitting scanning the pages and smoking a fag: no smoking bans in newspapers in those days, or daft drinking-on-the-premises taboos, otherwise there would have been a walk-out. Back then, walk into the news or sports desks, and you dandered into a Beijing-style smog.

So the rookie editor says to oul' hand George: 'George, what are we leading the back page with tomorrow?'

George doesn't even look up from the page layouts he's avidly perusing, takes a drag on his fag, and says: 'There was a big football derby between Linfield and Glentoran yesterday and it ended in a riot. Great pictures, both of the goals, and the fans fighting,' says George. 'That'll do,' he adds.

Not for the new editor, it wouldn't.

He stuns the sports room when he commands: 'I want the Oxford and Cambridge Boat Race to be the main story, with picture, on the back page tomorrow.'

'You what?' replies George, at last extracting the glowing cigarette from between his now pursed lips.

'You heard me,' says the new editor, turning to swan back to his newly furnished office. 'My son is going up to Oxford at the end of this school term. The Boat Race leads the back page.'

Now George Ace was a man of the world, and a man of the people. But he turned to me and Herbie and Eoin and says: 'What f*****g boat race is that man talking about?'

I told him – Oxford and Cambridge.

He asked: 'Where's that held?'

I said that it had been staged on the River Thames in London the previous day, Saturday … although I had to confess that I hadn't a baldy notion who'd won it.

'Right, cub,' he says to me (he always called me 'cub', right into my late thirties), 'isn't that that boat race where, at the end, they throw that wee w****r who sits at the back and pulls the strings to steer the boat into the water?'

I said it was.

'Right, if Mister New Editor wants the Boat Race to lead the back page tomorrow morning, he'll get it.'

With that, he despatched me to the old 'creed' room upstairs in the garret, where all the Press Association reports and big events – from the coronation to state funerals to the Wembley Cup Final to, well, the Boat Race – were sent across from the PA's Fleet Street HQ on the wires via big, old, rackety but still beautiful teletext machines.

I got the lads there to pull me about half-a-dozen prints of Boat Race pictures off the wires. I wanted action shots. If we were going to lead the back page with the Boat Race, we needed an all-action picture as the window on the page to draw in the punters. I garnered pictures of the oarsmen straining, their veins sticking out like tree roots on the sides of their sweating heads. I got pics of the boats going head-to-head on the Thames, neck and neck in the treacherous, choppy waters.

Back down at his desk, George was having none of them. 'No,' he said, 'no good. Get me a picture of what I was talking about there. That wee man they throw into the river at the end.'

I did as I was bid, came back down from the creed room, handed George the picture as requested, and he said to me: 'Cub, if you've filed all your rugby copy, away on home.'

I'd my reservations. But with George in that mood, to argue with him would have been like trying to ride the Grand National blindfold.

As I left, George himself was drawing the layout for the back page on a big, ten-column-wide, broadsheet page plan: it was pencils, pica rules, and rubbers in those days. Apples weren't computers and keyboards back then: they were fruit grown in the orchards of County Armagh.

By midnight that Sunday the paper would have been put to bed to run off the first editions. I was about to go to bed, too, when the phone rang. It was the office. The voice on the other end had an urgent request.

'Can you get a taxi and get down here quick, Jim?' he asked. 'We've got a big problem with the back page. It needs changed. We can't get the hold of the sports editor. You'll need to do it.'

I didn't even ask. I called a cab, and got down there fast.

The face of the printer who met me was as white as the Scandinavian newsprint on the huge reels waiting to go on the now-still presses. He handed me the proof copy of the back page.

I saw his problem.

The aforementioned Mr Ace certainly had acquiesced to the new editor's wishes and placed the Oxford and Cambridge Boat Race as, literally, the splash on the back page. But above the six-column picture of that 'wee w****r' being tossed into the Thames at the end, he'd put a triple-deck headline, in 96-point Bodini bold font (unheard of before in the grand old *News Letter*, which was, and remains, the bastion of Ulster unionism), which accurately, but outrageously, read:

WINNING BOAT RACE

CREW HOLD THEIR

COX ABOVE THEIR HEADS

I changed the headline and signed off the back page in about as long as it took the cox to hit the water from his lofty perch.

But there was hell to pay the next day: not least from the proprietor, who had to be informed, gently, why the print run had to be held and why the paper was late hitting the streets.

As for Mr Ace, he was still nowhere to be found … for the next week. Because the previous Friday, he had drawn advance expenses to head for a big horse racing festival in England. And, of course, there were no mobile phones in those days for your editor to contact you instantly.

I'd got George out of jail – and he went on the run, and stayed there until all bets were off on him getting the sack.

Recruited, or press-ganged, into the sports department by George, I went from reporting club matches – badly, some rugby aficionados claimed: I didn't digress then, and I still don't – to reporting Ulster's Inter-Pros and Ireland's international campaigns. I travelled, and stayed, in some style: all expenses paid (including beer money for 'entertainment'). Twickenham, Murrayfield, and the triple oval ball citadels of the old Cardiff Arms Park, Parc des Princes, and, of course, our own Lansdowne Road.

And there were the absolutely 'insider job' nights, which were completely off the record and couldn't be put in print then. Like getting most of a very bored All Blacks squad, who were on a tour of Britain and Ireland, smuggled out of the toilet windows of a hotel close to Belfast and squeezing them into a fleet of taxis to ferry them to a night at the dogs at the now defunct and demolished Dunmore greyhound stadium.

Getting those guys out was a bit of a gamble in itself. Getting them back in after Kiwi curfew time was quite another. But just like at the dogs, money changed hands: and the player who had been appointed nightwatchman, to make sure none of the Blacks broke the curfew, was palmed a few quid – no names, even now, no pack drill. But let's just say he turned a blind eye: and played a blinder for the All Blacks against Ulster the next day. As did his team mates. Even though they may have gone to the dogs, literally, the night before. But they came out of the traps on fire the next day, and even before half-time the odds were against the home side clinching a historic upset.

Aaaah, for rugby in the rare oul' times …

And there were even times when the press were actually allowed to travel on the team bus back to the hotel after the official post-match dinners. Those were swashbuckling occasions – in the company of the likes of Willie Duggan, Stewart McKinney, and a clan of other very colourful individuals. They were permitted to take a pint or two on the night before a match then, never mind the night after.

Indeed, I once witnessed, and was in the company of, an Irish winger who downed a couple of pints of stout in the Shelbourne Hotel on the Friday night before an international. I asked him why only a couple of pints.

He said that he couldn't have any more in case they acted as a laxative.

I enquired further. He told me: 'Jim, the couple of pints of Guinness will make me want to have a shite before the game. But just about.'

'But you know we will be playing ten-man rugby out there tomorrow?'

'I'll be lucky to see the ball, never mind get it in my hands even once. I'll be freezing out there. So I need to hold my shit in … just to keep me warm.'

Such were the days, as Willie John McBride immortally quipped, when the forwards were mere donkeys … and the backs were ballerinas. Albeit ballerinas busting for a shit.

Those were halcyon days – in spite of the carping from some parents, punters and players – for sports hacks like me.

Even the Irish press corps had a rugby XV. The 'manager' and mentor of that motley crew, who arranged the fixtures and selected the team to play against the French and other national press XVs, was the legendary Edmund 'Ned' van Esbeck, the rugby correspondent of the *Irish Times*. Ned had a nickname: 'the Pope'. Because whatever he wrote or opined about Irish rugby, it was deemed that his word, just like that of the pontiff, was infallible.

I played for that team – or at least turned up – a few times. We could handle ourselves – Colm Smyth of the *Irish Independent*, Bob Messenger and John O'Shea of the *Irish Press*, and a few feisty others.

Except for one Friday night in Paris when, at an eve-of-international dinner always arranged by our manager, Mr van Esbeck (who, as a Pioneer, never touched the stuff himself), we had more than a few too many post-grub goblets of that fine Gallic brain scrambler: Grand Marnier.

If you'd lit a match to our arses in the scrum the next morning, collectively we'd have ignited faster and burned longer than a rocket launched from Cape Canaveral.

But we beat Les Bleus of the French press, even though they'd a few ringers – recent ex-internationals who were now doing TV or radio commentary and were not, by any stretch of the imagination, fully paid-up members of the full-time press pack.

But somehow we survived. We got the job done, and the reports of the international match later that day got filed.

Somehow.

Covering boxing was a 24/7 part of the sports job, too. I was fit in those days, still playing rugby for the Malone

RFC Wednesday XV   – and proving more than a match for the best the British Army battalions then bivouacked in Northern Ireland (like the Scottish Black Watch regiment) could put out on a rugby paddock against us.

Meanwhile, I spent a week with the NI Commonwealth boxing squad at their pre-Games training camp deep in the bowels of Tollymore Forest Park at the foot of the Mourne Mountains in County Down. The legendary Gerry Storey, who had coached a legion of Irish boxing teams to the Olympics and other international tournaments, was in charge of the Commonwealth Games squad at the boxing boot camp – running hills, squat lifting tree trunks, sprinting up steep forest trails trailing tree trunks tied round our waists.

I use the word 'our' because Gerry permitted me to join in with the squad and write 'paper tiger' daily dispatches about how hard that regime was: as hard, in fact, as the boxers themselves, who seemed to be hewn out of the Mourne granite rock embracing the boot camp.

And it was that same boxing squad that I followed down to Brisbane for the Commonwealth Games staged on Australia's Gold Coast in 1982. I reported on their exploits there: and was even smuggled in – by Gerry, of course – to spend a few nights with them in the athletes' village.

Gerry might have been adept at smuggling me *in* to somewhere. But there was a famous occasion when he managed to smuggle himself *out* of his then day job on the deep-sea docks in Belfast.

As my old marathon running mate John 'Mo' Shaw tells it, he was working on the dock one day when Gerry says to him: 'John, I need to head off. If the foreman or anybody asks for me, tell them I'm away for a cup of tea.'

The cup of tea lasted for a week. Mo recalls: 'I said to him when he got back: "'That was some cup of tea – where did you go for it?"'

Without missing a beat, the imperturbable pugilist trainer replied: 'Cuba.'

In fact, Mr Storey had phantomed off – or a shorter word to that effect – with an Irish boxing team fighting in Cuba.

Some cup of tea, indeed …

As for Mo Shaw, he was an ex-amateur boxer of some renown, as was his brother, Eddie. And Eddie, who also became a good friend, was, of course, the cornerman who trained Barry McGuigan all the way to the featherweight World Crown at London's Loftus Road soccer stadium in 1985. Barry McGuigan was to become a friend, too, and still is. And his manager, BJ 'Barney' Eastwood, remains a charismatic and colourful acquaintance, who has always obliged when I needed an interview for either a newspaper or a broadcast story.

Indeed, the last time BJ did an interview with me it was for a radio profile of another Belfast boxing great, Rinty Monaghan. We met at the King's Hall, the setting for Rinty's rise to become a Lord of the Ring. I should have had something with which to thank Mr Eastwood. Instead, he went to his car, parked outside the arena, and handed me a bottle of single malt whiskey. Once again, that demonstrated Barney's sheer big-heartedness. Which is why it almost broke my heart when boxer Barry and manager BJ later became embroiled in a bitter legal battle in the Ulster High Court. The 'Clones Cyclone' lost the case, and it cost him a cataclysmic cache of hard, and hard-earned, cash.

Sure, these days, Barry has bounced back, and literally done the double, echoing with Carl Frampton almost exactly what BJ did with him on his way to a world title win over Eusebio Pedroza on that magical night at the Queen's Park Rangers' arena in London back in 1985.

But it would still warm the cockles of my heart – and I'm sure many thousands of others – if both men were to meet and have one final handshake because of what they shared in those glory days in the run-up to Barry's world title. There is one indisputable truth about that Eastwood/McGuigan/Shaw triumvirate. Their triumph, indeed their heroism, was hewn not just out of sporting sacrifice and prowess. They also sculpted a huge healing process for Ulster society as a whole.

Back in those days of that trio's sheer bravado and brio, our society was being blown apart at the seams by the terrorists. And those three men – packing out the Ulster Hall time after time, then the King's Hall – with hard men, Belfast hard chaws from the Shankill and the Falls and every other nook and cranny of the city, helped, in no small measure, to keep the fabric of our society from falling apart altogether.

I had moved on from reporting boxing by the time Barry fought, and won, against Pedroza in London. I was there all the same: as a fan not just of Barry, but of Barney, and of the late Eddie Shaw, too. I'd my mitts full covering rugby and boxing, and in the summer reporting cricket and athletics. But then I went for the high jump. I was offered, and accepted, the job of sports editor of the daily's sister paper in those days, the *Sunday News*. The Sunday paper is, sadly, now defunct. But that happened after my tenure with it: first as sports editor and later as editor. So it wasn't me wot done it, Guv ...

Still, while I said it was a 24/7 job reporting sport for those two papers back in Belfast, what happened next was not only a whole new ball game but a whole new shooting match.

And shooting was only one of *twelve* disciplines I went to cover, flying solo, at the Brisbane Commonwealth Games in 1982. Plus, I wasn't working for one paper: I was covering the games for two – the *News Letter*, which I had previously worked for, and the *Sunday News*, of which I was then sports editor.

The multi-deadline Brisbane brief was to cover a dozen disciplines – shooting, archery, swimming, athletics, boxing, the whole gamut – each and every day and night. Thankfully, my lifelong friend from schooldays at Annadale, Alan Moneypenny – who had managed the miracle of staging the British Athletics Championships in Northern Ireland, at the Antrim Forum complex where he was chief executive, the year before during the raw terror and trauma of the 1981 Maze jail IRA hunger strikes – had travelled to Brisbane, too, on official sporting business. He gave me a *big* hand out, knowing, as he did, that I was on the road every morning at 6.00 a.m. to cover the early-start sports spread around a myriad of venues, and often ending up not finishing getting my boxing reports filed until two the next morning.

Did I mention sports reporting being talked up as a dream job?

Aye, it was hard going. But worth it. Especially when the *Brisbane Courier* newspaper found out that I was running marathons at the time myself and sent a reporter and photographer to put a profile of me on a whole page.

The boxing squad KO'd me – with ribald banter that would have made a ringsider blush, it must be said – about that. But I still share a pint with the Big Lad, ex-Belfast Celtics and Ireland basketball player Mr Moneypenny and, unlike Ireland, where all our wars are merry and all our songs are sad, all our memories of that games in Brisbane are merry. And 'narry a one', as the Big Lad himself would say, is sad.

But there was, in fact, one sad moment at that Games.

One member of our athletics team travelled all the way down to Australia to compete in the high hurdles – and bizarrely injured himself in the warm-up for the very first heat. Months of blood-and-sweat training literally evaporating into muscle tear, if not tears, in the blistering tropical heat – after travelling every one of the tortuous 10,277 miles just to get Brisbane from Belfast in the first place.

A bonus was, of course, that he was a non-starter. So he didn't face the ignominy of finishing last. Which was exactly what happened to me on my competitive athletics debut. Mind you, I wasn't supposed to be participating in the All-Ireland athletics league club tie. I was meant, as usual, to report it.

The tie took place in the County Donegal border town of Letterkenny. A number of clubs from across the island were involved. One of them was a Belfast club, Annadale Striders, spawned from the sports department of my old school. One of the club's top officials at the time was 'Big Charlie' Johnston, also an ex-Annadale pupil. A car carrying Striders, athletes had broken down on the way from Belfast to the border. Other club members could double up on the track, but Striders were two throwers short in the field events: for discus and shotput.

'Right, McDowell,' says Charlie, 'I've just made you an honorary vice-president of this club. That qualifies you to compete. Drop your jacket on the grass,' he says, 'roll up your sleeves, we're on next. I'm tossing the shot, and you're throwing the discus.'

You didn't argue with Charlie Johnston. If I had, I'd have been swallowing the discus – or having it used as a suppository. And without anaesthetic.

Endgame: Johnston cruised the shotput event. McDowell finished last in the discus, and almost did in a disc in his back while spiralling around in the throw circle like a bruiser of a ballet dancer on speed.

A tragedy was to follow, though, which broke the hearts of all of us who knew and loved Charlie Johnston.

An IRA assassin on a motorbike shot him dead in Talbot Street, smack in the heart of Belfast city centre – 'in mistake' for his brother, who had been an officer in the reserve wing the RUC. The two brothers looked very alike. The mistaken identity murder occurred on 11 August 1981. A coroner was later to describe it as 'a most horrific, blood-chilling and sickening case'. I wrote an appreciation for the *News Letter* the next day.

I still visit the big man's grave, close to the most beautiful giant copper beech tree you'll ever lay eyes on, in Knockbreda parish churchyard, at the top of the Ormeau

Road in Belfast. And I take great pride in reminding Big Charlie that while he was gunned down by criminals, his son, David, who has also become a good friend of mine, went on to be a top cop in England. Putting criminals like those who gunned down his Da where they belong: banged up behind bars.

9

VAN MORRISON AND ME

I once worked as Van Morrison's minder.

He didn't know it then. And unless he's reading this now, I doubt he ever will.

It was during a long journalists' strike in 1979. I was working for the *News Letter* at the time. The strike, over pay and conditions, had been called by the National Union of Journalists (NUJ) across all Northern Ireland daily and Sunday newspapers. Most of the reporters and photographers in the Belfast papers, those who were members of the NUJ, walked out. The strike was to last seven weeks. We even printed our own strike newspaper. It went out in opposition to the evening newspaper, the *Belfast Telegraph*, which was still being published in skeletal form, in spite of the strike.

The strike paper was called the *Belfast Times*, to clash and compete with the 'BT' of the *Telegraph* title. It was published on a press then owned by the Peace People, an organisation set up to counter terrorism by the heroic Mairead Corrigan and Betty Williams, who were to later win the Nobel Peace Prize. Our distribution HQ was the famous hacks' pub just round the corner from the main newspaper offices, called Benny's Bar, or, to give it the name painted above the door, the A1.

We did our own distribution, sticking bundles of papers under our arms and heading out on to the streets to sell the paper on the pavements and at the main bus and train stations. But we were only a few issues in when a page one headline we ran bounced back to bite us.

An Ulsterman had been transferred to the world-famous Harefield hospital in England for what was then a very pioneering operation – a heart transplant. He had the surgery during the day and that night the hospital issued a bulletin saying it had gone well. The next day we ran an optimistic splash headline along the lines of:

BACON AND EGGS FOR HEART OP MAN

By lunchtime, when the paper was hitting the streets, the poor punter had passed away.

Time, as they say, waits for no man. And on that occasion it certainly hadn't waited for the publication of the *Belfast Times*.

It was around this time, during the marathon strike, that, for one memorable night, I worked as a minder for Mr Morrison. My brother-in-law at the time, Trevor Hanna, was in the music business. 'Van the Man' was scheduled to do a show, with his band, at the Whitla Hall on the Queen's University campus in Belfast. Trevor knew I was boracic lint, skint, from being on the picket lines and helping produce the strike paper, which was only a token publication. It was just about managing to pay the printers, with no pay for those of us pumping out the stories and pictures.

The Morrison concert promoters needed a minder to accompany the rock star in his hired limousine from where he was staying to the university show venue, remain side-stage while Van performed, and act as escort back in the limousine after he'd finished. I was, in essence, a quasi-bouncer – if not a full-blown one.

There was handsome money for the job. But there was one strict job criterion: Van was only to be talked to if he talked to me first.

He didn't.

The whole way there in the limousine, even at the interval in the five-star performance, and the whole way back. Not one word. That suited me. Because if the notoriously publicity-shy superstar had asked me what I normally did for a living, and if I'd answered him truthfully, I'd have been bounced right out of that stretch limousine even before my arse had hit the shiny leather upholstery on the back seat.

But Van did a real-life impression of Simon and Garfunkel's 'Sound of Silence'. And I kept my lips sealed and my trap shut and was grateful to trouser the few quid for the job. Also, this is the first time I've written about it. So you're reading a kind of exclusive: for what it's worth.

A real exclusive that I dug up for the *Sunday World* about the man now titled Sir Van reportedly made him angry when he was shown a copy of the paper as he strolled into the five-star Culloden Hotel near his Holywood, County Down home for Sunday lunch.

I could well understand why.

In 2011 I got a tip-off that Van – who was married to the former Irish model Michelle Rocco, with whom he has two children – had a lover. She was a 44-year-old Texan called Gigi Lee – his former tour manager. Gigi had a little boy, who'd been born in 2009. A birth announcement had appeared online which read: 'Gigi and Van Morrison are proud to announce the birth of their first son, George Ivan Morrison III. "Little Van", born December 28, 2009 – the spitting image of his daddy.'

It was very quickly taken down. Van Morrison strenuously denied the child was his.

When she was pregnant, Gigi had, sadly, been diagnosed with cancer. Van brought her back to Northern Ireland and set her up in a secluded house in County Down, deep among 'the rolling hills' he made famous in song.

Tragically, Gigi died, having been cared for in her final days in the Belfast Hospice. She was then buried – in secret. But I got a tip-off about the 'ghost' funeral. I went to the City Council offices in Belfast, which records births, deaths and marriages. You can request and get, for a fee, copies of all three sorts of certificate, even if you're not a relative of the person named on the certificate.

I got Gigi's death certificate, which proved that she had indeed died in Northern Ireland.

We tried to get in touch with the notoriously press-shy Mr Morrison. We eventually got a statement from his solicitor.

We ran the story as the front-page splash the following Sunday. But I had held back another tragic link to the story. I'd also been told, by the ultra-reliable source who'd tipped me off about Gigi's death, that the little boy the couple allegedly had together had also died. I didn't pursue that line.

The next Sunday, though, another Sunday newspaper led its front page with the story of the young boy's death from a debilitating illness. I understand that made Van Morrison even angrier than the first story about Gigi.

Did I feel sorry for the man? Of course. You'd have to have a heart of stone not to feel for him in the circumstances. By all accounts he behaved honourably in looking after Gigi in her final days. But like many other public figures I've reported on, he is just that. A public figure. And media coverage comes with the territory. There is a public interest in the lives of the famous.

But to be fair to Van, there were no follow-up complaints from him, his lawyers or indeed any member of the public about this alleged invasion of privacy. However, the notion of privacy is a spectre which casts a long shadow over every newspaper, and every newspaper editor.

The phone-hacking scandal that sparked the closure of the *News of the World* brought the subject of privacy into even sharper focus. Of course, that whole shocking saga centred on a series of criminal acts, for which Rupert Murdoch's News International media organisation paid dearly in terms of compensating the victims of the hacking, and for which journalists ended up in the dock in a court of law. And rightly so.

In the *Sunday World*, which is, like the now defunct *News of the World*, a red top Sunday tabloid newspaper, we would never have considered or condoned phone hacking. Our many contacts who supplied us with information – at every level of society, from the political sphere, the world of entertainment and the paramilitary and criminal underworld – were so good we never needed to.

But the preciously thin line between alleged invasion of privacy and publishing a story in the public interest always had to be trodden with the taut and fraught balance of a tight-rope walker.

And the word 'balance' is crucial here. Because what may be deemed to be balanced reporting in the eye of the publisher and public may equally be deemed to be imbalanced and invasive in the eye of the individual who is the subject of the story.

But public figures – politicians, pop, rock or movie stars, celebrities – all need, and feed off, the press when it suits them. They revel in the oxygen of publicity when it's good. However, it can't all be one-way and saccharine. And when it turns sour, the cry of 'invasion of privacy' inevitably crops up.

It is the duty of the press to point out hypocrisy in public life: it's in the public interest. For example, a politician who is known for moralising about the lives of others is revealed to have been less than fastidious in their own private life. Or someone who sits on a public body, making decisions that affect us all, who is shown to have behaved in a manner that raises serious questions about their own judgement. Public figures, in other words, who try to pretend they're something they aren't.

The inevitability is that if you're in the public eye, you're going to come under scrutiny from the press. And I firmly believe that such scrutiny is in the public interest.

In the *Sunday World*, our core journalism was defined by exposing paramilitaries, drug pushers and paedophiles and supporting the peace process. We also didn't patronise our readers by indulging in lecturing or hectoring them with long-winded editorials and opinion pieces. Instead, our maxim was simple: Write the stories and let the punters – the people who buy and read our paper – make up their own minds.

Tens of thousands of them did, and they made us the biggest-selling paper in Northern Ireland. Sure, I had to joust with the then Press Complaints Commission – since replaced by the Independent Press Standards Organisation – over a litany of complaints, including alleged invasion of privacy. Nevertheless, I can count the number of complaints found against us over twenty-five years on the fingers of one hand. So we were obviously doing something right.

The Van Morrison/Gigi Lee story was one of the biggest-selling editions of that year. And the rock star didn't bounce a writ in our direction claiming invasion of privacy, either.

I had once worked as Van the Man's bouncer: and after that Gigi story, I could understand that he probably wanted to bounce my baldy head off a wall.

My 1979 strike stint as a minder, and the later sad story of Gigi, were like the sandwich slices around a period in my life when I was bounced out of my chair as editor of a Belfast newspaper, before being blacklisted by the newspaper's bosses and unceremoniously sacked. That was in 1984.

The newspaper in question – now defunct, but that had nothing to do with me! – was the old *Sunday News*. I'd been appointed sports editor and then editor of the paper after working in news and then sport for its sister daily paper, the *News Letter*. The proprietor of both was the last in line of a family who had owned the *News Letter* for decades. And he was a feisty, old school, hard-headed Belfast businessman who didn't put the papers before profit.

This dyed-in-the wool stalwart of both the Ulster Unionist Party and the Orange Order marched to only one tune: making money. He was the most charming character with a bottle of gin in him. And the most kernaptious old bowler-hatted bastard when the gin was dying in him. He'd been a captain in the Irish Guards in his younger days. And he clung on to the military rank title back in civvie street. He was Captain O.W.J. 'Bill' Henderson.

For all the seventeen years I worked for him, two 'R' words dominated our tempestuous relationship. Rows. And mutual Respect.

Indeed, long after I left his employ – after he blacklisted me for joining and leading the 1984 strike: still the only editor, I believe, in either the UK or Ireland to do so – when I got that kicking from the UVF gang at the City Hall, his was one of the first letters through my door, in his usual spidery handwriting, inquiring after my wellbeing and wishing me well.

And when I attended his funeral, his wife and daughters greeted me at the church door with a warm embrace.

But the day he sacked me, 1 June 1984, I'd just given Lindy a warm embrace … as I left her in the maternity unit of the Royal Victoria Hospital in Belfast. Overnight she'd given birth to our first son, Jamie.

I left her at six in the morning and dandered, delighted, down the Grosvenor Road on the mile walk to the city centre. I caught a bus there heading up the Ormeau Road to Galwally, where we then lived. The bus was full of Ormo Bakery workers going in to start the day shift. I knew most of them. (I later filmed in the bakery while fronting a TV documentary for BBC Northern Ireland focusing on the history of *The Road*, which was the title of the half-hour film.) When they discovered I'd just become a Da again, the friendly banter flew.

So I got home. I was running marathons at the time. I pulled on the training gear, and headed out for a run across nearby Belvoir Forest Park and along the towpath on the banks of the River Lagan.

I was heading back up my own street with the usual bubble of sweat on the then balding, if not totally baldy, head, and I saw the postman standing at the gate of the house. I knew him. And, instinctively, I knew what was coming.

The sack.

'McDowell,' says he, 'I've got a recorded delivery

letter here for you. I need you to sign for it.' He produced a pen. I signed.

I opened it in front of him. It was my P45, formally informing me of the termination of my employment with Century Newspapers.

He asked me what it was. I told him.

'Ah well,' says he, slapping me on the shoulder, 'you're a fit enough bugger. You can always get a job as a postman.'

And with that, he was off up the street, whistling.

Me, I was left whistling into the wind. Wife in the hospital with our newborn son. Me unceremoniously sacked as editor of the *Sunday News*.

At the time, NUJ members in both the *News Letter* and the *Sunday News* had gone on strike (again) in a row over pay. What had caused Captain Henderson to give me my marching orders was that despite being regarded as management, and therefore not expected to side with the workers during industrial action, I could not face the thought of crossing a picket line past hard-working colleagues and friends. So I joined them.

The strike lasted a mammoth eleven weeks, leaving me skint and faced with signing on the dole.

But, as usual, I fought Captain Bill one last time. I used employment law and precedent to force him and his board to pay me severance pay. A number of other strikers had also been blacklisted and barred from the *News Letter/Sunday News* premises. Three of us decided to set up a freelance reporting agency in Belfast. We called it the Ulster Press Agency. The UPA for short. There was myself, Joe Oliver, and Brian 'Barney' Rowan.

For over eleven years – during which time Barney went on to become the security correspondent for BBC News NI – we worked hard, and long. But just as on the rugby paddock, we never looked back, and we never stepped back. We took the advice of another great Belfast freelance to heart. His name was Denis O'Hara. And right at the start he told us: 'Every half-crown counts. Never turn down any job any newspaper asks you to do. Because if you turn them down once, they won't come back ... ever.'

We never did. We worked round the clock, for both Irish and British national newspapers, and publications from Australia to America. We had to. It was the only way we had to put bread on the table and keep the roof over the heads of our families.

It was a not infrequent occurrence for any of the three of us to work a day shift for the *Irish Press* when someone was off on leave from their Belfast bureau, go in and work from teatime to midnight on a sub-editing shift on the *Irish News* back bench in Belfast, and then head for Broadcasting House, BBC NI's HQ in the city's Ormeau Avenue, and do the graveyard shift, covering any news breaking overnight – usually terror-related – until 8.00 a.m. the next day.

And then trying to grab some sleep before starting all over again.

As for the newborn babe, Jamie, he spent the first three months of his life strapped to my chest in a baby pouch on picket lines .... and sleeping on the counter of Benny's Bar while we held strike meetings there.

That eleven-year sojourn at the Ulster Press Agency was hard work, and often very diverse work. I even managed to double for a year as the tutor-in-charge of the journalism course at the Belfast College of Business Studies, while still putting in the shifts at the UPA.

But I almost got the sack from the agency from Joe's wife, Marie, who did our admin.

Marie, a feisty lady you didn't mess with, came in one day and asked me what were the strange tiny black flecks sticking to the inside of the glass coffee pot we used in the office.

Without thinking, and without looking up from the typewriter, I told her: 'Ach, that was me, Marie. I boiled water in it and used it to shave in this morning.'

You could have heard the shriek from our second-floor office in Belfast's Donegall Street all the way to the hills of Donegal.

That was another 'bouncer' moment.

I just managed to get out the office door before the coffee pot bounced off the wall behind me ... inches behind my fleeing bonce.

As well as covering the big news stories of the day and the ongoing stories of the conflict, during those eleven years of the UPA we also reported on politics. Or what passed for politics in Northern Ireland. This was the era of direct rule, and the closest our warring politicians came to face-to-face political debate was in the debating chamber of Belfast City Council.

Or as I came to think of it, the Bear Pit.

I reported on Belfast City Council business every day: from sub-committee meetings to full council meetings to the constant bickering and battles that erupted in what sometimes resembled the Colosseum in Rome.

Except the lions wouldn't have stood a chance with these 'coorse Christians' of councillors when they bared their teeth, screamed abuse, set off rape alarms to disrupt proceedings and even resorted to fisticuffs.

I wrote about some of their more extreme foibles and faction fighting in a weekly *Irish News* column. I had satirically dubbed the City Hall 'the Dome of Delight'. And my column, supposedly addressed as a missive to the secretary of state of the day (there were to be several during the years the column ran) was called simply: *Letter from the Dome of Delight*.

Some of the awful antics I witnessed and recorded are chronicled in the next chapter. Meanwhile, the Ulster Press Agency was to prove my springboard into once again being appointed as a newspaper editor.

In this case, northern editor of the *Sunday World*.

10

THE DOME OF DELIGHT

Built of Portland stone with the towers in each of its four corners topped, like the great dome in its centre, with copper that has aged to green, Belfast City Hall is truly one of the great architectural jewels of the city. It first opened its doors in August 1906. That date is as ingrained in me as the marble embedded in the City Hall's walls and floors. Because in 2006, BBC NI asked me to present an hour-long documentary marking the centenary of 'the Hall'.

As a Belfastman, I was honoured to do so. Although the good old Beeb didn't pay me as much as it cost to build the place. The cost of the construction work, around £370,000, was borne by the old Belfast Corporation – which later became Belfast City Council. This money is said to have come from the corporation's gas profits.

There certainly was plenty of gas expended during the years in the 1980s when I covered the council's heated meetings and often explosive debates in the 'Dome of Delight'. For reporting some of the shenanigans that went on inside the City Council chamber, and on the marbled floors of the hall itself, gave me, and the readers, more than a few laughs.

Journalists who reported the City Hall on a daily basis were known as 'working the Marble': in other words, stalking the marble floors in search of stories, many of which were readily supplied by councillors eager to either promote their own agenda, or themselves, or to have a go at opposition political parties and/or politicians.

When my colleagues Joe Oliver and Barney Rowan and I set up and ran the UPA, it was a big part of my job in the agency to cover the Marble every day. It was a rich source of stories in those days.

City Hall was nothing if not a bear pit of politics: Sinn Féin were on the rise politically at the time; the influence and representation of the main moderate unionist and nationalist parties, the Ulster Unionist Party (UUP) and the Social and Democratic Labour Party (SDLP), were waning; and Ian Paisley's Democratic Unionist Party (DUP) was rocketing on the coat-tails of 'the Big Man'. Plus, the middle-of-the-road Alliance Party was gaining ground, and there was a phalanx of splinter and small party councillors, as well as independents, vying for power, and press coverage, in the corridors of the Dome.

The 'Dome of Delight' nickname pricked the pride of more than the esteemed city fathers, aldermen and councillors. City Hall officials got a fair bit of stick in the column, too. There was one in particular whose brief included ensuring that the rubbish was collected from the streets every week. He had a particularly exalted title, and he *did not* like being called the Chief Binman of Belfast in my *Irish News* column.

In the chamber itself, the political exchanges were ragged and rough. There was verbal abuse, there were walkouts and there were occasional fist fights – one even taking place behind the Lord Mayor's chair on one infamous night.

At times, when Stormont was prorogued, or the power-sharing arrangements fell apart, Belfast City Council was left as the fulcrum and main stage for political debate in the province. Meetings themselves were often vicious, with speakers continually shouted down and rape alarms let off to drown out rival councillors' speeches.

But delightful flashes of pure farce also shone through.

Like the time then Lord Mayor Alderman Tommy Patton, a rough, tough ex-shipyard worker, was in his chair during a debate on redecorating the inside of the elegant domes. Tommy had had a few in the Lord Mayor's parlour before the monthly meeting, as was the custom. But he'd fallen asleep on the job. Then suddenly he sat bolt upright in the chair, took immediate stock of what had happened, and interrupted the debate by declaring: 'Aldermen and Councillors, I'm cutting this debate short now and I'm telling you, as Lord Mayor, that what this City Hall needs is a good coat of Durex.' Not Dulux. Durex.

Or the time there was a proposal to put gondolas in the big duck pond smack-dab in the middle of Tommy's council ward in the predominantly Protestant and unionist east Belfast. The bold Tommy was having none of it. He told the assembled city fathers: 'Them things will only outbreed all the local ducks.'

Frank 'Pootsie' Millar, a former street-fighter, was from Sailortown in Belfast, the home of many of the city's hard chaws.

The long-serving Alderman Hugh 'Wee Shuey' Smyth had become Lord Mayor in 1994, the same year as the big and most significant IRA and Combined Loyalist Military Command (covering the main loyalist paramilitary organisations) ceasefires were announced. To his credit, although he was a member of the Progressive Unionist Party (PUP – the political wing of the UVF, just as Sinn Féin is the political wing of the Provos), Hugh, who was also known as the unofficial Lord Mayor of the fiercely loyalist Shankill Road, even before the First Citizen of Belfast chain of office was officially conferred upon him, was one of the first loyalist/unionist politicians to welcome the Provo announcement.

DUP leader Ian Paisley, for instance, did not, and was outright in his condemnation of and opposition to it.

Traditionally, each new Lord Mayor has an inauguration dinner/ball, and it was, and still is, polite custom and practice to invite councillors of other parties to it. Selected members of the press, especially those covering the Marble, are also among the guests. I knew Hugh well. We had a good working relationship, and I know he personally abhorred what was to happen to me later in the UVF attack outside the City Hall. However, he'd invited Pootsie to his inaugural dinner, and he sat Alderman Millar beside me at table, with the instruction: 'McDowell, keep an eye on him. You and I both know he can be a handful when he gets a few half 'uns of Bushmills whiskey into him.'

Indeed.

Now Lord Mayor Shuey was a good oul' chanter. He wasn't exactly Charles Aznavour or Frank Sinatra, but he could sing. And one of his favourite songs was a eulogy to his home town of Belfast, with its reference to the Black Mountain towering over the west of the city and the Shankill, in particular.

Hugh had engaged a wee three-piece combo for the night. They were very well known in Ulster. And among their gentle repertoire they played some soft 'Irish' songs. But the aforesaid Frank Millar had never heard of them: or, at least, when he got the aforementioned half 'uns of Bushmills into him, he forgot he ever had.

Hugh eventually got up on the stage with the three musicians, and sang his favourite song – which brought a standing ovation, seeing as half the population of the Shankill Road were among the guests packed into the Great Banqueting Hall.

But suddenly, as Hugh was coming down the steps from the stage, and before I could get a grip of him, Pootsie was out of his chair and heading straight for Hugh. He met him, head-to-head, at the bottom of the stage steps and started guldering: 'Hugh Smyth, you're a friggin' disgrace, and you've brought friggin' disgrace on this City Hall.'

Although Frank was an ex-shipyard worker, too, the only 'f' word he ever used was that quoted above: but there was often enough venom in it to suffice for the other 'f' expletive.

Hugh tried to calm him down, as I hung on to Pootsie's coat-tails.

He asked the apoplectic Frank what he had done wrong, to which Alderman Millar replied: 'You're the first unionist, never mind the first Lord Mayor, to have brought an Irish ceilidh band into the City Hall in almost a hundred years of its history.'

And putting his hand on Frank's shoulder – which also possibly stopped him falling over, considering the amount of liquid anaesthetic Frank had consumed – the implacable Lord Mayor replied: 'Frankie, that's no ceilidh band. They're Barnbrack!'

The band was a well-known folk/pop music outfit.

Frank Pootsie Millar was, for once, silenced, and retreated, at somewhat of a kilter it must be said, back to his appointed seat at Shuey Smyth's Lord Mayor's dinner.

The Lord Mayor's once-a-year black-tie balls often sparked controversy – for one reason or another. But a reference to them, albeit in an oblique, jokey way, almost cost one Lord Mayor's Sergeant-at-Mace his job.

The main role of the Sergeant-at-Mace, all decked out in ceremonial uniform topped off by a top hat, was to accompany the First Citizen on all official functions – such as royal visits to the City Hall – and to be in attendance when meeting and greeting other distinguished visitors. He also accompanied the Lord Mayor in the procession into monthly council meetings, bearing the First Citizen's Mace: just like the Speaker's Mace in the Westminster House of Commons.

However, another part of the mace-bearer's duties in the old days was to conduct tours of the Dome for foreign visitors and dignitaries.

Now this incident happened during the darkest days of the Troubles and everyone needed a laugh. But not everyone appreciated it.

The Sergeant-at-Mace at the time was an extremely colourful character called Dermot McGarry. Now, Dermot liked what was called in Belfast parlance 'a wee swallie' – a drink. He was also overtly camp: and this in the epoch in Belfast before it was deemed appropriate for a gay man to come out.

So Dermot, or 'D' as he liked to be called, had a few enemies among the homophobic brigade in the City Hall, especially some Bible-thumping councillors from the DUP, whose leader, Ian Paisley, cruelly castigated gay people as sodomites. Indeed, some within the DUP, especially members of the Free Presbyterian Church, which the Big Man founded, still do.

One day Dermot was guiding a gaggle of VIP tourists from the USA around the Dome, pointing out, sometimes in his own flippant fashion, the artefacts of the beautiful building, donated by wealthy benefactors.

But then he came to the Great Banqueting Hall.

He pointed out that in spite of Belfast being blitzed by the Nazis during the Second World War, the City Hall had largely escaped intact, except for the east wing, where the visitors were now standing. Dermot explained that the damage had, of course, since been repaired and the wing brought back to its original excellence. Dermot added: 'And this, ladies and gentlemen, is the Great Banqueting Hall where, every year, the Lord Mayor holds his balls.'

Cheeky enough.

But he went on: 'And you know, ladies and gentlemen, every year the Lord Mayor's balls just get bigger and bigger …'

Now the Yanks are not renowned for their appreciation of sardonic humour. But this raised a laugh from all of the assembled group – except one.

For what Dermot did not know was that she was a Sister of Mercy over from the States, dressed not in her habit, but in civvies, as was her order's custom when sisters were travelling in public. And this nun didn't appreciate the innuendo. She was not amused. She reported the matter upstairs.

Dermot faced a disciplinary panel. And he saved his job, and himself from being sacked, by the moleskin of his shiny top hat: not by falling on his sword, but falling on his mace, and promising he would stop 'taking the P', as he called it, when taking tourists around in future.

Dermot, a smashing man, was later to end up being busted down the ranks, being ordered to swap his Lord Mayor's mace for a brush and relegated to sweeper-upper in the council's St George's Market, just 500 metres down the street from his beloved City Hall. That could have broken another person, especially one with Dermot's length of service and esteemed position as Sergeant-at-Mace. But D, typically, dusted himself down, and literally brushed himself up … and if not entirely starting all over again, just got on with it.

Before then, Dermot had had other 'brushes' with the City Hall hierarchy. Like the time a big gruff, bluff ex-Palestinian policeman called Dickson Gilmore became

Lord Mayor. He was known as Dixie, both inside and outside the Dome. And he'd a bald head like a dome.

He and Dermot once had a row (one of a few) in the Lord Mayor's parlour, just minutes before a council meeting was due to start. It was in front of almost all fifty-two members of the council, who were also gathered in the parlour, as was the norm, before parading into the debating chamber behind the Lord Mayor.

As Dermot was carrying the mace into the chamber, directly behind First Citizen Gilmore, he started whistling that great American Confederacy anthem, 'I wish I was in Dixie ...'

He was lucky to escape the sack then, too.

One final vignette regarding Dermot – now sadly passed on and much missed in the Dome, in St George's Market, and in the bars of Belfast he often frequented.

When he was about to be stood down as Sergeant-at-Mace by vengeful City Hall bosses (some of whom had wanted him sacked for a long time), a major Belfast daily newspaper decided to run a campaign in support. Now, remember that Paisley and his Free Presbyterian ilk referred to gay people as sodomites.

Well, the newspaper decided to call its campaign, 'Save Our Dermot'. Until, that is, one of their eagle-eyed staff pointed out that the shortened version of that was SOD. The ultimately futile but well-meaning campaign went ahead. But under another title.

The quaintly monikered Herbie Ditty was Lord Mayor of Belfast in 1992. He made a number of faux pas – Herbie would have called them fox paws – in his time in office.

Hanging outside the Mayor's parlour is a famous portrait of the 36th Ulster Division going over the top of the trenches at the Battle of the Somme in 1916. A group of German industrialists and VIPs, brought to Northern Ireland to try to attract inward investment and create jobs during the nadir of the Troubles, were being chaperoned round the Dome by an official guide. Lord Mayor Ditty happened to come out of his parlour just as the German visitors were being shown the painting of the Somme. He obviously didn't know who they were, and even if he had, Herbie would still have put both feet in his mouth.

In any case, he interrupted the official guide and butted in to tell the assembled visitors: 'See that, that's when our boys were about to put the cold steel into the Hun.'

Without another word, Belfast's First Citizen walked away, leaving the official tour guide ashen-faced and wordless. As the soccer commentators on TV say: 'There's no comeback from that.'

Another of Herbie's howlers was when his opposite number down South, the then Lord Mayor of Dublin, Gay Mitchell, paid what was meant to be a courtesy visit to Belfast. Initially, Herbie, a dyed-in-the-wool old-time unionist, refused to even meet and greet his Dublin counterpart, whom he referred to contemptuously as 'a foreign visitor'. But there was a bit of leaning from the Northern Ireland Office, who were ultra-anxious to keep all lines open to the Dublin government at the time.

Herbie did meet Gay Mitchell at the Dome. But he didn't exactly greet him. Instead, he informed him that 'furners' (foreigners) weren't welcome 'up here'.

And then, when Lord Mayor Mitchell presented Lord Mayor Ditty with a miniature bronze replica of the iconic Molly Malone statue that stands close to the bottom of Dublin's Grafton Street, Herbie handed Gay ... a tea towel, out of the City Hall's souvenir shop.

I later found out from my Dublin Council sources that the specially commissioned and cast Molly Malone statuette had cost around 1,800 punts (Irish pounds in those days, before the euro). The (albeit linen) tea towel bearing an imprint of the Dome itself had cost a couple of quid.

When I wrote that story and it appeared in print, Herbie was furious. That story of a demeaning snub to the Lord Mayor of Dublin, among many others I wrote about him, led Herbie to try to snub me in a *big* way – by banning me from the Marble and trying to prevent me doing my job as a journalist.

Needless to say, I paid no heed whatsoever to Mayor Ditty and his ban.

11

THE BEGINNING OF THE WORLD

I went from reporting the Dome of Delight daily, to another kind of domed – and almost doomed – building in Belfast. It was the Belfast office of the *Sunday World*.

It was perched high above a round, red-brick tower atop an old Victorian office block in Belfast's High Street: and almost right next door to the ultra-modern concrete block of office suites which at that time housed the HQ of the Policing Board for Northern Ireland .

Provo bombers targeted that edifice on a number of occasions. And the blasts caused so much collateral damage to surrounding properties, the saga was to work its way, almost inevitably, into the black humour lexicon of Belfast street 'sleggin' – or, put more politely, slagging off.

The reason was that the nearby Albert Clock, a grey stone pillar crowned by four faces on each side, had been erected as a memorial to Queen Victoria's consort, Prince Albert. But it was often buffeted, badly, by the blasts from the car bombs planted outside the Policing Board HQ, less than 100 metres away.

Thus, when a Belfast punter wanted to insult someone – like myself – who had less than aquiline features, he, or indeed she, would jibe: 'See yer man, he's got a face that's been hit more times than the Albert Clock.' Or, indeed: 'See yer wumman, she's got a face …'

In that respect, when it came to slinging insults, Belfast was anything but a sexist citadel. Both sexes got it with both barrels when the opportunity, or excuse, arose. And it's still the same now.

However, those bomb runs on the Policing Board headquarters often shook, but never shifted, the *Sunday World* office, or its staff. Often, staff were evacuated. But they were never directly targeted as a group.

Jim Campbell, the veteran journalist who set up the *Sunday World* Northern bureau and became its first northern editor, had been singled out. He was shot on his own doorstep and critically injured by the UVF. But he survived, bravely fought back, and returned to run the bureau again.

Both he and reporter Martin O'Hagan received serious individual threats against them. But the *Sunday World* staff had never been targeted collectively. That changed the day a bomb was carried up into the minaret-style tower that served as their office on the fourth floor of the Victorian-era building.

There was a creaky old elevator with folding concertina doors – dubbed 'the Cage', and not without reason – which ran, sometimes temperamentally, to the third floor. To reach the *Sunday World* garret on the fourth floor, Sherpa Tensing should have been on hand to climb up the narrow Everest-climb staircase, and then shimmy along the skinny corridor into the *Sunday World* bivouac at the summit.

Us UPA hacks knew that Himalayan-style hike by heart. At the time, we were filing about half a dozen stories a week – outside the rest of our freelance markings and jobs – to the *Sunday World*. And as those were the days of typewriters and hard copy knocked out on paper sheets, these had to be hand-delivered to the *Sunday World* Belfast bureau. So we were in and out of there frequently every week, and often went for a pint with the *Sunday World* staff.

It was a difficult place to get into. But if a bomb was ever placed in the snakes and ladders-style edifice, it would be even harder to get out.

And that's how it proved in October 1992, after loyalist paramilitary bogeymen had scouted out the building. They ferried in a potentially lethal firebomb – canisters of petrol strapped each side of a highly explosive device – and planted it in the aforementioned skinny corridor leading to, and right outside, the *Sunday World* garret office.

There was no fire escape at the front of the building, high above High Street below. There was no emergency exit at the back of the bureau.

There was only one way out when the alarm was raised: stepping over the primed bomb, single file, one by one, in the cramped corridor – and hoping that the bomb didn't detonate and turn the tower-like office, and all of the decent people in it, into a towering inferno.

The *Sunday World* folk got out. The bomb was defused by the Army's bomb disposal unit.

Jim Campbell had already been the victim of a UVF gun gang, and Martin O'Hagan was under increasing threat from the Loyalist Volunteer Force (LVF) – a threat that was, ultimately, to prove lethal. So decisions were made that saw both men leave the Belfast bureau and work from other sites.

That left a void in the Belfast office. Some staffers at the time thought the Northern bureau might be closed. There was also the threat that, if that happened, it would show that terror organisations had the power not only to censor the press, through the threat of the bomb and the bullet, but that they had the muscle to muzzle the sections of the press who were exposing them for what they were: sectarian killers and gangsters. To use the phrase Jim Campbell himself coined about the *Sunday World*, 'Telling It Like It Is.'

Representations were made to Dublin. The UPA were approached to marry and merge into the *Sunday World* operation in the North, moving into the office, still in High Street, to help steer the paper and team up with the extremely courageous and brave staff to tunnel our way through the turbulent times.

We did.

But the UPA, because of our own commitments built up over by now more than a dozen years as a national and international news agency, couldn't continue to straddle two horses at the one time. Plus, it was agreed between the various parties involved at the paper's Dublin HQ and elsewhere that a new northern editor of the paper should be appointed. I had been acting in that shadow capacity, anyway, dealing with the legal and other administrative functions of the Belfast bureau.

I applied for, and got, the job.

That started a quarter-century of being a very proud and prime part of the *Sunday World*, with its roll of honour of brilliant editorial, advertising, legal and promotional professionals spanning both Dublin and Belfast. A newspaper which, like everyone on it, fought the good fight: confronting terrorism, and terrorists, on our own doorstep for over forty years.

And the *Sunday World*, the People's Paper, is doing it still ... in spite of everything.

12
KING RAT

My new job with the *Sunday World* led, almost immediately, to a head-to-head meeting with one of the most cold, calculating, cruel and callous killers of the Troubles.

Billy 'King Rat' Wright.

Wright was a psychopath who used and abused the sectarian hatred bubbling through the veins of Ulster society to satisfy his own bloodlust. He originally rose to the rank of Commander in the UVF in the killing fields of mid-Ulster, where both republican (particularly the Provos) and loyalist terrorists were waging a vicious tit-for-tat killing campaign.

Based in the Lurgan and Portadown areas, he was regarded, even by the UVF, as a blood-crazed and out of control madman. On one notorious occasion he ordered his henchmen to pump bullets into a mobile shop in the Drumbeg estate in Craigavon. Three people in the mobile shop were killed: Brian Frizzell, who was 29, and two young girls, Eileen Duffy (19) and Katrina Rennie (16). All three were Catholics.

The UVF kicked him out – not so much concerned about Wright's Catholic victims, more worried that he was now outside their control – using the quaint militaristic sanction of court-martial. They even passed a death sentence on him, ordering him to get out of the country – or face the consequences.

But Wright faced them down. And he even formed a more ruthless killing machine, a terrorist splinter squad called the Loyalist Volunteer Force (LVF). It was this gang of drug dealers and sectarian killers who were later to shoot dead in cold blood, in front of his wife, our *Sunday World* colleague and friend, Martin O'Hagan.

However, it was while Wright was still in the UVF that he served a death sentence on everyone in the *Sunday World*: reporters, photographers, sub-editors, advertising staff, the whole gamut ... right the way through to van drivers who delivered the paper and newsagents who put it on the stands and sold it.

I know all about that threat.

Wright delivered it to me face to face, flanked by his main enforcer, Mark 'Swinger' Fulton.

We were publishing damning indictments of Wright and his cadre of killers in County Armagh. Father-of-three Martin O'Hagan, who was born and lived in the town of Lurgan, was spearheading the coverage. Wright wanted him, and the rest of us, gagged. I was told that it was 'in our interests' that I, the northern editor of the paper, should attend a meeting in an office above Woodvale post office, at the top of the Shankill Road.

At the time, there were certain people in the ranks of the UVF political party, the Progressive Unionist Party (PUP), who did talk to the *Sunday World*. Maybe at times it wasn't friendly talk, but the late David Ervine, later to become a city councillor and member of the Northern Ireland Assembly, was prime among them. Indeed, he was later to write a weekly column for the paper, and invoke the wrath of the hard men in the UVF for doing so.

However, I went to that Woodvale meeting thinking it was to be at a pseudo-political level. Instead, walking into the room, I got the psycho, Wright, right in my face. He sat among a group of men, some known to me, some not. Neither David Ervine, nor Hugh Smyth, another PUP man who later became Lord Mayor of Belfast, and who also talked to us, was there.

The preliminaries were short and to the point.

Wright took over. Swinger Fulton was so called because of his long, gorilla-like swinging arms. He just sat and stared at me.

King Rat impassively delivered his blanket death threat. Wright was a tall man, about six feet, with close-cropped hair and a then-fashionable goatee beard. He had the weird habit of always talking about himself in the third person – 'Billy Wright demands this, Billy Wright orders that, Billy Wright will do this'.

He wanted a certain story, which had been published the previous Sunday, retracted, corrected – according to his version – and no more stories to be written about him, especially by Martin O'Hagan.

No chance. He was told that.

He and Swinger seemed set to go to war there and then: on me. But they were advised that UVF HQ would have a final say in what would happen.

A third party, shadowing the meeting for the UVF hierarchy based at their HQ, known as 'the Eagle', further down the Shankill Road, intervened. He said there would be a twenty-four-hour deadline for me to discuss the situation with my colleagues and *Sunday World* bosses and to respond. I was to go to the Eagle at the same time next day to give mine, and the *Sunday World*'s, reply to the Wright ultimatum.

The *Sunday World* staff were gathered and waiting for me to return. I had phoned the office when I got out of the meeting, and said we were in 'soapy bubble' … again.

I told them the score.

Like me, they were adamant: we weren't bending the knee to Wright or the UVF. Just as we wouldn't allow any other of the sectarian slaughter merchants – the Provos, the INLA, the UDA, whoever – to point a gun at us and try to censor us, either. That's the message I was mandated to take back up the Shankill to UVF headquarters the next day.

It's wrong to say that I didn't sleep that night; I did.

That's one fighting facet that always surfaced among the *Sunday World* staff. When we were in peril – and we were, many times – we'd sink a few pints, and then get up and do our jobs.

The next day, I went up the Shankill and into the Eagle. Wright was waiting inside. You could bite the tension. But this time, it was clear that King Rat was not going to be let loose to hold another kangaroo court, with me in his dock.

Instead, we were both told we were going to an office down a narrow, dark corridor leading to a badly lit back room. I didn't fear the worst. The UVF weren't stupid. They knew that all our *Sunday World* staff knew exactly where I was going, and why I was there. They knew that if I wasn't back with them within an hour, the cops were to be called. The UVF weren't going to 'romper' (give me a beating) or shoot me, being aware of the consequences.

But as I was walking down that narrow corridor, I got a get out of jail card: again, played straight into my face.

Wright was walking in front of me.

You had to squeeze past another person coming towards you.

A man squeezed past Billy Wright. But he stopped, momentarily, in front of me. And nodding back at Wright, and clearly within King Rat's earshot, he said: 'McDowell, what are you doing with that mad bastard?'

The marker had been put down. By the aforesaid David Ervine. I knew then how the wind was blowing in that organisation for Wright: he was on the way out.

And I knew, too, that the UVF didn't want, at that particular time anyway, the death of any journalist, or journalists, coming to rest on their doorstep … especially as a consequence of any Billy Wright death threat.

Now, that wasn't because of compassion for the *Sunday World* staff among the UVF leadership. It was because of the heat, at that stage, such actions would bring on the racketeering and other gangster activities of the organisation.

Wright's threat was withdrawn.

Soon afterwards, Wright himself was stood down and expelled from the UVF. The final straw for the UVF's bosses in Belfast had been the murder of an innocent Catholic taxi driver, Michael McGoldrick, whose bullet-ridden body was found in his car near Lurgan.

Sickeningly, the man who would later be convicted of the murder, Clifford McKeown, told the court that the killing had been a 'birthday present' for Wright.

Cast out of one loyalist terror grouping, Wright now defiantly formed the splinter terror gang the LVF, and he took a posse of defectors from the UVF in mid-Ulster with him. His gruesome reign of fear continued. And it was around this time in 1996 that Wright passed a personal death sentence on *Sunday World* reporter Martin O'Hagan.

Wright ordered that if he himself was ever shot dead, Martin was to be murdered. Such was the power he held over his henchmen, they were prepared to carry out his orders ... even from beyond the grave.

A year later, Wright himself was murdered, shot dead by guns smuggled into Ulster's supposedly high-security Maze jail. It may have taken four years, but we would ultimately sadly discover that Wright's ghastly and ghostly death threat on Martin was to haunt our colleague, and all of us, from the grave.

13
STOP THE KILLING

Something big – even bigger than what was already being attempted – had to be done to try to stop the slaughter on the streets.

It was 1993. The run-up to Christmas. Eighty-eight people were murdered that year; sixty-two of those victims were civilians. Rivers of blood were still running into the drains. But rivers of feet were also letting it be known that the ordinary people, too often bearing the brunt of the bloodshed, had had enough.

Every time there was an atrocity, there would be a rally outside Belfast City Hall, and outside the Guildhall in Derry, and outside town halls throughout the province. Thousands upon thousands of people would turn up, their footfall sounding, in the reverent silence, like the flow of many rivers flooding through the city-centre streets. There would be appeals for peace from politicians and others, particularly the trade union people.

The Irish Congress of Trade Unions (ICTU) acted as the totem-pole on many occasions, calling for and organising the rallies. One of their bosses in Belfast was, until his retirement, Tom Gillen. We were having a pint one day, Tom and I, when we came up with a plan. All the rallies around the country were hugely significant and crucially important, but they were disparate: spread around the cities and towns. Tom and I talked about how we could get one single, solid, massive bloc of voices, representing all the people, to put the message across, once and for all, to the terrorists – to all of the terror gangs – that the killing must stop.

That became the slogan. Simple and direct.

STOP THE KILLING

But how could we convey that message to the mass of people out there? And how could we get one massive, unified response, so huge and so heartfelt and so headline-hitting that it simply could not be ignored?

Having a pint with us that day was a big-hearted Belfast man by the name of Paul McLaughlin. Paul originally comes from up the Whiterock, in the west of the city. He likes to banter that that's where Gerry Adams comes from, too – and that he has something in common with the Sinn Féin supremo: 'In spite of where we both come from, neither of us has ever been in the IRA,' he is wont to quip over a pint of stout.

The four quare fellas tossing this big idea around that day were Paul, Frank Johnston, both then PR executives with British Telecom (BT) in Northern Ireland, Tom Gillen and myself. The four of us decided to try to marry that STOP THE KILLING maxim into the ICTU peace rallies protocol, and have it become the main theme. ICTU big-hitters like Frank Bunting, another friend, helped realise that.

And also, crucially, we would need the help of more of the press to do so. In particular, we needed the backing of the two daily morning newspapers, which reflected the views of, and were read by, both sides of the community, unionist and nationalist.

The *Sunday World*, as a weekly paper that already boasted a cross-community readership, would campaign from a peace platform. And it would plug the STOP THE KILLING slogan on a slug under its masthead on the front page.

But in the run-up to the peace rallies, we needed both the *News Letter* and the *Irish News* to work together and plug away every day, carrying it on their front pages, too. Myself and my friend Alan Moneypenny, who was working in PR back then, called a meeting of the newspaper editors.

The then editors of both newspapers, Geoff Martin and big Tom Collins, embraced the project with both heads and hearts when we had head-to-heads with them and explained the theme. But we needed something else. And that's where BT came in, with both Paul and Frank in prime positions, because of their jobs, to deliver.

We came up with the idea of a phone-in peace poll, the first of its kind in Ireland.

A phone survey would be set up, with a special number to call. And people could ring it free of charge.

They didn't even have to say anything: folk would simply ring a special number and that would signify their support for the STOP THE KILLING campaign. That's where Frank and Paul came in. They had to sell the idea to their BT bosses at the then Churchill House HQ.

They did that – and then some.

The result? A twenty-four-hour phone line was set up – and over 160,000 folk responded and backed the peace poll. At the time it was the biggest response to a newspaper telephone survey ever recorded in the British Isles. As Frank Johnston said at the time: 'When you look at the size of Northern Ireland's population and compare it with the response, it's just incredible.'

And it was. So was its impact. Just a few days later, towards the end of November 1993, it was revealed that British government representatives were holding secret talks with the IRA. What a coincidence ...

Anyway, the drive and demand for peace eventually paid off, in a hugely symbolic way at least, less than a year later in the autumn of 1994, when both the IRA and loyalist terror gangs – the latter grouped together under the banner of the so-called Combined Loyalist Military Command – announced their big ceasefires six weeks apart.

And out of that unique phone-in poll, there was another prize, other than the eventual prize of peace, temporary as it proved to be, with the Provo bombing of London's Canary Wharf in 1996, but then cemented in again with the Good Friday Agreement two years later. The other prize was that the Americans, who were prime players in the peace process, with the likes of special envoy George Mitchell and President Clinton, recognised the joint decisions and stances adopted by Geoff Martin and Tom Collins, who flagged up the phone-in in their newspapers.

At a special presentation dinner in a hotel in Carrickfergus a few months after the significance of the telephone poll had sunk in, both editors were jointly awarded a special President's Prize for what they had courageously teamed up to do. And it was a proud moment, too, for Messrs McLaughlin, Moneypenny, Johnston, Gillen and McDowell. Since then, the last three of those have retired, allegedly, from their full-time jobs.

The first mentioned, Paul McLaughlin, eventually left his BT public relations post, but is now at the PR helm of an organisation that has done a power of good in combating one abiding legacy of the Troubles: bigotry and sectarianism. It's called the Northern Ireland Mixed Marriage Association (NIMMA). And it has led to Paul McLaughlin speaking out again, just as he did in helping to front up the STOP THE KILLING campaign. We are still friends. And at the time of writing, he points out that the latest research suggests that one in five relationships in Northern Ireland – marriages or partnerships – is mixed: Catholic and Protestant.

He said: 'Mixed marriage remains a subject that can cause division, irritation and certainly isolation – even today – and the sectarian-based society in which we live does nothing to address this. Someone has to. NIMMA continues to. Sectarianism, we are told, was yesterday's problem, if we listen to those who hold the reconciliation purse strings. These folk should visit the green and orange ghettos of Belfast and the one-denomination villages and hamlets in the Ulster countryside to get a feel for the separate living that remains the norm for most people there. They are a cold house for those who wish to marry or co-habit across that tribal divide.'

Just over a century ago, in a completely different context, W.B. Yeats wrote of a terrible beauty being born in the Easter Rising of 1916. NIMMA has staged a different kind of rising, and has created a beauty in its own right in combating the silent, and not-so-silent, evils of bigotry and sectarianism.

14

'YOU GOT ME SHOT'

Throughout the 1980s and 1990s terrorist violence was not the only scourge of Northern Ireland society. As the security forces struggled to deal with the sectarian conflict, a new breed of criminal was capitalising on the general lawlessness – and the increasing popularity of recreational drugs. Not least among these was ecstasy (E-tabs) and other party drugs, which were easy to transport and enormously profitable.

Some of the drug godfathers had paramilitary connections. Some were to fall foul of the terror chiefs. In the pages of the *Sunday World* we relentlessly exposed them all. Needless to say the backlash wasn't pleasant. And in my case that backlash was often very personal.

One Saturday, a top drug dealer walked out of the Topshop store in the pedestrian zone centre of Belfast. He spotted me walking towards him. He confronted me in the street, which was packed with Saturday afternoon shoppers. And they stopped, gaped and listened agog as drugs czar Brendan 'Speedy' Fegan pulled up the sweater he was wearing, bared his chest, pointed to two lumps on it and bare-facedly stated: 'McDowell, you got me these.'

The lumps were two slugs from a .22 pistol still lodged under the skin on his chest.

Just nights previously, he'd been shot and wounded by a gunman in a flat close to Belfast's Golden Mile. He'd been on the run. Not from the law, although for a long time he was wanted by the police, and by their Drugs Squad in particular. No, he was on the run from the Provos.

The IRA had formed a ruthless death squad, called Direct Action Against Drugs (DAAD). It was spearheaded by the one-time Provo officer commanding (OC) in the Short Strand area of east Belfast, Gerard 'Big Jock' Davison, along with his then main henchman Kevin McGuigan. It was set up ostensibly to carry out a purge of the first independent drug dealers importing E-tabs, cannabis and other so-called soft drugs into the province. DAAD was eventually to murder, in cold blood, more than a dozen drug dealers. Jock Davison and Kevin McGuigan were later to fall out: and both would die as they had lived, by the gun.

In 2015 Davison was assassinated in a rain-lashed dawn in the market area of downtown Belfast, where he was then living. A lone gunman simply walked up to him after he bought his morning newspaper, and pumped a volley of bullets into him. No one has ever been arrested for the killing. But the Provos held their own high-level investigation. That internal kangaroo court found, in his absence, Kevin McGuigan guilty. He was sentenced to death.

And, in turn, on a twilight evening in August 2015, McGuigan was also summarily executed outside his own home, in the Short Strand area of the city, just a few hundred metres from where Davison had been gunned down.

No one has ever been convicted of that very public killing, either.

But both Davison's and McGuigan's murders were put down to that fall-out between them, which ultimately proved fatal for both of those once-top Provos.

As for Fegan's very public fall-out with me, he tried to chide me that I took drugs, too. He blasted: 'You drink alcohol. That's a drug.'

I replied: 'Alcohol is legal. You know what's in a bottle. It's my choice as an adult to drink. You're peddling poison and you're peddling your poison to school kids. That's the difference.'

As people continued to gawp, he did a runner.

But he couldn't keep running from the Provos and DAAD. In his hometown of Newry, the writing was already on the wall. The graffiti read: 'Speedy Fegan – You're a dead man.'

They caught up with him on Sunday 9 May 1999. Fegan had spent much of the day in the town of Warrenpoint, on the northern shore of Carlingford Lough, in the shadow of the Mourne Mountains in County Down.

The nickname 'Speedy' was apt. He loved speed. Fast cars. Fast women. And, particularly, fast horses. He was a heavy gambler. He could afford to be. One truckload

145

of drugs he'd had to abandon outside the Sheepbridge Inn near the border town of Newry, when he realised the Drugs Squad were on his tail, had a street value of a quarter of a million quid.

But on that fateful Sunday in 1999, Fegan was to pay the heaviest price of all for his love of a bet – albeit a *big* bet – on the horses.

He owned a trotting pony himself. There's a stretch of coast road between Newry and Warrenpoint where Travellers used to meet to race their ponies and traps. Speedy decided to take them on with his own harness-racing horse. His steed wasn't up to speed with the Travellers'. He reportedly lost £10,000 punting that afternoon. But he was a swashbuckling loser.

He then did an all-or-nothing deal with one of the fittest-looking Travellers. He'd take him on in a foot race, he said, a sprint along the straightest part of road, with the winner taking all.

Speedy won.

He went to a nearby pub, The Hermitage in Newry, to celebrate. And it was while sitting on a stool at the bar that he paid with his life.

Two gunmen walked in. They were from DAAD. Fegan realised that instantly. He cried out: 'It's the Provies.'

Those were his last words.

One of the gunmen pumped a salvo of bullets into him as he tried, pathetically, to defend himself with a bar stool.

Although there was no court case, and no convictions, the two assassins were believed to be the two top men and founders of DAAD: Jock Davison and Kevin

McGuigan. They had stalked Fegan and watched him enjoying himself at the pony trotting all day. And then enjoyed themselves as they watched him dying in a pool of his own blood on a cold bar-room floor.

Fegan wasn't the first victim of their Provo-fronted killer crew. That had been Ulster's first real drugs baron: a champion ex-amateur boxer called Mickey Mooney.

Starting out as a hard-as-nails petty criminal, Mooney – later dubbed 'Moneybags' by the *Sunday World* – had seen, and noted, the explosion of disco drugs like ecstasy and cannabis, or 'blow', on the streets of Dublin, Cork and Limerick. He decided to get into that lucrative business himself. He set up his own team, which included his Sumo wrestler-sized sibling, Liam 'Fat Boy' Mooney. Their drugs business boomed. When anyone, like nightclub bouncers, tried to interfere, Mickey Mooney brought his boxing skills to bear. And if his flying fists didn't suffice, he had no hesitation in turning to the other 'f' word – firearms.

He once toured the pubs and clubs of Belfast's then bustling Golden Mile – which was making a mint after all the years of the city centre being a ghost town during the nadir of the Troubles – wearing a raincoat with the right-hand pocket cut out. Inside, he had a gun concealed in his hand: a snub-nosed Uzi sub-machine gun. And his message to the doormen was as staccato as a burst from the Israeli-made short arm. 'Don't interfere with my business,' he warned the dickie-bowed door stewards along the strip of clubs and pubs on the Golden Mile, 'and I won't interfere with *you*.'

But there were no bouncers on the door of the 18 Steps pub, in the heart of another part of downtown

Belfast, when DAAD decided it was time Moneybags went to meet his maker.

DAAD discovered that Mooney and his mob were meeting there every Friday evening. The bar, in the city's Ann Street, was a respectable pub, used by ordinary members of the public. That's why Mooney chose it: it was good cover.

But there was one fatal flaw in using that pub for drug dealers or any other underworld gangsters. It had only one way in, and one way out. That was up, or down, a narrow flight of eighteen stairs leading directly from the street below.

A DAAD assassination squad had been stalking Mooney. They set up a simple ambush. A spotter was placed in another bar in Ann Street, where he could see the door at the front of the 18 Steps. He alerted the killer when he knew the Mooney mob were up in the second-floor bar almost opposite. He then phoned the 18 Steps pub.

DAAD knew Mooney didn't use a mobile phone: at the time, mobiles were in their infancy, although they were later to become the favourite tool of drug dealers. The public phone in the 18 Steps was right at the top of the stairs, outside the door leading into the main lounge. So the DAAD stooge phoned the pub number.

Someone, maybe a barman, answered it. The caller pretended to be a criminal cohort of Mooney, and asked to talk to him.

The door of the bar swung open and the person who took the call shouted: 'Mickey, it's for you.'

The last move of any kind Moneybags made in his life was to walk onto the landing and take the phone in his hand. As he did so, his back was to the staircase. A DAAD assassin was lurking just round the entrance at the bottom. He only had to walk halfway up the 18 Steps to start shooting.

Mickey Mooney, Ulster's first-ever drugs godfather, never knew what hit him. His body crumpled like a deck of cards, the stooge who'd made the bogus phone call still on the line, listening to the ex-boxing champ breathing his last breath.

The rest of the Moneybags mob still in the pub panicked. They thought they were next, that the DAAD gunman would keep coming.

He didn't.

But there was still only one way for them to run, to escape. And that was over their crime boss's dead, or dying, body.

And they did.

15
FAT BOY

Mickey Mooney never gave me any bother. His brother, Fat Boy, did.

Until DAAD tried to dunder him in a doorstep killing at his own home. That cooled his heels, and he did a runner. But not before members of his gang plotted to burn down my house. With me, my wife, and my two young sons inside.

It was a veteran cop who tipped me off about the 'burn them alive' murder bid. He had put many drug dealers, and other criminals and terrorists, behind bars in a distinguished career in Ulster's CID. And he had a squadron of (sometimes squalid) sources in the criminal underworld. He had to have. It was, and still is, a prime part of a good detective's job: running informers, paying sources – and sometimes playing them off against each other, especially when they fall out.

Indeed, that is when the *Sunday World* got its biggest criminal scoops: when gang members fell out, sparked feuds, and started grassing on each other. That was their revenge.

Anyway, this senior detective got tipped off about the plan to firebomb my home.

My wife Lindy and I had lived in the same house for years. My daughter Faye and our two young sons Jamie and Micah grew up there. Eventually, because of the litany of terrorist and criminal threats, it began to resemble a police station. Security lights and CCTV cameras peppered the walls just under the eaves of the roof. We could, at the flick of a remote-control switch, get instant access to images on TV screens around the house, both upstairs and downstairs, if we suspected intruders, or didn't know the identity of someone at the front or back door.

The Northern Ireland Office at one stage ripped out the windows downstairs, and replaced them with bullet-resistant glass. On occasion, the police would put in a device called a Hawkeye, which provided immediate emergency response triggered by a small panic button panel that had to be carried inside the house at all times, including in the bedroom.

I was told on many occasions by police to change my movements, not to stick to a routine, and to always 'watch my back'. This was virtually impossible given that the children had to be taken to school each day, and myself and Lindy had to get to work.

Lindy was a journalist with the *Belfast Telegraph* – and no stranger, either, to panning the paramilitaries in her columns – before moving into radio and broadcasting.

At least she understood the dangers, and the safety prerequisites, imposed upon us.

However, the house we then lived in was an old dairy farmhouse, with a laneway about 75 metres long leading up to it. And there was, coincidentally, a great pub, the Four Winds Inn, just across the road from the front gate. In a way, I was the luckiest hack in the world – a pub just 100 metres from my own front door!

The house itself could not exactly be described as secure, though. After one early threat, police visited my home to give me advice on measures I should consider to make the place as safe as possible. One officer, an absolute gentleman called George Hamilton (not the one who went on to become chief constable), asked if he could take a quick look around.

'Certainly, go ahead,' I said.

He was back in about five minutes.

'What do you think?' I asked.

'Two words,' he said. 'Move house.'

There was little other housing around us when we first moved in. But then urban spread began to envelop us. We didn't mind. It was jobs for builders in Northern Ireland, an area of often chronic unemployment. And the neighbours were decent people. The whole district blossomed. And apartments went up, some quite close to us. Drugs godfathers had plenty of hard cash to splash.

This was how Fat Boy's gang came up with their grotesque plot. They planned to buy an apartment that would not overlook, but would have a good view of, our home and the lane leading up to it: the latter important so they could note when we were driving out, or, more presciently for their plan, driving in. They would plant their scouts in the apartment: not to live in it, so that few clues would be left, and the bare apartment could be quickly forensically swept after they had targeted us.

And when the time was right, in the dead of night, when they knew we were asleep in our beds, they were going to plant firebombs at our front and back doors.

As well as this, they planned to pour a trail of petrol right around the perimeter of the house, splashing the walls and doors as they silently stalked us in the dark. The firebombs would explode, the trail of petrol would ignite and engulf the house, and when we tried to get out … well, you can imagine, we'd be caught in a fireball.

Well, the veteran cop, thankfully, alerted me. And he made it his business to let the Fat Boy gang know – again, through his underworld sources – that he knew of the fireball plot.

The police, stretched at the time trying to cope with an avalanche of terrorist attacks and murders, simply didn't have the officers to try to carry out surveillance on the mob's apartment 24/7 and try to catch them in the act. And they couldn't take the chance of not being there – and the fireball inferno being sparked with us trapped inside the house.

The gang couldn't take the risk to go ahead, though, knowing that the police were on to them. Fat Boy and his firebugs aborted their potentially deadly plan.

Meanwhile the Provos, under the guise of DAAD, were still stalking Liam Mooney. Mooney, at that stage, was living in the drug dealers' haven of Carryduff, a commuter-belt suburb about six miles south of Belfast city centre. A gaggle of drugs godfathers lived there back then, some in detached homes. Fat Boy had his home fortified. He and his family didn't even live downstairs on the ground floor, in case of a bomb attack or a drive-by shooting.

The house had all the trappings of my own: bullet-resistant glass, security lights and cameras, special TV monitors inside. And the doors were specially reinforced, to stop either bullets or battering rams breaking through. In the Mooney house everything was upstairs – living room, bedrooms, kitchen, bathroom.

DAAD were wise to all of this. They had tracked Mooney and his main sidekick – Kevin 'Maxie' McAlorum – for a long time, even on the pair's frequent drugs-buying forays to Amsterdam and back. (DAAD and the police weren't the only ones on Mooney's trail. We once captured him and Maxie at Dublin airport coming off a flight from Amsterdam: they weren't pleased, to say the least.)

They knew they couldn't force their way into Fat Boy's mini-fortress. So two of them, having hijacked a workman's van, turned up on the doorstep – dressed as window-cleaners. But they weren't just carrying buckets and ladders. They were toting guns.

They rapped on the door to ask if the inhabitants' wanted their windows washed. Someone – it's still not clear who, but it's believed it was a woman – answered the door. The bogus window-cleaners barnstormed in past her.

Cries of warning rang round the house. And Mooney and one of his gang were able to flee out the back of the house, clamber over a fence – even with Mooney built like a brick shithouse – and escape over a field.

The wannabe Provo assassins panicked, and fled.

But even having escaped death by a hair's breadth, Mooney's insatiable greed became abundantly apparent. Because as he fled, he lifted a big bundle of banknotes in a bag. As he scarpered across the field, however, the bag split – and the money spread across the field like slurry.

Mind you, by the time Fat Boy eventually used his mobile and was picked up by his cronies, he was said to have smelt like manure himself. But it was his own manure, which had been deposited in the seat of his 48-inch-waist pants.

Kevin Maxie McAlorum had a son of the same name. But while the father escaped the attention of assassins, Kevin Jr didn't. Like father, like son, he was a drug dealer too.

As he left his child to school on a June morning in 2004 at Dunmurry, a commuter village halfway between Belfast and the city of Lisburn eight miles away, a gunman struck. As Kevin Jr pulled up outside Oakwood Primary School, his Audi A4 was rammed by a van. Kevin Jr died in a pool of his own blood at the school gates as children fled and parents looked on in horror.

This was a grudge killing by the INLA, ordered because they believed McAlorum had killed their leader, Gino Gallagher, six years previously. By dark coincidence, McAlorum, who had also made enemies in republican circles because of his close links with loyalist drugs dealers, was murdered the day after the funeral of Gallagher's father.

The drugs trade tended to be a family business. Another to fall victim of DAAD was one of the siblings of the original godfather, Mickey 'Moneybags' Mooney. Even as a tearaway teenager, Paul Mooney had been the victim of a punishment shooting. But then the Provos – aka DAAD – got really pissed off with him. And they carried out what was known in Belfast back-street patois as a 'six pack' – shot in the elbows, knees and feet.

He was left lying in screaming agony, with blood filling his designer sports trainers. But he survived, unlike other 'independent' drug dealers DAAD had in their gunsights. And they included some hard men in their own right – or wrong.

They included Paul 'Bull' Downey, also murdered in Newry, and Brendan 'Bap' Campbell, who survived an earlier DAAD murder bid, but then tried to exact retribution on the IRA by tossing a hand grenade at Connolly House – Sinn Féin's HQ in Andersonstown. He paid with his life when bullets were pumped into him as he walked into Plank's restaurant on Belfast's Lisburn Road, just yards away from the main police station there.

Then there was Edmund 'Big Edd' McCoy in Belfast, Christopher 'Cricky' O'Kane in County Londonderry and, finally, six years after DAAD was formed, Paul 'King Coke' Daly, gunned down in Stephen Street, close to the doors of the *Belfast Telegraph* in central Belfast, in 2001 – just three years after the signing of the Good Friday Agreement in 1998.

I took no joy in the cold-blooded killing of any of these criminals. I despised drugs dealers. But the place for them was in the dock in a court of law, being convicted, and being put where they belonged: behind bars.

They should not have been the victims of summary executions carried out by DAAD, itself a spin-off spawned by another killer gang, the Provisional IRA.

And for our part in the *Sunday World*, we weren't out merely to 'felon-set', or to set these drug godfathers up for attack. We had young families of our own growing up in this community – *our* community. We felt we had a duty to expose whoever was trying to prostitute and live off our young people by poisoning them with drugs. We felt we had a duty to protect those young people – *all* of our young people.

And, again, I had met many of these drugs dealers face to face. They were street smart; they had to be, running the drugs networks that they managed, making deals worth millions of pounds.

I often said that if they had come from a different background, rather than growing up in educationally deprived areas, many of them could well have ended up as prime business entrepreneurs. In other words, they were by no means dumb – even though they diced with death by continuing to deal in drugs with the likes of DAAD hunting them down.

16

THE KILLING OF KING COKE

We dubbed him 'King Coke': real name Paul Daly.

I was in the *Sunday World* office working on a bright, sunny Friday afternoon. Friday night in Belfast during the Troubles was always known as 'gelig-night'. And with good, or rather bad, reason. That was when the worst street riots, shootings and, particularly, bombings were apt to occur.

But by early most Friday nights, we liked to have the majority of the hard news stories going into Sunday's edition wrapped up, so that the lawyers could libel read them early on Saturday morning.

I was usually in the office around 6.00 a.m. on a Saturday, working through until the first edition came off the presses. And after that it was what we called the Doomwatch. With the first edition off the presses around seven o'clock at night, it was then the long haul until about 1.00 a.m. monitoring what was happening on the streets, in case there were any more major terrorist incidents. If so, we changed the front page and page 2 for the final editions.

But it was certainly a mayday call of doom I got on that Friday afternoon in May 2001.

'McDowell,' the caller said. 'There's been a shooting in Stephen Street, close to the *Belfast Telegraph*. There's a guy lying in the street dead. Local people say it's Paul Daly.'

It was. He was yet another murder victim of DAAD.

Daly had gone to visit relatives of his then partner, a petty criminal called Jacqueline Conroy, who ran a female shop-lifting ring. He went to get out of a courtesy car – he'd left his own vehicle in a garage for repair that morning – when the lone assassin struck. He was half in and half out of the car, and was helpless when the fatal shots rang out.

Jacqueline Conroy and Daly's young daughter watched as he died in front of their eyes.

I ran the 200 metres from the *Sunday World* office to Stephen Street, which was just off Belfast's main thoroughfare, Royal Avenue. I recognised Daly from the big, thick Timberland boots he habitually wore. He was covered by a sheet as he lay there in the street. An ignominious end to the man they called King Coke.

A former bar and nightclub bouncer, and heavily muscled bodybuilder, Daly had in the past threatened to use those boots on me because of what I'd been writing about him. That happened one winter's night in the snow. At that time, Daly had been living close to me at the Four Winds in south Belfast. The Four Winds district sits high on the fringe of the Castlereagh Hills. If snow falls anywhere in Northern Ireland in winter, it falls heavily there.

I was out pulling sleighs in the street with my two young sons. It was night-time, the street was badly lit and then suddenly, in the dark, Daly drew up beside us in his four-wheel-drive jeep: it was about the only kind of vehicle, apart from snow ploughs, that were moving in the area that night.

He stopped, wound down the window, and in front of the young kids, told me: 'McDowell, I'd like to get out of this and give you the kicking of your life, and then bury you in that f*****g snow.'

I ignored him. What else could I do?

He drove off, laughing. But the very direct threat was no laughing matter.

Daly had already asked for a meeting with me a long time before that – when he was just starting in the drugs trade. He'd seen others making big bread smuggling drugs into the pubs and clubs where he worked on the doors. He thought he'd have a piece of that action.

We nailed him in print almost as soon as he set up shop, flogging E-tabs and blow to teenagers out for the night. He sent word that he wanted to see me, and named the meeting place as the old Parliament Bar at the back of the cobblestone streets now known as Belfast's Cathedral Quarter. Ironically, the Parliament was one of Ulster's first openly gay bars, which Free Presbyterian zealots used to picket at weekends. There were no evangelical protestors there when I met Daly and one of his minders one lunchtime.

Sitting across from me at a pub table, both of the heavies told me they'd break every bone in my body if we continued to expose them. (Strangely enough, the breaking of bones, finger bones, was later to play a significant part in the life, and death, of Mr Daly: I deal with that shortly.)

I finished the pint I was drinking and walked out of the pub, having previously planted another colleague in the lounge bar to watch my back.

We continued to expose Daly. Not least, much later, when he was at the zenith of his drug-dealing powers, and he murdered a decent young man and, until his dying day, got away with it.

The lad Daly cold-bloodedly killed was Gerard McKay Jr. He was the son of an ex-British Army veteran called Gerry McKay. Like father, like son; Gerard Sr and Jr were good, law-abiding citizens. But Daly had found out that Gerard Jr drove a ready-mix concrete truck. The drugs overlord thought that would be a fool-proof method of transporting large consignments of ecstasy pills and blocks of cannabis. By this time, with Daly making big bucks out of drugs, he was also peddling cocaine, which would also need to be transported under the radar.

His plan was to wrap up the drugs in waterproof bundles – using bubble-wrap and sealed-up plastic bags – and put them in the big revolving drum on the lorry where the concrete was mixed. While cars and ordinary vans and lorries could be easily stopped and searched by police and specially trained sniffer dogs, King Coke thought police officers would never stop a ready-mix concrete lorry on a road busy with traffic and tell the driver to tip his squelchy and quick-drying load onto the tarmac.

However, Gerard McKay Jr made it clear he wanted nothing to do with Daly, or his drugs.

So Daly made it his business to get one of Gerard's 'friends' to get him access to Gerard's flat off a side-street on Belfast's Ormeau Road. He and the 'friend' arrived one night with a carry-out of Chinese food. They also had with them a one litre bottle of Evian mineral water. Daly had already laced the mineral water with eleven crushed E-tabs. The carry-out was spicy hot. Gerard reached for the bottle, and took a couple of slugs out of it. He didn't take drugs himself, so the dissolved E-tabs quickly took effect. Daly then pressed him, again, on the plot to load up the cement mixer truck with parcels of his drugs. Gerard still had enough of his wits about him to consistently refuse. So bodybuilder, ex-bouncer and bullyboy Daly grabbed him by the throat and started to throttle Gerard. The lad had to open his mouth to gasp for breath. And Daly kept pouring the drugs-laced Evian water down his throat.

The drugs killed Gerard McKay Jr.

After he passed out, it was a slow enough death. Enough time for Daly and Gerard's former 'friend' to hoover the flat to get rid of as much potentially incriminating evidence as possible.

What happened afterwards is confusing.

It was not clear then, and it is still not clear, whether the pair scarpered and got someone else to call the police anonymously from a public phone box and say there was an emergency at the flat, or whether Daly was still in the flat when the police arrived and was allowed to leave – without being questioned then or afterwards.

Certainly, one man who believed that Daly got away with murder is Gerard Jr's father, Gerry McKay.

He believed then, and still does now, that Daly was a police tout. And that not only did Daly clean up his son's death in the flat that night, but that Daly's handlers arrived, too, and also hoovered up any forensic clues and/ or evidence there may have been for the murder of his only son.

I too believe Daly was protected on that occasion because he was a tout.

Gerry McKay Sr and I became firm friends, and jointly continued to pursue Daly and his mob relentlessly. We even attended a court case where Daly walked free after being handed down a suspended sentence – after confessing to putting one of his former cronies into intensive care after almost battering him to death in Daly's own house.

In another bizarre twist, it was only eight days after King Coke's broad daylight murder that I was invited to go to Daly's home, a low-set, brown-brick bungalow in the plush Laurelvale private housing complex close to the Four Winds bar in south Belfast. The phone call came into the office on the Saturday morning after Daly was buried. It had taken a few days for the funeral to take place after his murder, given that a post mortem had to be carried out and that report then filed to the police and relevant authorities.

The surprise call – to put it mildly – came from Daly's partner, Jacqueline 'Jacqui' Conroy. She said she wanted to see me, urgently, and asked if I would come to her home. That was a big ask, and a bigger 'if'.

What if I was being set up for what was left of Daly's mob, and walking into a beating – or worse?

I decided to go. Conor McCaughley, a good lad and a Gaelic football coach as game as they come, in sport and in life, was our staff photographer. He said he'd come with me – just in case.

The plan was that I would go into the bungalow first, and Conor would wait outside in the car. If anything untoward happened – like me shouting or a shot being fired – he would be able to dial 999 and call the police before doing anything else.

Nothing like that happened.

Jacqui Conroy greeted me at the front door. In looks, she was never going to be a Mona Lisa. But, in any case, she wasn't smiling. However, she did want to talk to me about a picture: although not the one hanging in the Louvre in Paris.

First, however, I insisted on looking into every room – and every wardrobe or stand-up cupboard – in the prim and proper, if not pretty, house. I wanted to make sure I wasn't being set up.

She let me do all that.

Then we sat down in the living room, me on the settee, her on the armchair at the window.

'You know I was no friend of Paul Daly,' I said to her. 'So what do you want to see me about? Why am I here?'

'Because you met two bastards in a car in Donegall Street,' she said. 'They offered you an exclusive picture of Daly. Did you give them money for it?'

I had indeed met two hoods who were in a car a few days previously in Donegall Street, outside the John Hewitt bar, named after a famous Ulster poet. But the pair weren't there for rhyme or reason: they wanted what they called 'rent' money, for a picture of Daly on holiday in some exotic clime, posing in his bodybuilder's budgie-smuggler Speedos ... with an imitation AK-47 or Armalite assault rifle in his arms. I recognised them. They were both low-level drug dealers themselves.

Now, whether people like it or not, tabloid newspapers – especially when investigating and exposing crime – do pay for stories, and pictures, or information leading to them. It is in the public interest to shine a light on the dark world of the gangs and the godfathers. But there was no way I was going to pay money to these drug dealers: what for? So they could buy more of their poison and, just as I had told Speedy Fegan when he pulled me in public, feed it to even more children?

'No,' I told Jacqui Conroy. 'I didn't pay them any money for that picture. Never did, never would.'

I didn't bother asking her how she knew I'd had a visit from the two Daly picture pimps. Belfast isn't only a village, it's a microcosm when it comes to the criminal underworld. There are more prying eyes and touts around than you'd get in the Gestapo.

Anyway, I didn't pay.

She said that was 'OK'. And then she made me, and Conor, still waiting outside, an offer neither of us could refuse. I went to the door and called Conor in from the car.

Then Jacqui Conroy put her hand under the coffee table in the living room. She pulled out a biscuit tin, just like your granny used to keep old pictures in. And it was indeed packed full of photographs: quite a lot of them of Daly ... including the one of him flexing his muscles with the mock gun.

'Take what you want,' she said calmly. 'I've no more use for them'.

I soon found out why. In our whole time in the house she had shared with King Coke, Ms Conroy never once referred to him as Paul. It was 'Daly this' or 'Daly that'.

And until we asked could we take her picture, she never shed a tear. She said yes to our picture request, but said she wanted to change her blouse. When she came back for Conor to take her posed picture, she was also wearing black mascara. It was smudged, as if she was in mourning and had been crying.

The whole time we were there, including for the photoshoot, she never shed a tear. The reason? Daly wasn't only a cruel sadist meting out summary punishment on the streets. Jacqui Conroy showed me her hands. Almost every finger was injured, almost every joint swollen or gnarled. Daly, she explained, had been cruel to her, too. And in fits of misogynistic bullying rage had, at different times, broken almost all her fingers. No wonder she wasn't shedding any tears for King Coke.

17

DICING WITH THE DEVIL

The fireball inferno threat on my home and my family from Liam Mooney's gang was silent – and remained so.

The blanket death threat from Billy 'King Rat' Wright was overt, and in my face.

It was to be the same with Hugh 'Cueball' Torney, an evil republican killer who headed up a lethal terror gang labelled the INLA – for Irish National Liberation Army. It was one of a few such republican outfits – another was the so-called Irish People's Liberation Organisation (IPLO) – which ran parallel to the Provos and were steeped in sectarian murder and criminality.

By the time I came face to face with Torney, it was the latter he wanted to talk about. The *Sunday World* had been reporting on how his mob in North Belfast had started cutting into the drugs rackets. Again, it was the ordinary people in places like the New Lodge Road who had come to plead with us to expose the pushers who were peddling the drugs and poisoning their kids – in both mind and body.

It was the old *modus operandi*: Get them hooked, they'll stay hooked, then they'll owe us – and they'll repay the debt by either acting as runners and dealing for us, or acting as mules to move guns and bullets ... and then get hooked into the terror gang.

Angered by our coverage, Torney put the word out. He wanted a meeting. I knew why he wanted a meeting all right: because of what we were writing about him and his INLA criminal cohorts. But, just as with the meeting with Billy Wright and other head-to-heads with headers, I wanted to know if there was a threat and, if there was, to gauge the strength, veracity and direction of it. As *Sunday World* editor Colm MacGinty always said: 'Intelligence is power.'

I agreed to meet Cueball. But I tried to set my own terms. It didn't matter. The death threat still materialised ... from his own mouth. But it wasn't personal, against me. It was worse than that.

The meeting took place just a year before Torney himself was shot dead, dying in his own blood in a hail of bullets as the result of yet another vicious internecine republican terror gang feud.

I had arranged to meet Cueball and his colleague – who, like Torney, was subsequently murdered by his own – in the heart of Belfast, just in case. But Torney, who was being hunted by the (then) RUC and by An Garda

Síochána on both sides of the border, wasn't exactly prepared to meet in front of the City Hall. Instead, he chose an alleyway, a cross between a back entry and a sidestreet, which runs beside a well-known pub and a bookie's.

In Belfast, there is always a flow of people between a public bar and a betting shop: the relationship between swigging pints and punting on racehorses has always been close and intimate. So if Torney, or his co-terrorist, were going to do anything – well, at least there would be witnesses, if the cops ever caught up with them.

When I got there, however, Torney was standing outside the bookie's on his own, wearing a leather jacket with a bulge in the left-hand side. It didn't take a Mensa IQ to work out what was in there, and it wasn't a big, generous and compassionate heart.

The greeting was cool, and cautious. My intention was to get Torney to go to a pub I had already earmarked. A colleague had agreed to meet me there. But before I could suggest to him that we go there, two things happened.

He said that someone else was with him, and was in the bookie's doing a bet. This turned out to be another INLA killer, called John Fennell. Impeccably dressed, he even wore a Queen's University graduate's scarf.

But even worse, before Fennell came out of the betting shop, the second thing happened: out walked a well-known unionist politician – a prominent Belfast councillor, a self-styled man of the people who was partial to a pint and a punt, like many another five-eighth.

I could actually see Cueball, well, cueing him up. His killer's eyes turned mean and keen. His hand moved towards his half unzipped leather jacket, with the bulge on the inside.

I told Torney: 'You can't do that. Not here. Not to him. He's unarmed. And, anyway, if you shoot him here, there's myself and most of the punters who have just walked by us into the bookie's as witnesses.'

Torney looked at the councillor as he came towards us. He looked at me. He said: 'Then I'll just have to blow you – and any of them who come out – away as well.'

Astonishingly, the unionist politician did something so straightforward, it was almost unbelievable. But it probably saved his life.

He spotted me, walked straight up to me and, ignoring Torney – he wouldn't have had a clue who he was – said: 'Jim, I've a story for you. I need to talk to you.'

'Not now,' I told him. 'Away for a pint in that pub down there and I'll be back to see you in half an hour.'

The sweat was beginning to bubble on my brow. I thought: I am standing eyeball-to-eyeball with a madman, a megalomaniac, a psychopathic killer ...

But Torney suddenly just looked at me. He looked at the retreating politician. He pulled his hand out of the inside of the leather jacket. His mate, Fennell, had just walked out of the betting shop. And he said: 'Come on – where are we going to talk?'

The unionist councillor went for his pint – not knowing how close he had come to staring down the barrel of a gun: and to murder, his own murder. Let's just say that he was lucky to live so that I could later tell him the tale. And after the telling, suffice to say he thought so, too.

Anyway, to Torney I proposed the pub I'd already staked out.

Cueball went in front, up the stairs to the first-floor lounge – presumably to see it wasn't a set-up, to ensure I hadn't tipped off the security forces. As we walked up the carpeted steps to the lounge, I pretended to stumble. I knocked into the back of his legs. He stumbled, and grabbed the wooden bannister. At least his fingerprints are on that, I thought. If he shoots me, at least there will be forensic evidence.

Torney turned round and smirked at me. 'Nice try,' he said. 'But if I have to shoot you, no one will be in any doubt who did it.'

In the lounge bar, we went to a snug, a private benched-off area where we could have our own table. I ordered a drink, to make it look just like ordinary blokes in for a pint. Torney and Fennell ordered only orange juice. When the order arrived, Torney tore straight in.

And he didn't fire verbal blanks. Instead, he issued a deadly ultimatum. He bluntly stated: 'Let me make it clear. If another story appears in the *Sunday World* about the INLA being involved in drugs dealing, it will not be you who will be shot. It will be one of your reporters. The reporter will be shot through the side of the head, so that it will be a slow death. And then it will be you who will bear the responsibility of telling the reporter's family who shot them, and why the reporter died.'

Torney adjusted the bulge of the gun in his pocket. He slid it back inside his leather jacket, like a snake retracting its fangs. He really did exude the evil air of the Devil himself.

Suddenly, he just stood up, stared, drained his glass of orange juice – Fennell hadn't touched his – and they both walked out of the upstairs snug in the lounge bar, without even a backward glance.

Of course, the gutsy editorial team in the *Sunday World* were never going to acquiesce to that threat – or any other. They went on doing what they were doing.

Torney went on doing what he was doing too – waging bloody internecine war, fuelling bitter feuds. But about a year after he'd issued his death threat to the *Sunday World*, on 3 September 1996, the Grim Reaper caught up with him. He was cut down in a hail of bullets in the tinderbox town of Lurgan.

He and an accomplice were ambushed walking along the County Armagh town's Victoria Street. Torney was hit from behind, bullets blasting into his back. But he still managed to spin around. More bullets flew. Torney tumbled, to die in a pool of his own blood only seconds later. Rescuers who rushed to his aid turned him over to try to resuscitate him. It was too late.

Underneath his still-warm corpse they found a Beretta 9mm pistol. Strapped to his body they discovered a holster. To this day, I still wonder if that was the gun that Torney was carrying beneath the zip of his leather jacket when I met him up that alleyway in Belfast.

I may have thought that the Torney death threat to myself, and the *Sunday World* staff, died with his early demise. He was just forty-one when he was assassinated.

It didn't.

I'd taken my son to the Ulster Senior Amateur Boxing Finals in Belfast's Ulster Hall a few months after Torney's paramilitary-style funeral. I was sitting close to ringside. At the interval, I gave my son money to go and get a soft drink and a packet of crisps. As I sat alone, a single hood walked up to me. He stooped down, looked straight at me, and said: 'Hugh Torney remembers you – from the grave.'

They were haunting words.

Cueball may have fired his last shot, but it was clear the INLA killers he'd left in his wake hadn't. It was also clear that Torney's threat still stood, even though he was lying in his cold grave in the INLA plot – where the image of an AK-47 assault rifle is still carved into the communal headstone commemorating dead 'volunteers' – at Belfast's Milltown Cemetery, at the top of the city's republican Falls Road.

As for the man who'd sat stoically silent while Torney issued his threat in the downtown Belfast bar, he also came to a brutal and bloody end. John Fennell, the man with that Queen's University graduate's scarf hanging casually round his neck – he had never, of course, attended the Belfast seat of learning – said nothing throughout the encounter. But, like so many before him, Fennell was to find out that those who are linked by bloodlust find it all too easy to turn on each other.

By Christmas 1995 and the spring of 1996, conflicting INLA factions were waging another internal war. Torney had fallen foul of two proven bloodthirsty warlords: Gerard 'Doctor Death' Steenson and Gino Gallagher. They had once been his terrorists-in-arms, allies. Both of them were to die as they lived: by the gun.

But when Gallagher was gunned down in broad daylight on the Falls Road on the morning of New Year's

Eve, 1995, the finger was pointed at Cueball Torney. He'd believed Gallagher was gunning for him. So, in typical paramilitary feud style, he'd got his retaliation in first. And John Fennell, as Torney's number two, was in the frame for having set up the carefully planned killing of thirty-one-year-old Gallagher.

Plus, there was another clue. The lone gunman in the Gino hit wore a wig.

Cueball, on the run from anti-terror and murder squad cops on both sides of the border, and from rebels within the original INLA ranks, had taken to wearing wigs as a disguise. Indeed, while it was never proved, there were reports that he was wearing a wig (whisked away by his accomplice that day) when he himself was shot dead in Lurgan.

So both Torney and Fennell were in the gunsights of their enemies. And Cueball had certainly been served grim notice of what to expect.

Almost six months to the day before Torney himself died in a pool of his own blood, Fennell's body had been discovered bloodied and battered. He'd gone on the run after the Gino Gallagher murder, hiding out in a caravan park in County Donegal, almost 100 miles away across the border from his own turf in Ardoyne, in north Belfast. The mobile home park was close to Bundoran, a town on Ireland's Atlantic coast, embraced by breathtaking scenery.

But it wasn't the scenery that took Fennell's last breath away. It was being brutally and mercilessly battered in the head with breezeblocks after being kidnapped and tortured. Even Garda detectives hardened to the atrocities of the Troubles – on both sides of the border – were horrified at the sheer barbarity of the bloodletting, which they discovered, after a tip-off, on 4 March 1996.

And sources say that among the quiet man's belongings scattered around his murder scene was a blood-soaked Queen's University graduate's scarf.

And I wonder, again, just like the gun found on Cueball's corpse, was that the same Queen's scarf Fennell wore as he sat in grim silence while Torney issued that death threat in the Belfast downtown bar almost a year previously?

18
TERROR ON MY DOORSTEP

The son who'd been with me at the boxing match, when the hood resurrected the haunting 'Hugh Torney remembers – from the grave' threat, was my eldest boy, Jamie. All of my family – Lindy, my daughter from my first marriage, Faye, Jamie, now also a journalist with the *Sunday World*, and our youngest son, Micah – knew all about living with danger. They did it every day and night – especially at night.

Our house back then, in the 80s and 90s – we lived in it for thirty years until 2016 – was up a laneway in south Belfast. It was an old converted farmhouse and it was hard to find. That worked for us when the shadow of the gunmen and bogeymen, both republican and loyalist, loomed. So, too, as I've mentioned before, was the fact that with its array of security devices, it resembled a police station.

A visitor once remarked on how good the installation of all the windows and doors had been.

'Who were your glaziers?' he asked politely.

'The Northern Ireland Office,' I replied.

He didn't ask twice.

But we loved that house. Lived there for thirty years – almost half my lifetime.

Still, my children had to live with the omnipresent threat of something happening to me – or to them, because of me. And their mother, Lindy, was no slouch when it came to slagging off the gangsters and gunmen during her time as a reporter – she worked with the *Belfast Telegraph* for over twenty years – especially in her weekly column.

We were all acutely aware that at any time, day or night, danger could arrive on our doorstep. However, the worst threat one of my family faced came from a different doorstep. It came from a doorman on duty at a bar/nightclub in south Belfast, which was known as BT9 and was a supposedly safe zone in the city.

And again, a long time after he'd been at the Amateur Boxing Finals with me on the night of the threat from the grave incident, it was Jamie who was in the eye of the storm.

The *Sunday World* had been hammering two brothers who were big-time drug dealers, and had been dealing over a long period of time. They were linked, again, with the allegedly 'loyalist' drugs gang, the LVF (founded, as mentioned earlier, by Billy 'King Rat' Wright after he was kicked out of the UVF). But these boys were running their rackets out of south Antrim, rather than Wright's base of Lurgan in County Armagh.

Anyway, our son Jamie was at university by this stage. Like most students, he was keen to have a few bob in his pocket, other than what his Ma and Da subbed him. He had worked nights in bars around the city. He'd landed part-time shifts at night in this plush pub with its upmarket clientele in the heart of the leafy suburb of BT9. He thought he was safe grafting there, sometimes until 2.00 a.m.

So did we.

Until one Sunday, when I was coming home with friends – Bat'n'Ball, Ginger, Wee Geordie – from a greyhound coursing meeting at Balbriggan, which lies between Dundalk and Dublin. I got a call. A story 'contact' I knew well was looking for me. He knew someone close to the two LVF drugs godfathers we'd been panning in the paper. They, in turn, were close to a doorman who at the time was working security at a city pub/club where Jamie was working behind the bar.

The doorman – we later discovered he was in league with the 'loyalist' LVF! – told them about Jamie. So they hatched a plot to get at me by targeting my son.

My story contact told me to get home quick, and that if Jamie was at work that Sunday night – it was close to Christmas, the bar was extremely busy – to get him out, and home.

We managed to do that: and thwart a sick plot to not only kidnap our son, but to shoot and perhaps even kill him, stuff his pockets with money and drugs, and then put the word out on the street that this innocent young man, who was just trying to earn a few quid to get himself through university, was himself a drugs dealer!

The evil warped thinking was not only that we would be left devastated and grieving for a murdered son, but that the *Sunday World* would be discredited by the blatant lie – which, in some quarters, always sticks – that the son of an editor whose newspaper consistently crusaded against drugs barons was a drug dealer himself.

Evil is too soft a word for what that depraved duo of drugs overlords planned.

But just getting Jamie home safe wasn't enough. We decided that if this crew knew where he was working at night, it wouldn't be difficult for them to discover – if they didn't already know from Jamie talking to other people in the bar, maybe even the bent bouncer – where he spent his days. That was at lectures, doing his degree course at the University of Ulster campus at Jordanstown – right on the cusp of the drug gang's South Antrim turf.

So we decided that our son – with his agreement – should get out of the country. We explained to the education hierarchy what had happened, and it was arranged for Jamie to break off from the university course and go abroad for a while. He'd a good mate at the time, Matt. So both headed off to backpack around Europe for a while: until, back home, my contact could assure me that the heat was off.

Unfortunately, I couldn't go to the cops and try to get the gang, or the Judas bouncer who had betrayed our son, jailed. That would have blown the cover on the contact who had tipped me off about the audacious abduction bid, and put his own life in danger by doing so. So we sucked it up. And we in the *Sunday World* kept on sticking it to the two brothers and their LVF mob.

Jamie got stuck back into his university course when he came back from his enforced sabbatical. Fair play to him, too, he got his degree. And that hairy experience – among many others because I was his Da – didn't stop him sticking to the old rugby mantra, either: 'Never look back, never step back, and always – always – keep on the front studs.' That's why he followed his mother and father into this game: newspapers. It's why, as I write, he's part of the brilliant and multi-award-winning editorial team which is the *Sunday World*, both North and South in Ireland. And he's married to a lovely girl, our brilliant daughter-in-law, Lucy and both of them love their pretty, long-eared pooch, Lola.

Jamie's now mastered something that his oul' man could never get a grasp of: IT, and the online news production pipeline that all newspapers and broadcasters have to concentrate on. But before I butter him up too sweetly, just a rugby-ball-in-the-bowels caveat. Both he and his brother, Micah, grew up to be giants of men: in more ways than one. Both now tower over the six foot mark: Jamie hitting the tape at six feet four and a half; Micah, who is carving out a career for himself in London, an inch taller. And both are gym monkeys: something, even in the halcyon days of his albeit limited rugby past, their Da never was … too bloody boring pumping iron when you could be doing real weightlifting and hoisting a pint off the bar counter.

But even though they're big and bulked up, they were both backs, never playing in the forwards to get two cauliflower ears and a busted snozzle – never mind the road map of scar tissue on the baldy head – like this oul' grizzled geriatric, who played God's Game at number eight for thirty-seven years. And that's why they raise a smile when I still call both of them 'my ballerinas'. At least, I think they're smiling. Or maybe they're just gritting their teeth.

19
KIDNAP!

Hacks are supposed to write front-page stories: they're not supposed to appear in them. The rule is – you don't want to be the story. But thanks to a startling and unusual incident, I broke that rule.

It was a routine morning. I had just driven up to the gates of Belvoir Primary School in Belfast to leave my eldest son, Jamie, off to go into assembly. Jamie was about six at the time. My wife, Lindy, was in the car, along with our younger son, Micah, who was only a few months old.

I let Jamie out of our car, and led him through the school gates. A child with long blond hair was riding a pink bike along the pavement, heading towards the school gates. A bit behind, a woman, obviously the child's mother, was walking along the pavement. As I got into my car, which was parked on the other side of the road, I noticed a car cruising very slowly past the child (who, because of the long hair, I initially, but erroneously, took to be a little girl).

There was something odd about the snail's pace of the car, almost as if it was keeping pace with the bike. It slowed to a stop just a little way in front of the child.

And then suddenly – oh so suddenly – a man, a giant of a man with muscles bulging, jumped out of the back seat of the car at the pavement side. In one fluid, shocking movement he kicked the bicycle from under the child, simultaneously whisking him into his arms, and then bundled both himself and the wee lad into the back seat. The woman, still further back, let out one of the most blood-chilling screams I have ever heard. She started to run.

But the car revved up and took off at speed.

Two road repair men were working opposite the school. Like Lindy and myself, one of them had seen what happened. He did the only thing he could to try to stop the car. He threw the shovel he had in his hands at it.

It skittered across the road and as I took off in pursuit, I almost careered into it.

I was driving an ageing, beat-up, silver-coloured BMW 7 series at the time: a big, lumpy, grumpy thing, hard as hell to manoeuvre in tight spots, especially parking spots, if ever there was one.

As the front car sped off, I noticed a white plastic bag had been wrapped around the back number plate. Most of the number was obscured. But plainly visible was a G, indicating a Galway registration.

There were two men in the car. Old and all as my car was, I 'gave her the guttie'. The child had obviously been kidnapped. They had to be stopped. The question was – how?

The driver was heading south, making, as it turned out, for Shannon airport. But, as it later transpired, he didn't know the main roads to get him back onto the M1 out of Belfast, where he needed to get to in order to get back to Galway, where he had hired the car. So instead he took the back roads – narrow, twisting, hilly, bendy, scary wee roads towards Lisburn town, the nearest access link to the motorway.

I was going after him, hell for leather – horn blasting, lights flashing, red hazard lights on, doing anything to attract attention, hoping perhaps a passing police car would see us, or a member of the public might dial 999 to tell the police about two mad drivers hammering like hell at 70 miles an hour on a wee country back road. Remember, these were the days before mobile phones.

I had Lindy in the car and our wee son, Micah. Much as I wanted to stop the kidnappers, I didn't want to endanger their lives. Eventually, after about five miles of sheer driving madness and mayhem, Lindy decided that she and the child had to get out. I pulled over, quickly, into a roadside garage. Lindy got out with the child in her arms. She ran into the shop where a customer was talking on the pay phone. She asked him for the phone as she needed to call 999 and tell the police where we were and, more important, which route the kidnappers were taking.

Meanwhile I continued the chase, bouncing off kerbs and verges on the skinny road. That's where the damage was done to the old Beamer. But, thankfully, it kept going: and then some.

Class picture from Porter's Public Elementary School down Donegall Pass: no school uniforms here, as our parents couldn't afford them … and our schooldays were less than happy because of the cane-wielding principal, 'Bazzler' Todd.

At Annadale Grammar School, where the masters didn't have to teach us. We learned from them, about lessons and, more importantly, about life.

I could have wallpapered a room with these. My wife, Lindy, suggested the downstairs WC. The message that I was to be shot 'this morning' would have proved a sure-fire cure for constipation! But even then, we had to laugh. I think …

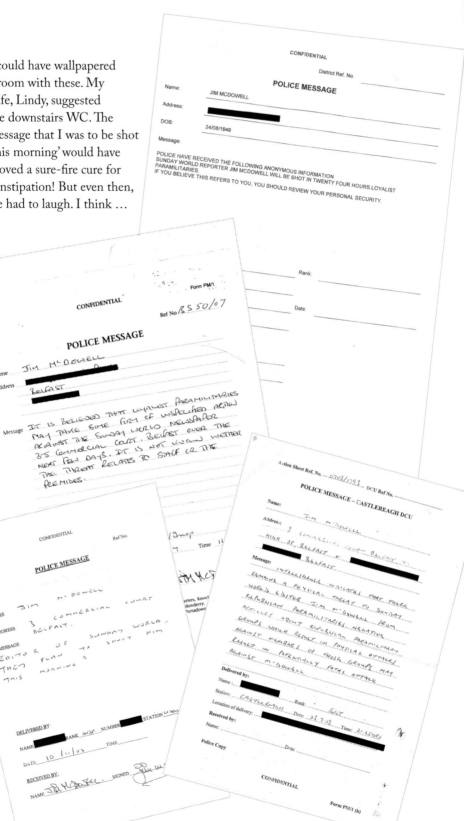

CONFIDENTIAL

District Ref. No. _____

POLICE MESSAGE

Name: JIM MCDOWELL

Address: ▬▬▬▬▬▬▬▬▬▬

DOB: 24/08/1949

Message:

POLICE HAVE RECEIVED THE FOLLOWING ANONYMOUS INFORMATION SUNDAY WORLD REPORTER JIM MCDOWELL WILL BE SHOT IN TWENTY FOUR HOURS. LOYALIST PARAMILITARIES.
IF YOU BELIEVE THIS REFERS TO YOU, YOU SHOULD REVIEW YOUR PERSONAL SECURITY.

Rank:

Date:

CONFIDENTIAL   Form PM/1

Ref No RS 50/07

POLICE MESSAGE

Name   JIM MCDOWELL

Address ▬▬▬ BELFAST ▬▬▬

Message IT IS BELIEVED THAT LOYALIST PARAMILITARIES MAY TAKE SOME FORM OF UNSPECIFIED ACTION AGAINST THE SUNDAY WORLD NEWSPAPER 35 COMMERCIAL COURT, BELFAST OVER THE NEXT FEW DAYS. IT IS NOT KNOWN WHETHER THE THREAT RELATES TO STAFF OR THE PREMISES.

CONFIDENTIAL   Ref No:

PM1

POLICE MESSAGE

NAME   JIM   MCDOWELL

ADDRESS   3   COMMERCIAL   COURT   BELFAST.

MESSAGE   – EDITOR   OF   SUNDAY WORLD,   THEY   PLAN   TO   SHOOT   HIM   THIS   MORNING =

DELIVERED BY:
NAME ▬▬ RANK INSP NUMBER ▬▬ STATION ▬▬
DATE 10/11/03   TIME

RECEIVED BY:
NAME JIM MCDOWELL   SIGNED ▬▬

Action Sheet Ref. No. 0303/1393   DCU Ref No. _____

POLICE MESSAGE – CASTLEREAGH DCU

Name:

Address: JIM MCDOWELL   3 COMMERCIAL COURT SUNDAY BELFAST 93
HIGH ST., BELFAST
▬▬ BELFAST. ▬▬

Message: INTELLIGENCE INDICATED THAT THERE REMAINS A PHYSICAL THREAT TO SUNDAY WORLD EDITOR JIM MCDOWELL FROM REPUBLICAN PARAMILITARIES. RELATIVE ARTICLES ABOUT REPUBLICAN PARAMILITARY GROUPS WHICH RESULT IN PHYSICAL ATTACKS AGAINST MEMBERS OF THESE GROUPS MAY RESULT IN POTENTIALLY FATAL ATTACK AGAINST MCDOWELL

Delivered by:
Name: ▬▬
Station: CASTLEREAGH   Rank: SGT
Location of delivery: ▬▬ Date 23.7.93

Received by:
Name: ▬▬ Time 21.25HRS

Police Copy   Date:

CONFIDENTIAL

Form PM/1 (b)

Form PM/1

Ref No ....

POLICE MESSAGE

(JOURNALIST)

Name ....

Address C/O SUNDAY WORLD
3 - 5 COMMERCIAL COURT,
BELFAST. BT1 2NB.

Message LOYALIST PARAMILITARIES ARE CONSIDERING
CARRYING OUT SOME FORM OF ATTACK ON
SUNDAY WORLD JOURNALIST.
THEY ARE AWARE HE DRINKS SOCIALLY WITH
RAYMOND McCORD IN A CITY CENTRE BAR
AT LUNCHTIME.

Delivered ....

Name ███████████████████████ Rank ....

Station LISBURN ROAD Date 8|8

Reference 534

District Ref. No. B169/10 9/8/10

POLICE MESSAGE

Name: JIM MCDOWELL

Address: COMMERCIAL COURT BELFAST

DOB:

Message:

POLICE ARE IN RECEIPT OF INFORMATION THAT CRIMINAL ELEMENTS INTEND TO CARRY OUT SOME FORM OF ATTACK ON JIM MCDOWELL AND HIS STAFF. THIS MAY TAKE THE FORM OF A PHYSICAL ASSAULT

THIS MAY REFER TO YOU

YOU ARE ADVISED TO REVIEW YOUR PERSONAL SECURITY

CMC Ref No. ....04/08....

POLICE MESSAGE – CASTLEREAGH DCU

Name: SON OF JIM MCDOWELL

Address: ███████████████████████

Message: POLICE HAVE RECEIVED INFORMATION THAT
MEMBER/S OF LVF INTEND TO CARRY OUT AN ATTACK
ON A PERSON BELIEVED TO BE THE SON OF JIM
MCDOWELL EDITOR OF THE SUNDAY WORLD. THIS
ATTACK MAY BE RELATED TO HIS EMPLOYMENT.

Delivered by:

Name : ███████████████ Rank .... Time:

Station: .... Date: ....

Location of delivery ....

Received by:

Name: .... Date: ....

District Ref. No.

POLICE MESSAGE

Name: Jim McDowell

Address:

DOB: 24/08/1949

Message:

POLICE HAVE RECEIVED THE FOLLOWING ANONYMOUS INFORMATION

Persons have a bomb which they are intending to leave at Jim McDowells house within the hour.

THIS INFORMATION WAS RECEIVED AT 2107HRS 25/01/10

Delivered by:

Name: ███████████████

No: ███████████ Rank: Sgt

Station: Castlereagh

Time: 1930 Date: 26-1-10.

Received by:

Name:

Signed:

Recipient Copy

Form PM1
03/08

Page 2 of 4
CONFIDENTIAL

Lindy and I are married in – where else? – Belfast's 'Dome of Delight', the City Hall. I still had (some) hair then …

The then Ulster Secretary of State, John Reid MP, visits our office for the unveiling of the memorial plaque to our murdered colleague, Martin O'Hagan, and assures me that his assassins will be caught. At the time of writing, sixteen years on from the callous killing, we're still waiting …

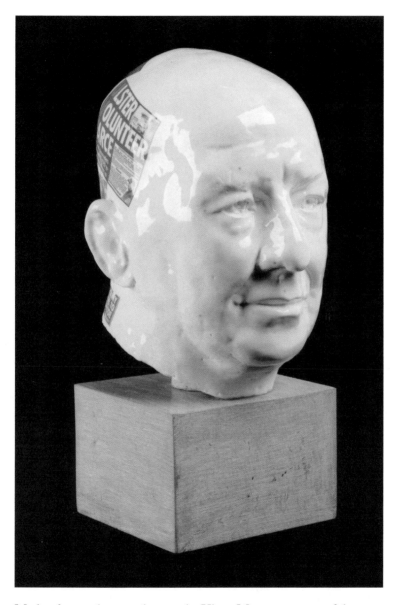

My head on a plate: on show at the Ulster Museum as part of the Royal Ulster Academy Annual Exhibition in 2016. Sculpted by the RUA's Bob Sloan and, with *Sunday World* headlines circling my baldy head, Bob appropriately titled it, 'Headlines'.

The great betrayal – 'Brigadier of Bling' Jim 'Doris Day' Gray (right) with his son Jonathan … Gray left him for dead in a hotel room in Thailand.

EXCLUSIVE INTERVIEW

SHOUKRI SPEAKS ONLY TO THE SUNDAY WORLD

By JIM McDOWELL

THE UFF boss blamed for trying to ban the *Sunday World* from loyalist areas has given an exclusive interview – to this newspaper!

In a bizarre twist, north Belfast UFF 'Brigadier' Andre Shoukri (above) contacted us this week.

He **DENIED** he was behind a terror campaign of threat and intimidation to stop ordinary people in loyalist areas reading this paper.

He said he had phoned to **REBUT** what was written about him in last week's paper – even though it is supposed to be banned on his own 'turf'.

But he point-blank **REFUSED** to discuss any details of any meetings he was at with either the UFF or the UVF.

And in another bolt out of the blue, Shoukri echoed the recent statement from the IRA when he said of the UDA/UFF: "We want peace!"

FULL BIZARRE INTERVIEW: Pages 4&5

'The Bookies Brigadier' Andre Shoukri sanctioned a UDA boycott of the *Sunday World* – then broke the self-imposed silence to berate me. So I put him on the front page!

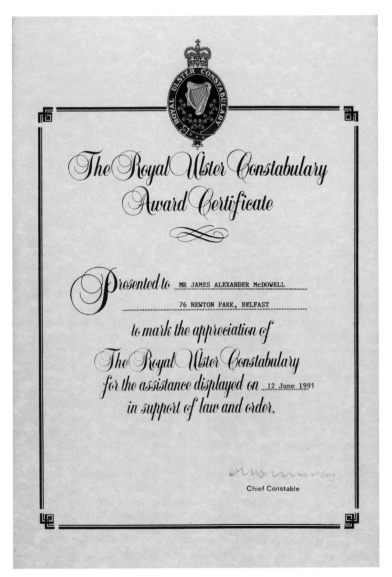

The Royal Ulster Constabulary
Award Certificate

Presented to MR JAMES ALEXANDER McDOWELL

76 NEWTON PARK, BELFAST

to mark the appreciation of
The Royal Ulster Constabulary
for the assistance displayed on 12 June 1991
in support of law and order.

Chief Constable

The citation from the police after the schoolkid kidnapping saga.

MR. JIM McDOWELL

SUNDAY WORLD

Proof that I was in the presence of Elizabeth Regina II. There was some verbal horseplay between myself and her husband, the Duke, over my Da running a 'cream cookies', or a bookmaker's betting shop.

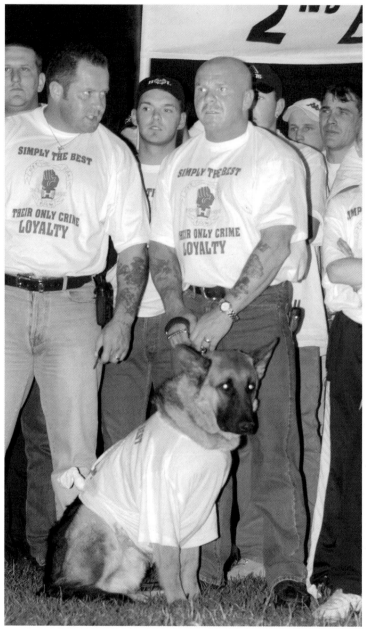

Shankill UDA/UFF godfather Johnny 'Mad Dog' Adair and henchmen from his infamous C Coy 2nd Battalion based on Belfast's Lower Shankill Road. Even his dog, called Rebel, is wearing a C Coy T-shirt proclaiming 'Simply the Best', and 'Their Only Crime (is) LOYALTY'. On the Shankill and elsewhere throughout Northern Ireland, the decent people turned that maxim around to state that as far as Mad Dog's mob were concerned, their only loyalty was crime.

The face of evil – Hugh 'Cueball' Torney. He even had a death threat delivered to me from the grave.

LVF psychopath and godfather Billy 'King Rat' Wright. Pictured here under a makeshift Orange arch in the Maze jail, where he was later murdered. He passed a death sentence on our colleague Martin O'Hagan … and it was carried out when Wright was in his grave.

Wright's assassin, former top Irish National Liberation Army (INLA) terrorist Christopher 'Crip' McWilliams. Like 'King Rat', he was a gym monkey behind bars, and was also a bit of a Svengali – he managed to get the weapons smuggled into the HMP Maze which were used to kill Wright in the back of a prisoners' transport van.

Gerard McKay Jr. His father Gerry Sr still believes his son was murdered by drug godfather Paul 'King Coke' Daly. And so do I.

Gerry McKay after making his case at the Stormont Assembly, supported by the late David Ervine and Monica McWilliams of the then Women's Coalition party, who later became the Human Rights Commissioner for Northern Ireland.

A mugshot of 'King Coke' Daly snapped while he sat in his Mercedes car before appearing in the dock for a court case – for hammering a fellow heavy and putting him in intensive care. Daly still walked free with a suspended jail sentence.

Daly's prostrate body, draped in a blanket, lies on the pavement of Stephen Street in downtown Belfast, just minutes after he was gunned down in broad daylight. Such gruesome scenes have since pockmarked the pavements of Dublin because of the Kinahan-Hutch gangs' bloody drugs vendetta.

The Milltown massacre perpetrator, Michael Stone. He's pictured putting on a bullet proof vest similar to the one he probably wore when trying to storm Stormont and shoot Gerry Adams and Martin McGuinness. Renowned as a stone-cold killer, he once told me that shooting a man was like watching a coat fall off a clothes hanger.

The morning after drug dealers firebombed the *Sunday World* Belfast office in 1999. I survey the damage.

The 'Mo Says No' moment. Then Secretary of State Mo Mowlem visits the office to show support and solidarity after the firebombing … but I wasn't there, because I was in Dublin for the Ulster European Cup rugby match. And Mo left me a note saying 'No' to my knighthood … some chance, anyway.

Drug godfather Liam 'Fat Boy' Mooney. A top cop told me his mob planned to burn our house down, with me and my family in it.

Fast bucks, loose women, flash cars – and instant death. Drug godfathers Brendan 'Speedy' Fegan (left) and Brendan 'Bap' Campbell on their way to the races in Dublin drinking beer in the back of a chauffeur-driven luxury limousine. Both were later to be summarily executed by gun-toting assassins.

Baby-faced IRA gunrunner Conor Claxton, jailed in the USA for smuggling guns to the Provos … while the Ulster Troubles were supposed to be over.

And then, a stroke of luck. The police by this time had been fully alerted: by the road workmen running into the school to raise the alarm, and by the school, of course, and the child's mother herself. The kidnappers' car was speeding along the M1 towards Dungannon and then Enniskillen, and on across the border heading back to Galway and then Shannon airport and back to the States. But an off-duty cop driving along the motorway had seen the car hurtling past him at high speed. He had no idea what was going on, but he decided to give chase.

At one point he pulled alongside the kidnap car, holding up his police warrant card towards his passenger side window, giving the clear message to the kidnapper, and his accomplice, to give up.

Meanwhile, the man in the car was also holding something up against his car window. A sheet of paper, obviously too far away for the policeman to read.

And then suddenly the car slowed, pulled into the hard shoulder and stopped.

The policeman pulled in behind and stopped too.

The kidnapper stepped out of his car.

This brave officer was unarmed at this point and had absolutely no idea what was going on. The Troubles were still going on at the time. Policemen were terror targets. It could have been an ambush.

He approached the car slowly. The door opened. The driver stepped out, walked towards him and then ... fell on his knees!

He was still holding the piece of paper, crying, begging the policeman to let him go.

He was the little boy's father.

It turned out he and the boy's mother had lived together for a time in New York, where he came from. She was from Belfast. The pair hadn't married, but when they'd split up the break was amicable and the pair shared the care of their little boy. However, the mother then decided she wanted to move back to her native Belfast. Under New York law the father was able to apply for custody (as an unmarried father, he would not have had the same rights in the UK at the time). The mother, though, had taken the child with her back to Belfast and had enrolled him in Belvoir Primary School in the south of the city, where our son Jamie also attended.

The father now apparently decided that the only way to get the boy back was to snatch him. Conveniently, he'd managed to talk a bodybuilder friend – the big guy who'd done the actual snatching – to join him in this foolhardy enterprise. At the speed he was driving, he could have killed himself and his own child. He could have killed us all.

While all this was going on, I was still some way back. In car chase terms, I am no Steve McQueen. I promised myself that the next time I watched Steve McQueen in the movie *Bullitt*, I'd rather take a bullet than try to emulate him in that famous car chase.

Still, there's always a sting in the tale of a tail-to-tail car chase.

First, when Lindy jumped out of the car with Micah at the small country garage and got on the public phone to the police, she gave them all the details of the getaway car, where we'd chased it, where she was now, the route

I was heading after the kidnap car; and, presumably to help helicopter cops identify our vehicles, she was asked what sort of car I was driving. Her reply? 'A silver BMX.'

Now, as the officer pointed out, there's one helluva difference between a tiny bike that wee boys do wheelies on and a silver BMW doing 70 miles an hour.

Some months later I attended the court case, where the American father was tried for the snatch attempt. I got to talk to him and he seemed like a decent man – albeit one who hatched a daft and extremely dangerous plan. The mother seemed like a good woman, too. The judge treated the father mercifully on hearing that both parents had agreed to work together to resolve their differences.

It was one of those incidents where you think, if only they'd done that in the first place. At least this story didn't end in tragedy, as it so easily might have. For my efforts, I ended up on a couple of newspaper front pages the next day, instead of writing them. And I was awarded a commendation, which was presented to me in one of the main police stations in Belfast, Castlereagh, which was also the main terrorist interrogation centre at the time.

Fitting, or what?

Trevor Ringland, who played rugby for Ulster, Ireland and the Lions, is a lawyer and a man of immense integrity and commitment. He has done much to heal the wounds of a still bleeding, and oft-times still bitter, community in Northern Ireland. I am privileged to know him and respect him so much. Ditto his Da, Adrian.

Adrian was a top cop, now retired, in the RUC and, after the transition, in the PSNI. After the kidnapping court case – the father was free to return to the States, rather than being locked up in a Northern Ireland jail with the consequent expense to the taxpayer – the police decided to give me a citation. So I was invited to go to Castlereagh police station in east Belfast to receive a framed copy, signed by the then Chief Constable. It was a bit of a relief to be going there *not* for the purpose of being handed another PM1 certificate, warning me of yet another threat from paramilitaries.

Lindy and our still very young boys went with me. When I walked into the room where the presentation was to be made, who was the senior police officer assigned to hand it over? Adrian Ringland.

I hadn't known he'd be there. And he hadn't known the identity of the Jim McDowell who was being accorded the honour.

When I walked in, to be offered a warm handshake, his words to me were: 'McDowell, if we had known it was you, we wouldn't have recommended this citation – we'd have gone for the George Cross!'

He was kidding, of course. Still, it was lovely, and a privilege to receive the citation.

And Adrian did me another great favour that day. Our lads were intrigued by the place. So I asked if they could be fingerprinted. Adrian obliged. An old-fashioned ink finger-printing pad was brought up and the boys still have those fingerprints, dabbed on official police parchment with their full names, birth dates and address recorded on it, as two of their prized, if perhaps, dodgiest, possessions.

Sadly, the oul' car hadn't come out of its trip so well. My back road racing had banjaxed both the gear box and the clutch. It cost as much to repair the jalopy as the thing had cost in the first place.

Would I do it again? Of course. But it would be better if Steve McQueen was still around – and he could do the driving instead of me!

20

BENNY'S AND THE LIFE OF BRIAN

During the very dark days of the Troubles, evenings were often leavened by pints of room-temperature porter in Benny's, the hacks' and printers' bar in Waring Street, at the back of the *News Letter* printing presses.

Brian Keenan had just been released as a hostage in Beirut. He had been working as a teacher in that city when he was kidnapped in April 1986. After a period kept in solitary isolation and chained to a radiator, Keenan had been joined by a fellow captive, journalist John McCarthy. Keenan's long ordeal, and the tenacious campaign waged by his sisters in Belfast to secure his freedom, had moved the hearts of millions. His release made global headlines. Keenan's old mates, Jackie Redpath from the Shankill and Frank McCollum from Ardoyne, were flown over in a private jet to Lebanon by the Foreign Affairs Department in Dublin to bring him back to Ireland.

Back in Belfast, the freed hostage was now trying to adjust to normality (or what passed for normality in Belfast). Jackie Redpath phoned me one Friday evening. He said that Brian, still a bit frail from his ordeal, wanted to come into town for a pint. Benny Conlon's Guinness, still served at room temperature, had a priest's collar the Pope would have been proud of. And it had so much body, you could use a knife and fork to eat it. Brian Keenan had liked having a pint in the skinny wee pub when he'd worked for Belfast City Council as a community development officer, before becoming a lecturer in Lebanon. Like many others, he found it quirky – to say the least.

The back wall of the bar leans so far forward, pieces of cord had to be strung along the shelves to keep the bottles of spirits from sliding off. The bar counter tilted in the other direction, towards the back wall. When a pint was served with the froth running down the glass, you had to have the reactions of a Grand Prix racing driver to grab it before it slithered and slipped away from you, heading for the floor on the other side of the antique teak counter.

The sliding door into the gents was the door off an ancient Belfast tram. And the wall facing the counter was lined with beautiful, albeit nicotine-stained, oak panels, which were said to be rejects from the carpenters' shop when they were fitting out the *Titanic* for her ill-fated launch in 1912.

So, quirky indeed.

And the same adjective could be used to describe most of its clientele: Thack the Hack, Smarty Marty, big Nicky the Blueman, Wee Sam the Postie, Jolly Roger Oscar… and that doesn't even start to paint the picture.

But it was Thack the Hack's wife, Maggie Thackway, who almost gave Brian Keenan a heart attack the night Jackie Redpath brought him down for a quiet pint.

When Jackie had phoned me to say that he was bringing Brian down the town and into Benny's, he'd asked me, not unreasonably, to tip off any fellow reporters who might be having their regular drink after work to give Brian a 'bye-ball': in other words, the emphasis really was on a *quiet* pint.

There were to be no requests for interviews, and the pub visit was to be completely off the record. I passed this on to the press posse in the pub that night. They all agreed, unhesitatingly. The Belfast man had been through enough: he deserved a pint in peace.

And so it happened. Jackie and Brian came in and dandered down to the back lounge, with everyone just saying 'Bout ye, Brian', or 'Good to see you back, Brian', and, unanimously, just quietly wished him well.

It was noticeable, however, how pale, thin and wan the ex-hostage looked. He had the complexion and demeanour of a shroud, albeit a shroud sprouting a beard. Little wonder.

So Brian and Jackie settled in to sup their pint, unmolested, left alone.

It turned out to be the quiet before the storm walked in – in the form of one Margaret 'Maggie' Thackway. Maggie is a lovely lady, and the greatest of company. But quiet she isn't. That night she was looking for her other half, Thack the Hack – our good friend Cyril Thackway, a brilliant if volatile newspaperman, sadly now deceased. He was standing right down at the bottom of the bar, where it opened up into the back lounge.

Maggie first spotted Thack, who was doing his best to look sober. But she forgot him as soon as she clocked Brian – who she later claimed she'd known and worked with in some capacity.

Spontaneously, she guldered out, 'Ooooh, Brian' – and made a dive straight for where he and Jackie were sitting. And before anyone could pin her down and point out the quiet pint protocol, Maggie had planked herself on the startled, just-released Hezbollah hostage's knee, loudly exclaiming: 'Ach, Brian, love, sure I hardly recognised you without being chained to a radiator.'

To be fair to Mr Keenan, he mustered a waxen smile … as two of us hauled Maggie off him and away back up the bar.

Fair to say that Maggie was never offered a job as a diplomat at the United Nations in New York after that.

And fair play to Brian Keenan. Through his books and life, he went on to teach the rest of us very valuable lessons about the survival of the human spirit in even the most harrowing and horrifying of extreme, life-threatening circumstances.

He also taught us about what that simple word humility really means.

Frank McCollum, as mentioned previously, flew in an Irish government jet with Brian Keenan's sisters to bring the Belfast man home from his Beirut hellhole. Frank had worked with Brian in Belfast City Council and was a top union official in the City Hall. He was also the kindest and gentlest man, but when pushed, he didn't take any s**t. Indeed, he was at one time the chairman of a social club in his native north Belfast, in the mini-metropolis of Ardoyne. Only problem was, he got into a digging match with someone he took umbrage with. And Frank had to bar *himself* from the club courtesy of his part in the pugilism.

Still, it was the compassionate and caring Mr McCollum who I once met in the saddest of circumstances. It was two days after the infamous IRA Shankill fish shop bombing in Belfast on Saturday 23 October 1993. Nine innocent people died and almost 60 were seriously injured when a bomb carried in in a cardboard box blew up. One of the two Provo bombers, Thomas Begley, was also killed. The other, Sean Kelly, was critically injured, and was eventually sentenced to nine life terms, only to be released early under the terms of the Good Friday Agreement in 1998.

The Ardoyne cell of the IRA had planned and executed the bombing in the mistaken belief that the loyalist terror godfather Johnny Mad Dog Adair, whose killer C Coy UFF (the UDA-linked Ulster Freedom Fighters) which was based on the Shankill, was holding a meeting in a room above Frizzell's fish shop that Saturday. They weren't. But loyalists, and especially Adair's murderous mob, were slavering with bloodlust – sectarian bloodlust – after the Provo bomb blood-letting.

The drugs and death-dealing outfit C Coy had a tit-for-tat maxim spawned in reaction to IRA atrocities.

Based loosely on the one-time Fred Flintstone slogan, it ran: 'Yabba-dabba-doo, any Fenian will do.'

So three days after the Shankill bombing, on 26 October, Mad Dog despatched a murder mob armed with high-powered assault rifles. They went to a Belfast City Council cleansing depot, known in Belfast parlance as a 'binyard', on Kennedy Way in Catholic west Belfast. They riddled the binyard, and a Portakabin in which the workers were having their morning tea break, with rapid-fire bullets. Two men died, cut down in the merciless cascade of fire. They were Mark Rodgers, 28, and James Cameron, 54. Five other people were wounded in the attack.

I was still working with the Ulster Press Agency. We were covering for three newspapers that day, and I rushed to the scene. Just as on that awful Saturday on the Shankill, it was again carnage. I kerned what information I could from workers, bystanders and folk who'd heard the shooting and, inevitably, the screaming. Then, this being the days before mobile phones, I had to make a run for it and find a pub, shop, house – whatever – where I could cadge the use of a landline and start filing copy: again, off the top of the head. There were no shops, pubs or garages nearby. I ran up a street, and randomly knocked on a door.

I'll never forget this. A lovely woman came to the door. I told her who I was and what I was. She let me in and allowed me to use her phone in the hallway. I filed the first copy to the English paper, then made another transfer charge call to the Dublin paper we were on shift for that day, and had just started filing another holding story to the *Cork Examiner* (now titled *The Irish Examiner*), for which we were the Northern 'stringers'.

I was standing out in the hallway of the house, where the phone sat on a small table. The woman had gone into the living room, holding the hand of a young child. A knock came at the door. I thought the woman hadn't heard it over the sound of my voice on the phone. So I answered the knock. Standing on the doorstep was Frank McCollum.

He was as surprised to see me as I was to see him. We just stood and looked at each other. And then it hit me: hard. Frank McCollum, City Hall union official, the fatal terror attack on the City Council binyard just down the street, two good working men lying dead...

The woman was coming out of her living room at this stage. Frank just said to me: 'Jim, one of the men lives here...' Frank had come to tell this lovely woman her husband was one of the two murder victims. I turned around and looked at the woman. I will never forget the black cardigan she was wearing. I had already put a fiver under the phone holder, intending to tell the woman that although I had made transfer charge calls, it would get the child something.

I just stared at her now. I put the phone down back on the reviever without speaking to the copytaker still waiting on the end of the line. I nodded to Frank – a good lad, who understood that I was only doing my job, and that I hadn't known and couldn't have known when I knocked that door that this kind woman had just been made a widow, in the most harrowing and cruel circumstances. Just like the innocents targeted   solely for sectarian slaughter on the Shankill, too, a few days earlier. Frank and a couple of colleagues who were with him to bear the bad news stood aside as I left the house.

As I walked away, I heard the keening, the anguished cry of the woman, as Frank, however gently, told her that the love of her life who had left for work that morning wouldn't be home. Ever again.

And do you know, outside of actually being at the scene of atrocities within minutes, and witnessing the bloody and brutal scenes there, the worst part of covering the Troubles was just that: witnessing the grief of wives, husbands, brothers, sisters, fathers, mothers, sons and daughters when they had been told that someone who loved them, and they dearly loved, was dead. How they had been taken from them, by bomb or bullet.

It would be wrong to say that woman's keening – that grief so heavy it feels like carrying a bag of coal in your very soul – still haunts me. But it still hurts. How could it not?

As reporters, we are trained to be – and our Code of Conduct stipulates this – impartial and objective at all times. Rubbish. Maybe when we're reporting on courts and councils, or politics and parliament.

But not when it comes to the indiscriminate – or the discriminate, those deliberately targeted – murder of innocent people. Your own people. The people, many of whom you know, in a country as small as Northern Ireland, or Ireland.

Then, you *report* accurately. But you *write* from the heart. That's how it is. Yes, there were people who were jetted in from the big broadcasters' HQs in London – BBC,

ITN, Sky, whatever – when there were huge atrocities which made headlines in the UK and worldwide.

They were known by us as blow-ins, but not derogatively. They were good pros, doing their job to the best of their ability.

But they didn't live here. They didn't live with the death and destruction and the desperation and the desolation of the bereaved every day. Reporters here in Northern Ireland did. We were, and still are, part of that community. And when that community bled and mourned, we bled and mourned with them. We translated the red blood pouring down the pavements into the black ink printed on the white pages of newspapers.

We didn't always do that impartially or objectively. Because we were part of it. And anybody who says they did is either a liar or a fool.

Or just doesn't have a heart.

21

DUNDERED BY A DODGY CHOPPER

It was a combination of a clatter of pints of stout and a swirling helicopter that ended my rugby career, which, to be honest, was spiralling spectacularly downwards anyway.

Guinness were launching their next big thing – Guinness Cold, an attempt to mimic the American market where, such was the demand for chilled drinks, you could stick beer on a lollipop stick and the Yanks would still lick it.

To me, there was nothing wrong with Guinness draft the way it used to be served in Benny's Bar, where stout used to be pulled, and sold, at room temperature. Indeed, journalists and TV crews covering the Troubles from round the globe used to gather in Benny's, where Billy Swail, the father of snooker ace Joe, took longer than his son took to clear the table to pull a pint of the black stuff. It was that good: liquid gold, black gold.

Still, the geniuses at St James's Gate down in Dublin decided to go for the American dream: ice-cold beer.

Now, there's only two things that the Yanks have contributed to the culture – and it is a culture – of buying a beer in a bar. One, the aforesaid alcoholic icicle in a glass. The second thing? Bloody bar stools. And both are bum deals.

Now, especially if you suffer from the oul' Duke of Argyles – piles, or more politely, haemorrhoids – you slip or stagger off one of those stools after a heave of bevvies, and you're walking like John Wayne just had a Texas cactus planted in his pants. Not that John Wayne didn't have a funny walk anyway.

Guinness decided to take a press posse on a magical mystery tour around Northern Ireland in the hope of positive PR coverage for their new beverage. Only thing was, they didn't tell us what we were doing on this Tour of the North until they bussed us from their aptly named Apollo Road headquarters to what is now the George Best City Airport.

There, we were introduced to a platoon of pilots – and to a shiny fleet of tiny helicopters in which we were all going to fly off to a special lunch destination.

Now, I'm not afraid of dying. I just hate flying. I really hate flying. Unlike driving a car, you're not in control. Your life is literally in the hands of some man or woman up front in the cockpit – and if they've had a cockfight with the old man, or woman, the night before, God only knows what kind of mood or shape they're in.

So planes are bad enough for me. But a tiny helicopter that seats just five people? And one of them is the pilot? Shit. Never mind John Wayne's underpants. I had a hundredweight of coal in mine when I saw what we were travelling in.

Still, a few pints had been had at Guinness HQ beforehand. It was too late to save face … or lose it. I had to go. But there was another salient, and very sobering, factor.

Lindy was working for the *Belfast Telegraph* at that time. She had been despatched by her news/features desk to cover the press launch, too. She knew all about my trepidation about airborne trips. At first, she offered to go up in the same helicopter as me. But on second thoughts, it was agreed that we wouldn't do that. This was my idea. If one chopper went down and one of us was killed, at least there would be one of us left for the kids, I told her.

She rolled her eyes dismissively. 'Don't be so damned melodramatic,' she said.

Melodramatic? Some people would call it foreboding. It was more. It was a premonition. And a premonition – almost – of doom.

We took off from Belfast. The group of helicopters followed the scenic route round the Mourne Mountains, up the shores of Carlingford Lough, and headed cross-country for County Fermanagh and lunch at Florencecourt, a stately pile where the late, great Jean Jamet, the company's northern commercial director, was to give us a presentation of what the new Guinness Cold was all about.

Well, to sub-edit this horror tale, I alighted from the tiny helicopter – to call it a flying shoebox would be to do disservice to any well-heeled leprechaun – and did a Pope John Paul. I went down on my knees and kissed the manicured lawn.

Then we had lunch, with, of course, more Guinness. And then came the official PR presentation from Monsieur Jamet, who, incidentally, had been a half-decent rugby player in France in his day.

At the end of his spiel, Jean asked: 'Any questions?'

'I've only one, Jean,' says I. 'Where's the nearest taxi depot 'til I get a cab back to Belfast – because I'm not getting in that helicopter again!'

However, after another few pints of Dutch courage, I relented, and got back in the chopper.

And therein lies a tale: well, a tail, actually, of the helicopter, and what happened to it.

Because, before take-off, Guinness had given us all these padded black flying jackets with the Guinness logo – a huge pint of the cold stuff – emblazoned on the back. A couple of the press pack found these uncomfortable to wear in the helicopters, so two of them were folded up and put into the small luggage compartment in the side fuselage of our chopper.

Now, it wasn't known at the time, obviously, that there was a fault in the catch that was supposed to secure the little luggage cubby-hole.

Shortly after we were airborne again, and over one of two big expanses of water called Upper and Lower Lough Erne, we heard a massive *crack*: like the axle of a car breaking. To use an aeronautical term, the chopper started 'feathering', that is, swirling round and round like a whirling Dervish.

The pilot, Malcolm – to whom all aboard owe their lives – was an ex-RAF Iraqi war veteran who had switched to commercial flying after leaving the service.

It wasn't immediately clear what had happened.

We were all wearing earphones so that we could hear, throughout the flight, what Malcolm and the other pilots were talking about to each other. One of the other choppers reported seeing 'something like a pair of geese' fly straight into the tail rotor.

It wasn't two geese, or any other kind of bird. It was two of the puffy, thick Guinness flying jackets, which had flown out of the luggage hold when the faulty hatch had sprung loose. They whirled straight back into the whirlybird's tail rotor, got wrapped around the drive shaft, and the drive shaft sheared and flew off into a field some 1,500 feet below us in the County Fermanagh countryside. Technically, we were out of control. We should have died.

Hero pilot Malcolm issued a mayday. Immediately, air control at Belfast International Airport, and the Army air corps, in those days stationed at St Angelo aerodrome near Enniskillen, came on line. Malcolm told them what had happened and, more crucially, what was happening. We were going down.

We could hear everything that was being said.

But as Malcolm struggled to try to control the fairground ride-like spin, the four of us passengers remained remarkably calm and composed. We were staring death in the face: and we simply stared back. We didn't blink.

In the back seat were Joe Kearney of the *Irish News* in one window seat, myself in the other, with broadcaster Barbara McCann wedged between us.

In the front passenger seat, beside the pilot, was Brian Duffy, then MD of Guinness in Belfast. And as that stricken helicopter bucked and bellied out and spun and then bucked again – just like a bull in a rodeo – those of us in the back seat put our arms around each other.

Brian pushed his right arm back through the gap in the front seats, and with our free hands, we grasped his, in an instantaneous, but very human, act of solidarity. We all knew we were in 'soapy bubble' – bad, bad trouble. We knew we could die. But there was no panic. There was no hysteria. We simply clasped each other tight, let Malcolm do what he was doing, and no one – *no one* – even mentioned dying.

Instead, embraced by hands and arms in this mini-rugby scrum, we team-talked each other. We spoke of how we were going to walk away from this. How we were going to survive – not perish. What I now call the most profound celebration of the human spirit I have ever encountered – in spite of what I have done, seen, reported and endured – prevailed.

And there was another very special manifestation of human compassion and caring that occurred up there, while we spiralled towards potential disaster.

The PR presentation stopover at Florencecourt – we were meant to be flying on up to the official opening of a new hotel in Derry City – was also used for refuelling the helicopters. But that meant that we had an almost full tank on board. When we hit the deck – and we knew it was inevitable that we would – that could spark a fireball, with all lives lost.

So Malcolm jettisoned the fuel. Then, to try to get a straight, dead drop – so that the chopper would land as flat as possible and not plunge nose-first into the ground, or crash on its side – he also turned off the main rotors above our heads as we were sitting holding each other in the cabin.

There was complete silence.

We were, of course, all thinking about our families – our wives, our children, our brothers, our sisters, our friends.

And then Barbara McCann whispered some of the most unselfish words I have ever heard.

It was a simple little prayer: not about herself, but offered on behalf of her mother and father, Brendan and Sylvia – Brendan, himself a veteran press photographer during the Troubles, who was no stranger to danger, and his lovely wife Sylvia, a friend whom all of us in the Belfast press corps knew well.

In that silence, Barbara's selfless Christian plea was: 'Dear Jesus, please look after my mother and father.'

Just seconds later, pilot Malcolm managed to belly-flop the helicopter on to a soft crash landing, in a field. Like the veteran, ice-cool fighter pilot he had been, he had just kept working at the controls, wrestling with the joy stick until he managed to *thunk* us down almost flat, without nose-diving or turning turtle to what would have been our certain deaths.

And after the longest two minutes and thirty-six

seconds of all our lives – that's how long it was since the tail rotor blade had snapped and sheared off – we were still alive.

But three of us – Barbara, myself, and pilot Malcolm – were in searing pain. We had broken our backs, Malcolm in two places.

Joe and Brian had somehow escaped serious injury. They were able to get out and tend to us as two Army helicopters with medics on board, which had been shadowing us from their St Angelo base, touched down. Plus, one of the other two PR trip helicopters had also landed.

Lindy was on that one. As she ran across the field, I was by that stage hanging half out of the one of the rear doors of the crashed 'copter. The medics needed to get to Barbara first. She was in a bad way.

I was lying half out on the grass, ashen-faced – of course – and with blood running down my chin and on to my chest. I had bitten my tongue, badly, on impact.

Seeing that sight, Lindy thought I was dead. But the military medics were getting to work on the three of us.

Then, 'Jippo' Ballantine from the Downtown Radio station, who'd also been on the helicopter with Lindy, ran up. He grabbed my hand.

As the medics lifted me onto a stretcher, I winked at him and babbled through a bubble of blood still on my lips: 'That's the last time I'm going to a lunch with you ...'

It was going to be all right.

And it was. The Army whisked us to the local Erne Hospital, from where we were raced, with sirens blaring, to the City Hospital in Belfast and its special neurological unit. A good fellow there, consultant Nigel Hamilton, looked after us from then on in.

But on the way up in the ambulance, I had begun to gag because of the special, precautionary surgical collar that had been strapped round my neck as I lay, my whole body also strapped and immobilised on the ambulance stretcher.

And when the X-rays taken at the Erne hospital were handed over in the City Hospital, there was an anguished gasp and an angry question: 'Who loosened the collar on his neck? His neck is in a mess!'

I had to quickly explain, as best I could – in the very straitened circumstances – that the mess my neck was in had nothing to do with the chopper accident. The damage to discs and vertebrae up there were the cumulative legacy of almost forty years in a rugby scrum!

And that sporting syndrome was to spark another quandary. There was a suggestion, at one stage, that a piece of bone might be taken out of one of my hips and inserted into a split in one of the vertebrae in my lower back. I gave that a bye-ball, explaining to the fantastic, though somewhat flummoxed, medical staff who eventually got me back on my feet (albeit I had to wear a full-torso plaster of Paris for nine months) that I didn't fancy them delving deep into one of my hips.

Because after all those years training for and playing rugby, and after all the years I'd spent pounding the pavements to train for and get round eleven marathons, I was very dubious indeed as to what kind of state they'd find my hip bones in!

Eleven days after being rushed to hospital, I was out.

I was weak. I had that plaster stretching from my Adam's apple the whole way down to my lower waist. But along with the rest of the other four on what could have been a very fateful day, we were, at least, alive.

The day after I got home, I was out walking, although I couldn't even bend down to tie the laces on my training shoes. A couple of weeks later, I was jogging again.

I'm still jogging.

The back, after all these years, is still flexible enough for me work up a sweat jogging five mornings a week, added to giving myself a good daily rollickin' on the rowing machine – just about the time it takes to row, and win, the Oxford and Cambridge boat race. But, at my age, the only Blue I get for that is blue in the face.

Malcolm, the pilot, to whom we all owe our lives, recovered well, and the last I heard he was working as a chopper pilot for a police force in England.

Barbara, or Babs, McCann, had a rougher time. She was a keen golfer, and the back injury badly affected that. But she continued to work as a journalist, and a bloody good one at that, and at the time of writing is working for Ulster Television in their Belfast HQ.

We phone each other for a yarn, only sporadically, but we certainly make sure to phone each other every year on 21 October – the anniversary of our very own annus (helicopter) horribilis.

I was still in the hospital, embarrassed – well, you would be, wouldn't you, if it took three nurses to roll you on and off a bed pan, with your own weight plus the plaster of Paris weighing as much as a bag of coal, every time you needed a shit – when something happened that left me with a *really* red, rather than a blue, face.

People were very kind to me. 'Get well, Big Lad' messages flowed in, visitors abounded – fellow hacks from the press, politicians, ordinary punters, as well as those Christian gentlemen who preach from the pulpit every sabbath, they all came to see me. Quite a lot of clergymen from different churches, actually. Maybe, as in rugby, they thought they saw the opportunity for a conversion.

One day, towards the end of my hospitalisation, two dog collars turned up. At the same time. They sat on each side of my bed. Unfortunately, I couldn't move my head on the pillow at that time, so I was getting the message from both gentlemen (and they are gentlemen) in each ear, at the same time.

And then, to my relief, I heard the guttural tones of this boomin' Belfast voice coming up the ward. It belonged to an oul' mucker of mine from the Cregagh Red Sox rugby genre, Willie Duncan, the former Ulster and Ireland rugby player.

'Thank God,' I thought, 'the Good Lord has saved me from the clergy!'

Not only that, he'd a six-pack of stout tucked under his arm. Our mate, Ronnie Bingham wwas with him.

'Jimmy,' says Willie, 'we know you busted your back on that Guinness trip, so we brought you a few cans of Murphy's [another black stout] instead.'

I don't know what the clergymen thought about this: but they probably got the message that it wasn't for taking Holy Communion while they were there.

Anyway, the very welcome visitor launches into a yarn

about how everybody at the rugby club was asking about me. And he says, in fact, that at the 'do' in the club the previous Saturday night, just a few days after the 'copter crash, he got so fed up with people asking about me, he commandeered the microphone at the interval, when the band were taking a break, and announced that I was still alive, and on the mend.

And then, with the two clergymen still sitting on either side of my bed, he came out with a killer line.

Willie says to me: 'Jim, I also just told the folks on Saturday night that you'd been dundered by a dodgy chopper.'

I felt like calling for the screens, the bed pan and those three nurses yet again.

I managed to squint to one side of the bed. One cleric was rising out of his bedside chair, saying merely: 'Goodbye, Jim. I'll say a prayer for you.' And, glancing sideways, he says: 'And I'll say a prayer for your friend as well.'

I managed a glance over the other side. The other cleric had his head between his knees – laughing.

Never mind the helicopter accident itself, that one-liner from the redoubtable rugby man – in front of the two dog collars – almost did for me.

22
MO SAYS NO

Ulster were the first Irish team to win what is now the rugby European Championship.

That was on the famous day of 30 January 1999. I was there. One of 49,000 fans, mostly from Ulster, who watched David Humphreys and his heroes with the Red Hand on their jerseys beat French side Colomiers 21-6 at what was then called Lansdowne Road.

I was both working and watching the game that day. And according to then Secretary of State for Northern Ireland, Mo Mowlam, that cost me a knighthood.

I'm sure the irascible political peacemaker – as Secretary of State she banged the heads of the party leaders together, with special US envoy George Mitchell, to forge and hammer out the Good Friday Agreement of 1998 – was only kidding.

But I never got to ask her before she tragically died from cancer.

I write 'irascible' because the dyed-in-the-wool Labour Party veteran could be both feisty and funny in the blink of an eye.

The first time I met her, I was chairing a series of chat shows for BBC NI television. The idea was that the series would run for six weeks and comprise panels of half a dozen young students, both Catholic and Protestant, meeting and questioning prominent politicians, police officers and other prime figures in the province's life. I was the facilitator, sitting in the middle of the students, channelling the questions, ad-libbing the links and, if necessary, keeping the students 'on message' according to BBC protocol. Among the interviewees were Gerry Adams, the late David Ervine, then a Stormont Assemblyman, PSNI Chief Constable Sir Ronnie Flanagan and, of course, Secretary of State Mo Mowlam.

The series stirred up quite a flurry of controversy: not least when one of the young lads, Ruairi McKenna from Ballymena, asked the Sinn Féin president, in front of the cameras, if he'd ever been in the IRA. Adams almost swallowed his pipe. He hesitated, and then denied he'd been in the Provos. I think that was the first time the question had ever been put to him in public. And, of course, it has been the subject of some very forensic picking-over ever since. Not least when the *Sunday World* published a picture of Gerry at a republican funeral wearing a black beret.

But Ruairi wasn't stopping there. He then posed the next logical question to the man who was head of Sinn Féin: 'Why not?'

Then there was Sir Ronnie Flanagan, a former Ulster rugby player himself, who sparked a ruckus during his interview when, questioned by another student, he claimed the IRA were implicated in a murder when they were supposed to be on ceasefire.

And then there was Mo. The Beeb flew all of us – the panel and the crew – to the Labour Party conference in Bournemouth to do the interview there. It was a pretty straightforward, par-for-the-course political update, with no upsetting of the political applecart: on either side.

Except for the start.

The mischievous Ms Mowlam was sitting in an armchair as the countdown to my front-of-camera intro started, prompted by an autocue. The producer was leading me in: 'Ten, nine, eight, seven…' until, out of the corner of my eye, I glimpsed Mo moving her hand up and down and making a very rude gesture. At me. Silently, she was smiling and giving me the w****r sign.

Instant collapse of intro. The students were in stitches. And we had to do it all over again. Luckily, it was being recorded, put in the can. Otherwise, we'd have been off the air. Probably for good.

Another time we crossed paths, it wasn't for public consumption.

I'd asked her to be a guest at a lunch in Belfast organised by our then managing director Michael Brophy for senior editorial staff and members of the board of Independent Newspapers. Michael asked me to 'spring a surprise'. I did. I didn't even tell him beforehand who the guest would be.

Mo was enmeshed in the pre-Good Friday talks at Stormont. She arrived late and was a bit out of breath. She was the only woman round a thirteen-person lunch table upstairs in Michael Deane's Michelin-star restaurant. As soon as she was introduced and sat down, she immediately doffed the bandana she had taken to wearing on her head after the hair loss caused by her cancer treatment.

There was some sort of vegetarian starter for the lunch. Mo, in spite of her medical condition, declined. 'I don't eat health food,' she quipped.

But she did get stuck into politics, and a phalanx of Ulster politicos, during a no-holds-barred question-and-answer session with the other folk around the table. And never mind the vegetarian starter, she used some very fruity language indeed, while explaining that immediately after eating, she had to hurry back to Stormont for another series of make-or-break meetings.

That also meant that while everyone else at table was having a jar, she couldn't.

I took her arm to escort her down the stairs to the front door, where her security escorts were waiting with her ministerial car. As we got to the first landing, she stopped, swivelled, looked me straight in the eye, and bluntly stated: 'McDowell, never again invite me to a lunch where I cannot imbibe f*****g alcohol!' I never did get to invite her to another lunch.

But the day she knocked my knighthood on the head, she had invited herself to our *Sunday World* office. She knew, and had been briefed, of course, about all the bother we'd been through with the paramilitary bogeymen: the loyalist boycotts, the threats from drug dealers and gangsters. But what prompted her visit to our office was that it had been targeted by drug dealers for an arson attack. That happened late on the night of 28 January 1999 – two days before Ulster's Heineken Cup Final in Dublin.

Chris Moore, one of my best friends, an outstanding, award-winning TV and newspaper journalist and author, and the principled and unrelenting pursuer of the evil paedophile priest Fr Brendan Smyth, was out for a meal and a drink that night. He knew where our office was, of course, as he'd put in a couple of spells working for the *Sunday World*. I was at home when Chris phoned me. As usual, he didn't waste words.

'Jimmy,' he told me, 'your office is on fire.'

Not quite. But firemen were at that stage breaking in the door to douse a blaze in the office hallway. The drug dealers had squirted fuel through the letterbox and lit it. The blaze was confined to the hall and bottom stairway because of fireproof doors. But the whole downstairs premises, which served as our office, was a bit of a mess with scorch, smoke and water damage.

Within days, we had discovered who the arsonists were. We also learned that one of them was badly burned by a blowback from the petrol fumes when they burst into flames. We didn't send him a bunch of flowers or a card wishing him a speedy recovery.

Alerted by Chris's SOS call, I spent most of the night at the office. Next morning, Secretary of State Mowlam phoned me. She said she wanted to pay an official visit to the office to show solidarity and support for our staff, and the newspaper. I thanked her, said we would welcome that, and asked her: 'When?'

She replied: 'Tomorrow.'

Tomorrow was Saturday. The day of the big match in Dublin.

Two of us, myself and big Richard 'Sully' Sullivan, an avid Ulster rugby fan – as is his brilliant son, Jacob – were supposed to be going to Dublin not only to watch the game, but to fill no fewer than eight pages of the northern edition of the paper with colour stories and picture-led features on the Ulster fans down there.

However, Sully, who has since taken over from me as northern editor of the paper, had to cry off at the last minute. That left me to do the interviews and file the stories to fill those pages – albeit puffed out with a portfolio of pictures – on my own.

Mo hadn't dropped a bombshell in my lap when she phoned. She'd dropped a rugby ball.

I asked her, politely, did she know what was happening in Dublin the next day, Saturday. She seemed surprised. I told her about the Ulster v. Colomiers final. I told her a posse of the main politicians from the North would be there, Gerry Adams among them. I told her protocol probably dictated that she should be there, too.

She paused. I heard her say something to one of her advisers. She said she'd phone me back in a couple of minutes. She did. She said she was now going to the game, too. But she would visit the office first, around ten o'clock the next morning.

I then teed up a drop goal myself. I told her: 'Secretary of State, I won't be in the office tomorrow morning.' I explained to her that I had to go to Dublin that night, Friday, to be up and on the job to fill eight pages from early the next morning. Plus, I told her honestly, I also wanted to be at the game to see Ulster make European and Irish rugby history.

I explained that because of the cross-border convoy of fans going south on the Saturday, there was no way I could be in the office at ten for her visit, and then make it to Dublin by road to get copy for four pages filed before the game, with another four pages to fill with (as it turned out) jubilant celebrations afterwards.

She said she would phone me back in a few minutes.

Apparently, the plan was that she and her entourage would travel the 100 miles south by road, too, after the gee-up visit to our office. It changed.

She came back to me. 'We'll both be in your office at ten. Then we're going to fly down. You can fly with us.'

She'd arranged a helicopter to get to and from the game. An offer from Ms Mowlam I couldn't refuse? You bet I could. After the chopper crash three years earlier, there was no way I was climbing back into one again so soon.

I told Mo so. She understood. At least, I thought she did.

She did indeed kindly visit the office on the Saturday morning at ten o'clock. The rest of the staff were there. I was in Dublin.

It was a smashing wee do, and a real boost for morale from Mo, with Karen, our old friend and boss of the Duke of York next door, even coming into the pub well before opening time and providing trays of sandwiches and buns, and pots of coffee and tea. And other refreshments …

I tried to catch up with the Secretary of State later in the day by phone, to thank her. It didn't work. But I got back into work myself the following Monday morning. Not even hungover from the celebrations in Dublin on the Saturday night, and the open-top bus victory parade for the Ulster lads back in Belfast on the Sunday.

A more apt diagnosis was 'hung under'.

I could barely lift my then balding, if not completely bald, head. But one of the best memories of the weekend was in the early hours of the Sunday morning, standing on a table in the swanky Berkeley Court Hotel in Dublin with a high-ranking official of the Colomiers rugby club, and trying to teach him, in front of a packed and very pissed but pleasant audience, the words of 'The Boys from the County Armagh' in French. 'Les Garçons de la Countée Armagh' just doesn't have the same ring, does it?

So when I got back into the still smoke-stenched and soot-blackened office on Monday morning, there was an envelope sitting on my desk top. It had my name on it. Handwritten. Obviously from Mo.

There was a note inside, on *Sunday World*-headed notepaper, also handwritten. Referring to my (albeit unavoidable absence) for Ms Mowlam's visit there on Saturday morning, the content was succinct and straight to the point, as you would expect from a Secretary of State.

She said how much she'd enjoyed coming into the office and meeting the staff, how much she'd appreciated the refreshments, but she'd been disappointed I hadn't been there to greet her. '*So you can forget about the fucking knighthood,*' the note ended.

It was a classic case of not Ulster Says No, but Mo Says No … to me. Not that I cared. I laughed. It was meant as a joke: Mo was jesting. I think.

So instead of working, I went for a cure.

Because while I was having a few pints in Dublin having got the job done, and filed enough copy for the four double-page spreads in the paper, the editor, Colm MacGinty, had posted one of the best sub-headlines ever on the front page of the northern edition of the paper to greet the exultant Ulster fans heading home on the Sunday morning. It read, simply:

SALUTE THE SONS OF ULSTER

Even on the Monday, I still needed to raise a glass or two to that. Plus, we saluted Mo's kind, considerate and important gesture of solidarity, putting a picture of her with the staff in the paper, too.

But there was one final experience with Mo that I didn't quite salute. Until afterwards.

I'd gone to the police sports ground in Belfast – dubbed colloquially by the cops themselves Sin City: I never asked why – to watch the NI police play an English police XV in the semi-final of the British Police Cup. I was in the company of some class cops: Tim McGregor, then president of the home rugby club, the late Kevin Sheehy, and Philip 'Bogey' Boyd, a club stalwart and former flanker, also since passed on.

Ronnie Flanagan, the retired chief constable of both the former RUC and the PSNI – he was the only man who could have married the former into the latter under immense pressure, both politically and even within his own force – was at the crunch cup game, too. He was to be the guest speaker at the clubhouse after-match dinner. But as the match drew to a close, he took a phone call. It was from Secretary of State Mowlam. He was needed at Stormont, to sign a proscription order effectively banning and declaring illegal two wacky, but potentially dangerous, loyalist vigilante organisations. He'd have to go to Stormont Castle and stay there until the banning orders came into effect at midnight.

He told me I was taking over as guest speaker at the dinner. Cold. No background. No research. No names. Nothing. But I did OK.

Until I came to the end of what I was saying.

It was then I brought some old Belfast sleggin' – bantering – of the peelers into play.

The venerable members of both the RUC and the PSNI, because of the colour of their uniforms, especially when decked out in riot gear, were caricatured by the initials BBs. That doesn't stand for members of the Boys' Brigade.

So I ended what passed for my speech by saying that of all the games of rugby I'd watched and reported upon, including that famous day on 30 January 1999 in Dublin, I'd derived most pleasure from that afternoon's match.

'Because,' I explained, 'I'd never before enjoyed, for a whole eighty minutes, the sight of two teams of black bastards kicking the shit out of one another.'

The remark was greeted with a gale of laughter from the Ulster cops.

It had to be explained to the English bobbies, over pints afterwards, what I was talking about.

Still, they gave me and Club President Tim McGregor a genuine bobby's helmet each in appreciation.

It, too, was black in colour.

And as they say, if the hat fits, wear it.

23

THEY HAVEN'T GONE AWAY, YOU KNOW...

Sometimes getting a good story, or a great story, is down to being in the right place at the right time. Just plain luck, in other words.

I've stumbled across a few stories in my time almost totally by accident. Like the time, driving through Belfast in the early evening, I saw what at first appeared to be nothing more than a traffic accident in the opposite lane. Police Land Rovers surrounded a van that was parked haphazardly with its back doors wide open. What made me realise that this was something more than a smash or a breakdown wasn't just the number of cops on the scene but the fact that those now searching the roadway at the rear of the van were kitted out in white forensic suits. I eased my own car around and parked up.

Witnesses at the scene described how a badly injured man had fallen from the back of the van. The thing is, he hadn't got his injuries from the fall. After an altercation in a nearby pub, he'd been surrounded by a bunch of men armed with iron bars, brutally beaten, bundled into the van and driven off, presumably for further punishment. Somehow, though, he'd managed to free himself and leap from the moving van.

Just before I'd come along ...

By far one of the biggest stories I ever came across by dint of being in the right place at the right time was connected to republican terrorism. But I chanced upon that one not in a Belfast street, but on the other side of the world.

In July 1999 I was on holiday in Florida with Lindy and our two boys. We used to stay in a great old hotel at the beach in Fort Lauderdale called, appropriately enough, Ireland's Inn. Named not for the country but for the man who owned it – a real gentleman called Jack Ireland. It was a world away from the pressures of the job in Belfast, a place where I didn't have to keep looking over my shoulder or sitting with my back to the wall, constantly watching who was coming into the place.

On a few occasions when I had been advised by security sources that threats against me were particularly serious and it would be an idea for the family and myself to get offside for a couple of weeks, it had been Fort Lauderdale and Ireland's Inn that we'd headed for. I saw it as literally a safe haven. A world away from Northern Ireland, the Troubles and anything to do with paramilitaries.

And then one morning ...

I have always been an early riser. I still like getting up with the dawn, and sometimes even before that, to head out for a run to clear the head. At that time I was putting in a fair few miles every day, running along the glorious beach in that part of south Florida. Then I'd head back to the hotel, picking up the local newspapers on the way. Among these was the Broward edition of the *Miami Herald*.

That particular morning there was a story on page one that, for obvious reasons, immediately caught my eye. Three people were due up in court in Fort Lauderdale that day, charged with running guns to Belfast. For the IRA.

Now the peace process, encouraged not least by American President Bill Clinton, was still at an early stage, the Belfast Agreement having been signed only a year previously, in 1998. Unionists had long been suspicious about whether the IRA were fully committed to the process, questioning their sincerity. It wasn't by chance that when the rock band U2 had played a free concert in Botanic Park in 1997, as part of their contribution to encouraging political enemies to engage in talks, that they chose to do a version of 'Suspicious Minds'.

The agreement had called for all arms to be put beyond use, but the paramilitaries, including the Provos, still hadn't decommissioned their weapons. To put it mildly, then, the idea that the IRA were still actively acquiring guns was, well, a bombshell that could torpedo the fledgling peace process.

I took the newspaper up to Lindy and we decided that we would go along to the court hearing to see what we could learn about the case. A friend agreed to look after our two boys while we were away. We chose from our holiday clothes something that wouldn't look too out of place in a courthouse and headed downtown.

A couple of press photographers were standing outside the building and we decided to ask them for some guidance on which court the hearing would be in and where reporters could sit. I started to explain where we were from to the first cameraman. 'Ach, God, ye're from Belfast!' he exclaimed. 'So am I!'

He was a freelancer based in Florida and covering the case for local papers. Since Lindy and I had both brought our press accreditation, we were allowed in and shown where to sit – right at the front of the court.

Before the hearing began the defendants were marched in to sit just in front of us. Marched is probably the wrong word. Shuffled would be closer. In court cases at home the accused, when being held in custody, are escorted into the dock by prison officers. I've seen prisoners who've been handcuffed. But nothing like this. It was a scene straight from an American prison movie. The defendants were all dressed in orange jail jumpsuits and chained at the ankles and hands, with another chain running between.

Before the court were Conor Claxton, 26, and Anthony Smyth, 42, both originally from Belfast, and Smyth's lover, Siobhan Browne, 34.

Browne, a stockbroker, lived in a posh apartment in upmarket Boca Raton. She was, to put it mildly, an unlikely IRA gun-runner. Previously married to a rich Israeli, she'd met Smyth in a local Irish bar. Within a short time he'd moved into her classy apartment. Although Browne came originally from Cork, she was now a US citizen – something that was of crucial importance in the gun-running operation. It meant she was able to buy the guns in the first place.

Smyth had introduced her to Claxton, who, he said, had just arrived from Belfast. He had also persuaded her to allow the younger man to move into the apartment they shared. He talked to her about the IRA. Browne claimed she had no interest in the organisation and only agreed to buy the guns because Smyth had asked her to. She was buying them under her own name and also using an alias.

But she was being monitored. The agent who busted the case wasn't from the FBI, but from America's Bureau of Alcohol, Tobacco and Firearms.

The agent, Regina Lombardo, had spotted the fact that Browne was buying a serious number of guns – the court was told 'over fifty', although the FBI believed that the wider operation involved many, many more. These weapons of death were being posted back to Ireland hidden, sickeningly, inside children's toys.

As the trio came into court, Claxton seemed to revel in the spotlight. In a statement he'd admitted buying the guns for the IRA. (Back in Ireland, the IRA denied they'd sanctioned the operation. But they would say that, wouldn't they?) Claxton said they'd be used against British soldiers, police officers and loyalist paramilitaries. He taunted his US interrogators with the comment, 'You didn't get all of us.'

Smyth, a big bulky man, sat sullen and silent, his eyes fixed straight ahead. As Browne was led in she kept staring at her lover, seemingly trying to catch his eye. At one point she even tried to reach out to touch him. A warden put paid to that, striking her arm hard with a baton. Browne looked devastated.

All three were given jail sentences, as was a third man, Martin Mullan, who was also brought to trial. But it was the potential impact on the peace process that made this such a massive story. At home, republicans tried to deny that the plot had anything to do with the IRA. But the FBI and the American prosecutor, Richard Scruggs, were adamant that the operation had been driven by the Provos.

The Americans were impressively well briefed on the various republican terror outfits. An FBI agent I spoke to and a Miami journalist with impeccable security contacts also argued that the gun-running operation had been much, much bigger and had stretched to other parts of the USA, including Philadelphia and California, and even to South America.

Meanwhile, back in Belfast ...

Not surprisingly, news of the gun-running operation had almost scuppered the peace process. The IRA were supposed to be on ceasefire. Here was shocking and incontrovertible evidence that they were, in fact, acquiring a fresh and significant arsenal. There were allegations of behind-the-scenes moves in both the UK and US to play down the seriousness of what had been uncovered. The reverberations were felt for years. When a UTV documentary in 2000 aired a claim by prosecutor

227

Scruggs that the plot had indeed been sanctioned by the IRA leadership, to use his own phrase, 'everyone went apeshit'. Scruggs said in a later magazine interview that he'd taken surreal phone calls from Washington in the aftermath as pressure was put on him to retract.

As for the guns that got through ...

In 1999 the Ulster Freedom Fighters (UFF) terrorist Johnny Adair had been allowed out of jail on leave. He'd been serving his sentence for directing terrorism. Adair and his then wife, Gina, were at a UB40 concert in Botanic Park when he was hit in the head by a bullet fired from a gun that is believed to have been smuggled in by the Claxton operation.

The shot merely grazed him. A bad aim? Or had the gun been 'modified' by security forces – the FBI or MI5, perhaps – who were aware of and monitoring the gun-running plot?

I don't know for sure.

But, to reiterate the infamous words of Gerry Adams, many believe that the IRA 'haven't gone away, you know ...'

24

THE MURDER OF MARTIN O'HAGAN

Martin O'Hagan could be the feistiest of characters. That was one of his strong points. He would take on any 'marking': the newsroom term for a job. Just before he was murdered, he even volunteered to go to Afghanistan to report on the impending war in 2001.

Back home, however, he enjoyed the more off-beat markings as well. That led to more than a few laughs. Like the time he discovered a few Thai hookers were running a brothel at a house in Ventry Street, off Belfast's Dublin Road. He was wired with a special recording device, which also had a two-way link back to the *Sunday World* office, so we could hear what was going on, just in case he got into trouble.

Well, he did … of sorts.

Martin played the girls perfectly, as if he was an ordinary punter just there for one of them to turn a trick.

But then, in the best tabloid style of the time, just when it came to 'doing the business', he pulled out his notebook and pen and came out with the classic undercover hack's line about being there to do a story.

Well, the ladies of the night went bananas.

As we listened, the Thai hookers got into a right old tussle with Martin, trying to wrest his notebook from him and trying to strip him, not for sex, but to search him for any recording devices. Thankfully, their pimp wasn't around at the time, otherwise we'd have been round to the brothel, which wasn't that far away from us in the city centre.

However, at one stage the hookers had grappled Marty to the ground. And then we heard him coming over the wire exclaiming: 'McDowell, there's one of them sitting on my face!'

To which I replied: 'Martin, there're punters who would pay a lot of money for that.'

Even Martin managed a chuckle at that.

He extricated himself safely from the scene, made his excuses and left, as they say. But the hookers had commandeered the *Dad's Army*-style wire-rimmed spectacles he always wore. The next thing we heard on the wire was the intrepid reporter telling us he was outside the house again. And after that came the anguished cry: 'Oh the dirty wee hoors.'

For what the torrid Thai hookers had done was bend Martin's wire specs in two … and posted them out through the door to him, through the letterbox, as he stood rearranging his clothes in the street.

Needless to say, Marty made mincemeat of the Thai tarts in the paper the following Sunday … and the brothel was banged up, in a different way, with its doors shut for good by the Monday.

Marty was feisty in another way, too. There are malicious people who say that Martin and I didn't get on. Bullshit. There were times when we had rows, especially if, as editor of the northern edition of the *Sunday World*, I had to 'spike', or stop, a story for legal reasons. That was my job. It's called editorial discretion.

Martin wasn't the only reporter whose stories I had to spike down the years. That often led to rows. But anyone who thinks a newspaper office, especially one like the *Sunday World,* where, because of the dangers inherent in their jobs, journalists are always living on the edge, is a kindergarten, is either a fool or doesn't know what they're talking about. Indeed, there were times when, having done the legwork and written stories myself, our libel lawyers advised me to either change it to get it in, or to spike it. And I've done both with my own copy.

But after rows in the office, as in most newspapers, it could be, and most times was, resolved over a pint in a pub. And that's where I was when Martin O'Hagan, all five feet four inches of him, feisty as a bagged ferret, literally ran to my aid.

I was in Barney O'Neill's pub having a pint when a convicted Provo bomber who'd been released from jail walked in. He and his mate were on the rip. They were ordering and downing what they were calling Ballymurphy brandies. Ballymurphy, in west Belfast, was an IRA hotbed. A Ballymurphy brandy was slang for a glass of cheap sherry, Bristol Cream, as I recall.

Anyway, your man, the ex-bomber, didn't like the *Sunday World*. Not many of them did, right up to the top of the IRA or Sinn Féin, including Gerry Adams – who, of course, was never in the IRA. So when he spotted me in the bar, he made it as clear as the spark on a detonator that he didn't like me. A digging match spilled out on to the street, as it does.

The scrap was soon over. A couple of good guys in the pub gave me a hand – or in this case a fist – out. However, news of the pub punch-up spread with the speed of a bullet: Belfast may be by name a city, but it really resembles a village when hot news hits the streets.

I went back to my pint in the bar, taking care that the blood still streaming from my snout – the Ballymurphy brandy thug had head-butted me – wasn't seeping down into the creamy head of my pint of stout.

Just minutes later, the swing door of Barney's burst open, and Martin O'Hagan came barrelling in, as out of breath as a marathon runner hitting the wall. He'd run the whole way from the then *Sunday World* office on the other side of the city centre when he heard about the scrap. He had hurried the whole way to the pub to give me a hand out, too. So much for me and him always being at war ...

And as he was to say of me afterwards, when sharing a pint with a mutual friend of ours, 'McDowell may be a big bastard at times – but he's our big bastard.'

And nowhere was that proved more than when Martin's lovely wife, Marie, would come into town from their County Armagh home town of Lurgan on a Friday afternoon, and the three of us would go for a jar together, most often to the Duke of York pub, where a very accurate caricature of Martin hangs on a wall to this day.

If only he and Marie had been in the Duke's the night he was murdered, instead of having a jar where they did.

The evening before he died, Martin left the office as usual and headed for the car park used by the *Sunday World*. He arrived just around the same time as Lindy was picking up our car. They stood and chatted for a while and Martin mentioned that he wanted to go to Afghanistan, where events were at that time spiralling towards war.

Lindy laughed. 'Jaysus, Martin, things are bad enough back here. You'd get shot out there for sure.'

Martin laughed with her as they said goodbye and got into their cars.

The next night I got the phone call.

It was late on that black Friday evening when Brian 'Barney' Rowan phoned me at home. Barney had worked with us running the Ulster Press Agency, before leaving to become the security correspondent for BBC NI. It wasn't unusual for us to exchange information after a terrorist shooting, bombing or other atrocity, especially when deadlines were looming.

I'd heard there'd been a shooting in Lurgan, Martin O'Hagan's home town. Nothing unusual about that. The County Armagh town was a hotbed of strife: and it still can be, with dissident republicans on the loose, despite the Good Friday Agreement.

Barney was phoning about the shooting, fatal as it proved. And then came the bombshell. Barney sounded unusually tense.

'Jim,' he said, 'what age is Martin O'Hagan?'

Alarm bells didn't start ringing in my head, as the cliché goes. Big Ben started bonging instead. I didn't really know Martin's age off the top of my head.

Then Brian said that although the police at that early stage weren't giving the victim's name, they were saying that the man 'down on the street' was aged fifty-one.

Brian then told me where the shooting had occurred. It was the road in which Martin lived with Marie and their three daughters. Both the age and the address synched. But I still didn't want to even countenance that.

'Jim, I think it's Martin,' said Barney quietly.

It was.

Lindy and I got into the car. We went to Lurgan, to the quarantined spot on the road that the police had cordoned off with plastic tape. The police knew who I was. I ducked under the tape.

Martin's body was still warm on the ground, the blood that had poured out of the bullet holes in his back pooled liberally on the tarmac.

I was white with shock and horror. And burning red with rage.

And then, even worse, just at this point an LVF mob haemorrhaged on a corner close to the fresh murder scene. They began an obscene, sectarian chant, the main crass chorus of which was '... another Fenian dead'.

Despair was subsumed by searing anger. I went to move towards them. The police at the scene were already stretched, coping with the immediate aftermath of the murder. A uniformed officer put his hand on my arm. 'Sir,' he said, 'do you want a riot erupting here, with bricks and bottles flying over this lad's dead body?'

No. Definitely not. Not with the terrible task still to be faced.

Going to the nearby O'Hagan home, to put my arms around a weeping widow who'd just witnessed her husband being shot dead in front of her. Martin had been gunned down just 100 metres from his own front door. He died a hero, protecting Marie from the LVF assassin's flying bullets.

He'd been at his favourite pub that night, Fa' Joe's in Lurgan town centre. ('Fa' is short for 'Father': that's how the locals referred to the one-time owner, and the name stuck.)

Marie was with him, enjoying a few Friday night drinks. It was only about half a mile from the bar to their home, a leisurely stroll. They decided to walk, as they often did.

But there was a spotter in the bar. A terror gang scout. He used a public phone in the pub to call his LVF boss as soon as Marie and Martin left. Two brothers were waiting in a stolen car. One had taken over from Billy Wright as godfather of the mid-Ulster LVF after King Rat's murder in jail. Indeed, known as the Piper, he had been the lone bagpiper at the terror czar's funeral.

The brothers, one of them, ironically, born a Catholic from a different marriage from his kin, had worked out a meticulous plan with their cohorts in a flat in Lurgan earlier that day, when the murder weapon had been produced and loaded. The elder brother, the Piper, was to be behind the wheel for the Chicago-style drive-by shooting. The designated gunman was his younger brother. Martin probably heard the car speeding up. Shooting started. He threw himself across Marie, covering her with the front of his body. A salvo of bullets tore into his back, killing him almost instantly.

Billy Wright's orders from the grave had been fatally and cruelly fulfilled.

King Rat had veered erratically from being evangelically Christian (allegedly), especially when incarcerated in jail, to being a junkie. After he himself had been ambushed and assassinated on a prison bus by INLA godfather Christopher 'Crip' McWilliams and two other INLA henchmen, John Kennaway and John Glennon, on 27 December 1997, he was found to have smuggled-in drugs in his system. But whether it was a religious vision or a drugs-induced premonition, Wright himself knew he was, at some stage, going to meet a violent end.

And I was later to learn, after Martin's murder, that Wright had used Old Testament language to order that killing as revenge for his own death. He told his killer cohorts: 'If anything ever happens to me, it is to happen to Martin O'Hagan tenfold.'

On the black Friday night of 28 September 2001, Wright's vengeance on Martin O'Hagan was exacted ... from beyond the grave. That meant that Wright would never face justice for the murder of a journalist, unlike the killers of another investigative journalist Veronica Guerin, in Dublin.

And, much to my chagrin and regret, the LVF killers who stalked and shot dead our colleague Martin have never been brought to justice, either.

In spite of us naming them numerous times in the *Sunday World*, often on the front page.

In spite of one of their LVF Lurgan mob, the evil Neil Hyde, turning supergrass, or police informer, and threatening to nail the drive-by killers in court ... only for the case to be withdrawn.

And the reason why Martin's killers are still free on the streets and have escaped jail, in spite of being convicted of other criminal charges down the years?

I believe they were touts – for whatever undercover security agency – and therefore, because of what they know of the 'dirty war', or because of what they have threatened to disclose, they are deemed 'untouchables'.

But not by me, or the *Sunday World*.

We will continue to name and shame the death-dealing LVF killers until their, or my, dying day. After all, those who campaigned for justice for Veronica Guerin succeeded. And we are (still) asking for nothing more, nothing less.

Simply justice for Martin.

25

THE LONG FIGHT FOR JUSTICE

In September 2008, two brothers, Drew King and Billy King, along with three others, Nigel Leckey, Mark Kennedy and Neil Hyde, were charged in connection with Martin's murder. Drew King, Neil Hyde and Nigel Leckey were charged with the murder. Robin King was charged with attempting to pervert the course of justice. Mark Kennedy, a Catholic, was charged with helping to conceal a getaway car. We hounded their court appearances thereafter, taking pictures as they strutted in and out of the courts.

However, in July 2010, once again, and to our great dismay, the charges against all five who were originally in the dock were dropped.

But their court appearances sparked a series of security incidents. At one stage, when I was reporting on proceedings at Craigavon Court, close to the LVF base in Lurgan, County Armagh, police had alerted me that a carload of hoods, who they suspected to be LVF henchmen, was waiting just outside the court precinct for me to drive out. They advised me to wait until they had moved the suspects on.

Death threats – those PM1 forms I had to sign – were delivered to me by the police. The police protocol was that they didn't always specify it was the LVF. The PM1s instead usually referred to 'a loyalist paramilitary organisation'. But myself and my staff, a number of whom also received PM1s, had no doubt where they were coming from at the time: the LVF. But there were others – many others – over the years from a range of terror gangs, both loyalist and republican.

Threats and abuse – just the other day, as I walked towards the Europa Hotel in the very heart of Belfast, two hoods ran past me and one of them, a big brute of a slabber, bellowed at me in the middle of the crowded street. 'McDowell, you're f****d!,' he roared.

Passersby gaped at me in horror. As usual, I shrugged my shoulders and told them: 'Just another satisfied *Sunday World* customer.'

They laughed.

However, there was one incident, at Craigavon courthouse, which was less easy to shrug off. Another *Sunday World* reporter, Hugh Jordan, then crime correspondent, and myself had gone to cover yet another hearing featuring the main LVF godfather charged in connection with Martin's murder. A posse of his heavies, including his chief enforcer – a *very* undesirable individual dubbed the Mohican, an ugly ogre whose 'sports' were badger-baiting and cage-fighting – were either in or loitering outside the Crown building.

My company car, a big black brute of a Toyota Land Cruiser – we dubbed it 'the Taliban' because the make is apparently a favoured vehicle among Afghani tribal chiefs – was parked at the front of the courthouse, in the official court car park, fringed by security cameras.

There was a break in proceedings on the benches inside. Hugh Jordan and I walked out past the security sangar at the front door of the heavily wire-cordoned complex. Suddenly, we heard a number of loud cracks rifling through the air. We ducked down. We thought we were being shot at.

But then Hugh pointed and exclaimed: 'It's your car!'

An LVF crew had been beating up the jeep with a crowbar and hammer. They then disappeared through a hedge running around the perimeter of the car park. Over three thousand quid's worth of damage was caused to the Toyota.

But when I later went looking for CCTV footage of the very public vandalising of the vehicle – which I was assured would be recorded on a central PSNI hub compiled elsewhere in Northern Ireland – I was told there was none. The CCTV cameras – covering a Crown courthouse where suspected terrorists and other dangerous and violent criminals often appeared, mind you – weren't working or covering the courthouse car park that particular day.

Did I previously mention LVF touts?

Meantime, the corollary of the car attack was that when I went to report subsequent court hearings concerning the LVF overlord, the police had to meet me as I drove off the M1 at Craigavon and escort me to the courthouse. They drove with me, in armour-plated cars and Land Rovers, to the gated secure compound used by judges and court officials at the back of the brown-brick building.

And then I entered the courtroom itself by the same semi-concealed door in the back wall of the room as was used by the judges, for security reasons, as they walked the few metres to their seat on the bench.

I sat down at the press desk: the courts there weren't big enough to merit press galleries. Armed police, and sometimes 'Ninjas' – specially trained anti-terror cops, known as Mobile Support Units (MSUs), heavily armed and kitted out head to toe in black combat outfits, just like the ninjas of kids' video fame – would also sit in the court, close to the LVF godfather and his goons, glaring at me from a few feet away.

And after the hearings, it was the same safety-first routine. A police escort until well away from the precincts of the court, but always keeping an eye on the rear-view mirror driving the 26 miles back up the motorway to Belfast: just in case.

After the charges were dropped against the five men, we continued to write about them. Drew King, in particular. He tried to shut us up – ironically, by using, or, in his case, abusing the law.

We had by this time written acres of newsprint about him and his drug-dealing gangsters. A reliable source started supplying us with a very potent stream of inside information, including the claim that the police had missed one vital clue on the night of Martin's assassination. The source told me that a second getaway car being used by the killers – the first one had been burned out – crashed into a grass bank close to the O'Hagan home in the blind panic to escape. A headlight and sidelight were smashed. Glass littered the ground.

But the LVF source later told me that his then LVF boss had ordered another couple of his henchmen – who the source named – to drive another car back to the crash scene the next morning, in full daylight. There, they swept up the glass splinters – which could have supplied a vital forensic clue to murder squad cops investigating Martin's murder.

We were also getting a stream of pictures of Drew King sourced to us, especially images of him flaunting his wealth, sometimes on sun-splashed foreign holidays.

He tried to do us by taking us to the Ulster High Court and, through civil proceedings, accusing us of unlawfully invading his privacy. King brought the action against the *Sunday World* for alleged misuse of private information and for harassment. He wanted the judge to place a reporting restriction upon us and ban us from writing about him in the future. He even wanted the judge to award him damages against the paper.

The judge threw out his claim.

But not before I had to give evidence under oath in the witness box.

King was all Mr Innocent in the courtroom. He claimed that despite playing the bagpipes at the funeral of Billy Wright in 1997, he hadn't known that it would be a paramilitary procession. (You would think he might have noticed it was when he showed up on the day.) He said he'd received death threats from five separate sources, both loyalist and republican.

When it came to my turn to take the stand his lawyer asked me: 'As far as you are concerned, you believe he murdered Mr O'Hagan and you think he has forfeited his right to a private life?'

'That's right,' I replied.

King's barrister argued that a number of reports in the *Sunday World* had been 'a gross invasion of Mr King's personal life and his family's private life'.

I told the court: 'It's no more a gross invasion than the bullets that went into Martin O'Hagan's back were a gross invasion of his right to life.'

I also pointed out that despite having been named in the *Sunday World*, King had never sued for libel. We believed our coverage was in the public interest, I added, because we believed King was 'a major figure in a sectarian killing machine'.

In his summing up of his judgment, Mr Justice Weatherup also referred to the point that King had not sued for libel: 'I make no judgment on the truth or otherwise of those allegations ... But I proceed in noting there is an absence of challenge to the allegations that are being made in this particular action.'

Referring to the claim of harassment, the judge added: 'Overall, on the question of whether or not this series of articles constituted reasonable conduct, I am satisfied that they did, and did not amount to harassment.'

As I said in later media interviews, this was a landmark ruling in terms of freedom of the press. I added: 'Martin O'Hagan was murdered for doing his job. Today's judgment allows us in the *Sunday World* and every other newspaper to continue to do our job to seek justice for those who are the victims of murder.'

King didn't get a brown penny. But then again, he didn't have to pay his legal costs, either. Because of the European Human Rights Act. Under that Act, criminals, killers and paramilitaries could get legal aid if they tried to argue that the press, by reporting their crimes, was allegedly invading their privacy, harassing them, or putting the lives of themselves, or their families, at risk. In other words, the bogeymen were using taxpayers' money to try to gag the press, and stop newspapers like the *Sunday World* reporting their activities in the public interest.

The Lurgan godfather tried it on once, and failed, although at no financial loss to himself.

But this was a vagary of the law, loaded against the free press and prostituted by the parasite Ulster paramilitaries, which became a tool to be used by other terror gang bosses.

And as one judge was to predict from the bench after throwing out another godfather's case: the whole 'gagging' business under the European human rights laws had, and still has, the capacity to bankrupt newspapers ... although the *Sunday World*, and other press organisations, continue to fight, and win, such gagging cases. Because although the plaintiff is bankrolled by legal aid – that's you and me, the public, paying for it – the crime bosses taking these cases have 'no visible means of income'.

So when a newspaper tries to chase them for costs: zilch, nothing, not a penny.

And the newspaper that has fought and, rightly, won, these cases has to pay its own instructing solicitors, as well as their briefs – their junior and senior counsel, or barristers. And if a case runs for days, even though it has been proved to have no merit and is thrown out, the newspaper or broadcaster can be left with a bill, each time, of up to £40,000.

As the learned judge presciently observed, that really has the potential to put newspapers in serious financial peril, if not bankrupting them completely. And all because of ill-thought-out and pernicious European legislation that is weighted entirely in favour of the criminal when it comes to legal aid, allowing criminal elements to make an ass of the law.

26

BEATING THE BULLY BOYCOTTS

They couldn't silence the *Sunday World* with guns and bombs, but loyalist paramilitaries thought there was another way they could destroy it. They tried to slap a blanket ban on our newspaper: not once, but twice.

Both times, it was a blatant, ugly and brutal attempt at censorship. They didn't like what we were writing about their killing and racketeering gangster mobs. They knew we were exposing them to all the people: but especially to the people living in the areas they thought they ran and controlled. And those honest, decent people who read our newspaper looked on us as champions of their cause. Both they, and we, had a common cause: to get the fascist jackboot of the paramilitaries off their necks.

So it was that the first time we were put under the cosh of a crude censorship coup, it was the Ulster Defence

Association (UDA), the largest Protestant (although they'd no right to that name) organisation that tried it on.

One Saturday, they plastered the loyalist parts of Belfast – and other towns throughout the province – with mini-posters warning people to stop buying the *Sunday World* and to stop reading it. Simultaneously, they tried to castigate and set up *Sunday World* staff … for allegedly setting up loyalists!

Nowadays, what they did would be classified as a hate crime. I'll let you judge for yourself.

On the first Sunday morning of the boycott – strange, isn't it, that the 'loyalist' UDA should use a word and tactic first made famous by Irish nationalists? – this poster appeared on doors, walls, and the shop windows of newsagents throughout Ulster. I have a framed copy. Because when we were told about it, we went out to see it for ourselves – and my wife Lindy tore it down from the window of the first newsagent's shop we visited, in east Belfast.

In stark black and white were the lies that the UDA employed to try to spark a boycott – which failed spectacularly when the ordinary, decent people of places like Belfast's Shankill Road simply snubbed it.

The potentially deadly document they posted read:

BOYCOTT

For years now the Sunday World
Newspaper has singled out and set up
Loyalists for assassination.
More recently they have added fuel to the
feuds within loyalism and where there

wasn't any, they have tried to start
new ones. The time has now come to
send a message to the Editor and the
people behind these lies. We have
tried to resolve this matter amicably
but to no avail. Therefore we are
asking for a total boycott of this
newspaper within all
Unionist/Protestant areas.
Stop the demonisation of the loyalist
Community.
BY
ULSTER WATCH COMMITTEE

The last four lines made particular mockery of the boycott stance the loyalist paramilitaries were trying to foist on people – the ordinary folk who bought the paper every week and welcomed us championing the cause of exposing the gangsters, racketeers and, yes, killers in their midst.

These folk didn't have a voice. We gave them one.

Those last four lines shouldn't have had a full stop in them. They should have more accurately read: 'Stop the demonisation of the loyalist community by the Ulster Watch Committee.'

No full stop needed. The ordinary people knew who was demonising them and their communities. It was the paramilitaries using the so-called Ulster Watch Committee as a front.

As for the 'lies', there were four prime porkies in the Nazi-style propaganda poster that would have choked a pig.

1. The *Sunday World* never 'singled out and set up Loyalists for assassination'. The loyalist gun gangs did that themselves, in a bloody series of internecine feuds over the years.

2. The *Sunday World* never did, and never needed to, 'add fuel to the feuds within loyalism', or 'tried to start new ones'. Loyalist paramilitaries were pretty adept at sparking and fuelling their own feuds: one between the UDA and UVF, in 2002, claimed eight lives on both sides in just a few short weeks before it fizzled out.

3. We weren't telling lies, we were reporting the truth, and were respected within our own industry for doing so – as evidenced by the *Sunday World* winning either the NI Sunday Newspaper of the Year Award or the Daily Newspaper Award six years in a row.

4. There was no attempt to 'resolve this matter amicably'. Paramilitary godfathers issued thinly veiled threats and tried to order myself and others to meet them, warning of 'the consequences' if we didn't. We point-blank refused: on the basis that we might end up staring point-blank down the barrel of a gun if we did. So much for resolving the matter 'amicably'.

So this, the first boycott, was on. It went on for weeks.

We faced it down. Threats were made to newsagents warning them not to put the paper on their Sunday news-stands. Bundles of papers were hijacked outside shops and burned, or thrown in rivers. And as all this supposed boycott was going on the bogeymen allegedly orchestrating it were still sending bundles of the *Sunday*

World to their 'soldiers' and 'volunteers' who were behind bars in jail.

Still, with the help of some very valuable and good friends – not least a corps of men who delivered the papers – we won through. And I'll never forget one early Sunday morning incident when we were determined the papers would get through, especially into the loyalist hotbed of east Belfast.

My good friend Paul Gibson, manager of the delivery firm, and another brave man, Willie the van driver, drove in front of me while I shadowed them in another vehicle. If there was an attempt to hijack their van, then at least there was a getaway car: mine. Plus, I wanted to show a bit of solidarity with the delivery drivers.

We drew up to the door of one newsagent's. Paul took a bundle of papers to leave in the shop. The person behind the counter saw him coming, met him at the door, and told him: 'Sorry, we can't take those papers.' The lad carrying the bundle simply dropped them at the door and bluntly stated: 'You ordered them – whether you sell them or not is your business, not ours.'

That riposte summed up the spirit of everyone – the vast majority of newsagents who defied the boycott order, the delivery drivers, the advertisers, the ancillary staff – but most of all the *Sunday World* staff, from the editorial floor right up to management level, who defied, and eventually beat, the boycott. A boycott that was, in essence, an illegal act ordered by illegal and proscribed organisations.

We wondered, at the time, how the British government would have reacted if a mainstream newspaper in any English, Scottish or Welsh city – the *Liverpool Echo*, the

Glasgow Herald, the *South Wales Argus* – had been overtly threatened in this way.

Regardless, in the end we did what we always did, and still do. We took it on, fought it, and won ... with the backing of the honest, decent people of Northern Ireland who wholeheartedly supported us.

Down the years I have witnessed many moving examples of readers expressing their gratitude to the *Sunday World* for exposing the gangsters holding their communities to ransom. (One of the cards I received after retiring as editor – and which I will always treasure – is signed simply: 'From the Good People of East Belfast'.) One example that touched me especially around the time of the boycott involved a little old lady – with the heart of a lioness.

There's not really a London-style cenotaph in Belfast. There's just a grand, elegant war memorial in a Garden of Remembrance, at the side of the City Hall. But everyone in the city still calls it the Cenotaph. And as in other cities throughout the UK – and in Ireland now, too – people gather there every Armistice Sunday to remember those who fell in the two World Wars, to pray and place poppy wreaths.

I go there, too: have done since my Da used to take us three brothers, as youngsters in short trousers and knee socks, with our hair Brylcreemed down. (That's back when I had hair: now, my philosophy is that I was born baldy, I'm going to die baldy, so to hell with the in between.)

It was during that first boycott that I went down to the Cenotaph, as usual, to hear the playing of The Last Post, and observe the two minutes' silence as the clock struck 11.00 a.m. And as I was walking away afterwards, this lovely wee woman with a poppy on the lapel of her coat and wearing her go-to-church Sunday best, complete with hat, came up to me and grabbed my arm.

She says: 'God bless you, Mr McDowell. And you never mind them bad boys – you just keep doing what you're doing in that paper.'

I thanked her, had a quick yarn, and then asked her if she needed a lift home, as my car was parked nearby. She thanked me, but said I couldn't give her a lift home as 'it would be too dangerous'. She explained that she lived in the heart of the Lower Shankill housing estate in west Belfast – the home turf of Johnny 'Mad Dog' Adair and his notorious 'C Coy' – C Company, 2nd Battalion of the Ulster Freedom Fighters (UFF) – the even more militant wing of the UDA. And, of course, it was the UDA who were the main muscle behind the boycott against us.

In any case, she added, she had to call at 'the hospital' on her way home. I asked her if she was ill, and again offered to drive her to hospital if she was.

No, she explained, it was just a quick visit to the city's Mater Hospital, just across the Crumlin Road from where she lived.

Now, the Mater Hospital, as the name suggests, was the old Catholic hospital in Belfast, although it always was, and still is, open to patients of all religious or political persuasions.

I asked her why she was going there. She said to get the papers, and the *Sunday World* in particular, from the hospital shop. And not only that, she had a shopping bag with her. She was also going to get copies of the *Sunday World* for her neighbours – they couldn't get it themselves because of the boycott banning their usual newsagent from selling it on the Shankill.

So here was this beautiful elderly lady from a UDA stronghold, bravely defying the bully boys – and even going to a Catholic hospital to get the banned *Sunday World* and smuggle it back into the housing estate where she and her good neighbours lived, under the bogeymen's very noses. I could have hugged that wee woman. I probably did …

We overcame that first boycott way back in 2003. And we went on to become the biggest selling newspaper in Northern Ireland – probably as much because of it as in spite of it.

But it wasn't a case of once bitten, twice shy for the loyalist bully boys. They came back to try to have another bite at us. This time they slung their banner over a common cause: the Loyalist Commission. And this time it wasn't only the UDA, it was the lot: UDA, UVF, Red Hand Commando and the LVF (before the latter split away and sparked another bloody feud with the UVF).

This time, even though all four outfits were still proscribed by law, and therefore illegal, they tried to put up a democratic façade. This was supposedly about 'helping loyalists find their way'. About easing them into politics.

Among those voices in the Protestant community sounding a note of scepticism back then was the Church of Ireland primate Robin Eames, who noted that loyalists would be judged by their actions: 'By that I mean an end to the drugs scene, the end of the beatings, the end of the intimidation and, above all else, the end of instilling fear in their own community.'

The loyalists had big town hall-style meetings, attended by some politicians who should have known better. And they were fronted up by a clergyman who definitely should have known better. His name: the Rev. Mervyn Gibson, then a Presbyterian minister, but who, in his former life, had been a member of the RUC's Special Branch, whose 'speciality' was supposed to be hounding and locking up all terrorists, both loyalist and republican.

He was also a top Orangeman, and, at the time of writing, still is.

Nothing wrong with that, in itself. Half of my family were in the Orange Order; good men, who were proud of it. It was their heritage, and mine. Even though I was never a member myself, I respect the Order. Still, the Rev. Gibson, clergyman and ex-RUC officer, decided not only to meet with paramilitaries of the likes of Johnny 'Mad Dog' Adair, Jim 'Doris Day' Gray from the UDA, 'Winkie' Irvine from the UVF, and other peons of the loyalist paramilitaries, like John 'Coco' White, among others, he actually chaired their commission. I'd my own view on his actions then: he was a publicity-seeking windbag. Nothing has happened since to change my mind. He is still strutting around, fronting the Orange Order protests over their parades being banned from certain areas. And his florid face still flounces out of our TV screens whenever controversy flares over any issue hinting of 'loyalism'.

Anyway, we beat that boycott, too.

Partly because, goaded by Gibson's abortive efforts to gag us, I put him on the front page, bannering the headline over his picture with the blunt and accurate accusation that he was trying to gag the *Sunday World*.

But during this whole fatwah being perpetrated on the free press – and freedom of speech – this so-called Loyalist Commission was agitating for a meeting with the then Chief Constable of the PSNI, Hugh, now Sir Hugh Orde.

They got it, too. And I was standing having a teatime pint after work when I got a phone call to tell me that the whole shebang of shameless apologists for the paramilitaries, including the Rev. Gibson and, indeed, a posse of paramilitary godfathers themselves, were heading to the Brooklyn HQ of the police for a meeting with the Chief Constable.

I phoned a taxi and headed straight for the PSNI HQ. I was too late to see the Gibson-led delegation going in, but I was waiting for them coming out. There were very senior leaders of the paramilitaries there, the top brass of the bogeymen. There was an impromptu press conference at the gates of the cops' HQ, as other media outlets had also been tipped off about this strange summit.

I got stuck in. I slung quick-fire questions at them.

'Why did you spark a boycott of the *Sunday World*?'

'Why are you putting the lives of my staff, and their families, in danger?'

'Why are you threatening and trying to silence the free press, and the freedom of speech?'

I knew that the cameras of UTV – their newsroom had also been tipped off about the so-called secret meeting

– were there, recording every word and gesture. I was trying to face down the whole posse – in public, in the car park of police headquarters, at that.

And they all ran away!

They spurned me. They blanked my face-to-face approaches. They actually scurried off and got into their cars. They hadn't the balls to even try to brazen out their censorship stance – especially in front of the rolling TV cameras.

UTV, thankfully, ran the footage on their next news bulletin. That allowed the ordinary Joes, the public, to make up their own minds.

Once again, we beat the loyalists on that boycott.

At the time I'd gone to the then Secretary of State, Labour MP Peter Hain, and got him to sign a petition condemning the illegal and evil boycott. And to the leaders of all the main democratic political parties in Ulster, who did the same. A gesture for which I, and the *Sunday World* staff, were and are grateful ... even though probably all of them had reason to take umbrage, at one time or another, at our coverage of the antics of politicians in their parties.

We had battled our way through another boycott. And it was one that had almost cost lives. Not our lives in the *World*. But two innocent staff working in a newsagent's shop close to Carlisle Circus in Belfast.

Carlisle Circus sits right on the interface between the loyalist Lower Shankill estate and the republican New Lodge Road. The UDA were, and still are, embedded in the Lower Shankill: it was the lair of 'Mad Dog' Adair and his notorious C Coy crew until they were forced out and into exile – by their own former 'comrades-in-arms' in the UDA, otherwise known, in street parlance, by those who abhorred them (especially in the loyalist areas they thought they controlled) as the Wombles.

But on the Sunday morning in question, the innocent staff in the newsagent's were serving customers – bread, milk, cigarettes, groceries – at the front of the shop, unaware that two UDA thugs had walked in and gone straight to where the newspaper stand was, with all the Sunday papers, both Irish and British national, on display. Their prime target, however, was the *Sunday World*.

The two arsonists sprayed the stand with petrol, lit a match, set it alight – and then the cowards scarpered. The shop went up in flames. The assistants, of course, didn't know what was happening – until they were almost overcome by smoke inhalation. Somehow, they got out. But they could have been burned to death. Or smothered to death by smoke.

That's how far the firebombers – and the UDA godfather who sent them out – were prepared to go. They were prepared to murder entirely innocent people in order to intimidate others. But their campaign failed.

It failed because decent people were prepared to stand up to the bully boys and their threats. It failed because the *Sunday World* staff, despite all that had happened in the previous few years, despite the murder of our friend and colleague Martin, despite knowing how very real the threat was, refused to be cowed.

Our answer to the bully boys ...

The next Sunday the *Sunday World* was once again on the stands.

27

STONE COLD KILLER

'It was just like watching a coat slipping and falling off a coat hanger.'

The spine-chilling words of loyalist serial killer and the Milltown massacre murderer Michael Stone. He was out on licence from a jail sentence of almost 700 years after confessing to the murder of six Catholics in a sectarian slaughter spree spread over years. He was only captured and caged after the murder of three mourners at the Milltown funerals of the 'Gibraltar Three' in March 1988. That trio were Mairead Farrell, Danny McCann and Sean Savage, who'd been shot dead by British undercover SAS agents while plotting to bomb British troops on the Rock of Gibraltar just over a week previously.

That triple killing – republicans dubbed it a shoot-to-kill execution – triggered huge controversy worldwide, and was the subject of an equally controversial TV documentary entitled *Death on the Rock*. But one fact was indisputable: Farrell, McCann and Savage were all IRA volunteers, and members of an active service unit (ASU) from west Belfast that both the Spanish and British intelligence agencies had been tracking for months. The British government claimed justification, stating that the Provo ASU had been planning to detonate a car bomb during an army band performance on the Rock.

All three were given IRA burials on the same day, with their black berets and black gloves atop tricolour-draped coffins. A huge cortége, led by Gerry Adams and Martin McGuinness and the entire leadership of the IRA-spearheaded republican movement from throughout Ireland, followed the triple funeral from St Agnes's Catholic church, down the Andersonstown Road in Belfast, to the gates of the cemetery at the big roundabout at the top of the Falls Road.

I was reporting it. You couldn't only feel the tension. It hung over the whole baleful proceedings like a black cloud, matching the black flags hanging from lamp-posts along the route.

The final destination, and the Gibraltar Three's final resting place, was to be the unmissable, striking and very distinctive rectangular republican plot in Milltown, which also held the remains of IRA 'heroes' like the hunger striker Bobby Sands.

The huge hive of mourners were swarmed around the commemorative plot. Knots of the press gang from all over the world were encamped as close as they could get. Stone, wearing a Belfast duncher cap and with a kind of fisherman's bag slung over his shoulder, had slipped on to the periphery of the graveside gathering.

The fisherman's bag was bunged with hand grenades. Stone hurled those first, straight into the middle of the mourners.

Panic erupted. People were down. There was murder, there was mayhem. And no one knew where the deadly grenade attack was coming from.

Until ice-cold killer Stone broke cover. He'd tossed all the grenades he had. He had to escape.

He started running along the big slope that runs the whole way down Milltown graveyard, from its gate on the Falls Road down to its perimeter running along the M1 leading south to Dublin. He was dodging between headstones. He pulled out a handgun.

The mourners' fright had now turned to fury. Snaking lines of them were chasing Stone along the winding, skinny paths between the rows of graves. Stone was running and stopping, running and stopping. Each time he stopped, he fired off a fusillade of shots at his pursuers.

But still they went after him.

He ran along a perimeter fence of high railings. He was getting closer and closer to the boundary at the bottom of the cemetery, where he could clamber out onto the hard shoulder of the motorway. But those chasing now had a hound's scent of a kill. And they were hounding Stone like greyhounds chasing a hare.

They were intent on assassinating the lone assassin.

They almost did.

They caught up with the killer as he ran along the hard shoulder. And Michael Stone almost met his Maker – that is, if his Maker wanted to meet him – on the verge of the M1. He was surrounded. He was taking a pummelling. One of his guns was wrenched off him.

But then he was rescued.

Scores of heavily armed police and soldiers had been monitoring the Milltown proceedings. Cops in armour-plated Land Rovers sped along the motorway. Stone was hauled from the crowd. But at a cost.

He'd taken a serious hiding. His back was so badly injured, he'd to walk with a stick for a long time afterwards. But he was alive, and because of his 'bravado' in carrying out the one-man murder mission in Milltown, his name was now to be etched into loyalist terror mob folklore as deeply as any chiselled into the headstones in the cemetery he'd so discreetly, and easily, infiltrated at the funerals of those republican icons, the Gibraltar Three.

Stone murdered three people and injured around sixty at Milltown. But that tally wasn't enough for him. He later claimed in an interview with me that he murdered a fourth victim that day.

Milltown cemetery sits on the edge of what is known as the Bog Meadows in west Belfast, which in turn sits tight on the hard shoulder of the motorway. Stone still insists he shot dead a fourth man, one of his pursuers, there. He claims that that victim slumped into the swampy bogland and was later spirited away by the IRA for a secret burial.

Stone alleged that this shooting occurred well away from the eyes of any of the reporters or TV crews covering the funeral and the resulting atrocity. He said his fourth victim may even have been a senior Provo, and the IRA didn't want to acknowledge that.

Now this may be the wholly phantom vision of Michael Stone, labelled a 'crazed killer' and 'madman'. But that's the relevance of the quote at the start of this piece. I asked Stone what it was like to kill a person in cold blood.

He referred, again, to his (maybe phantom) victim in the Bog Meadows. He described how he fell. And, with eyes as cold as the marble on a Milltown cemetery headstone, he told me: 'It was just like watching a coat slipping and falling off a coat hanger.'

No wonder when my old friend and colleague Martin Dillon wrote his definitive book on this loner of a loyalist serial killer, he titled it *Stone Cold*.

The day of the Milltown massacre, the UPA – for which I was working – had 'markings', or assignments, to cover for three different newspapers – one in Ireland, two in Britain. But a horde of hacks arrived in Belfast, too. I knew most of them from them having come to cover big stories before. Some of them were hardened hacks. But some hadn't ever been in the firing line. Literally. I had a posse of press round me heading for the Gibraltar Three funeral, and we corralled at the cemetery.

When Stone first started hurling his grenades, and they started exploding, some of the lads from across the water 'just didn't get it', as they say. Indeed, one even turned to me and said: 'Jim, someone's letting off firecrackers.' Myself and a few other local reporters grabbed him and a couple of others by their coats, and dragged them down behind headstones. Then the screaming and shouting started, almost simultaneously with Stone starting to shoot. They quickly realised what the score was: and it wasn't what we in Belfast call squibs (fireworks) going off.

I checked I'd no dead or injured hacks on my hands, then I followed the mourners chasing Stone down the slope of the cemetery. But I was working on a very tight deadline for two papers. Again, there were no mobiles back then. It meant taking in as much as you could, making a break for it, and trying to phone copy back to the offices you were working for – off the top of your head. This was the way even for a 'holding' story, so that the news desks could see how big it was, and decide whether to put another edition, or editions, on the street.

Stories like these, tragic and shocking as they were, were almost dictated by rote by seasoned reporters in those days. It was almost automatic. Just like gunfire. A phone. A copytaker on the other end of the line, and staccato eye-witness accounting.

In this case, it was something along the lines of:

A crazed loyalist gunman went on a bloody rampage at the funeral of the Gibraltar Three today.

The assassin struck as mourners – including Sinn Féin chiefs Gerry Adams and Martin McGuinness – were among thousands of mourners at the graveside.

First reports say three people are dead, with scores more down and injured, some seriously.

Howling and horrified mourners at Milltown cemetery in the IRA stronghold of West Belfast scattered as hand grenades exploded in their midst.

The lone assassin fired at angry mourners who pursued him out of the cemetery.

*He seemed to have been caught by those chasing him
on the motorway, and was being beaten when police
arrived and apparently rescued him ...*

That was the type of 'holding story' we filed, until we got
back on the scene and gleaned more details.

That's what I had to do now.

The nearest place I could think of getting access to a
landline was the Falls bus depot, right opposite the gates
of Milltown cemetery. A real character, an Austrian called
Werner Heubeck, ran the buses in Belfast at the time. He'd
even been known to carry bombs off 'his' buses himself,
when they were planted on board, especially in so-called
proxy bombing incidents where his drivers were ordered
at gunpoint to drive a bomb to a certain target.

On the day of the Milltown massacre, Werner – we
knew each other well – was again on the front line with
his workers, his drivers. He stood behind the high, spiked,
padlocked gates of the bus depot with a line of drivers,
defiant, in case there was a post-funeral riot (as there
often was) and rioters tried to break into the depot and
hijack buses to use as burning barricades.

Werner, who wore an Austrian-style soft hunting hat
with a feather in the band, had lost too many of his buses
that way already.

There was no note-taking here: no time. You saw it,
you got to a phone, you got through to a copytaker, you
gave her or him the catchline – usually just one word,
'Ulster', was sufficient: it meant, literally, trouble, i.e. a
Troubles story – and you started filing right off the top of
your head.

So I told Werner, quickly, what had happened down in the graveyard, and told him I needed a phone. He ordered one of the drivers to prise open the gates, let me squeeze through, and I headed for the inspector's cabin down the yard. I got there, made a transfer charge call to the first newspaper, as usual, and was about four or five tight paragraphs into filing the story when I felt a tap on my shoulder.

Mr Heubeck, Austrian hunting cap with feather perched on his head, was standing there. I paused on the phone.

'Mr McDowell,' he pronounced in his still strongly accented English, 'I hope *I* [and he put heavy emphasis on the second 'I'] am not paying for these phone calls?'

And this in the midst of me filing a story of multiple murders happening right on the doorstep of his depot.

I put my hand over the mouthpiece. I told him that they were all going through the operator, and that they were transfer charge calls: he wasn't picking up the bill. I also thanked him for the use of the phone, and then told him what to do with himself.

As I resumed filing copy, he turned on the heels of his soft suede shoes and strode off … back to the padlocked depot gate to once again stand guard over his precious buses. I did say that the man who kept Belfast's buses running throughout the nadir of the Troubles was a colourful character. And then some.

It goes without saying that Michael Stone was a much, much darker, deadlier character. A complex man, even by the standards of Northern Ireland's many twisted murderers. Sectarian serial killer, certainly. Psychopath?

Probably, like many more who found the Troubles an excuse for bloodlust and bloody murder. I met and talked with him a number of times when he was out of jail and back on the streets.

Lindy, who at the time was working for the *Belfast Telegraph*, got an interview with him when he was behind bars, in Her Majesty's Prison Maghaberry, about ten miles south of Belfast.

It was well known at this stage that Stone had taken command of the UDA prisoners on 'the wings': the areas of the jail that were segregated for loyalist and republican prisoners, and were then split up again into what factions of loyalism and republicanism the inmates represented – the UDA, say, or UVF on the loyalist side, the Provisional IRA, or the INLA, say, on the other. He was also seriously into pumping iron, weightlifting – as were other jailed loyalist heavies, the likes of Johnny 'Mad Dog' Adair and Andre 'The Bookie's Brigadier' Shoukri – and he had the Hulk Hogan look to go with it. Plus, he fancied himself as an artist, and was wont to put paintbrush to palette behind bars (more about this later).

Our two boys were off school at the time and Lindy and I were both hoping to spend some time with them. Unusually, there was due to be an eclipse of the sun that day. An interesting spectacle which some doom-mongers, especially in the fanatical Bible Belt sector of Ulster, were claiming heralded the end of the world.

So we took them with us and drove to the prison.

Lindy went on in for the visit – formal interviews by journalists weren't permitted, and visits had to be arranged by name only – and myself and the boys, still young at the time, watched the eclipse from the prison car park. When scudding clouds obscured the sun, we nipped into the Quakers' Portakabin, where they served tea and biscuits for folk and families waiting to go into jail visits. We could follow it, where it was happening throughout the UK, on the TV in there.

However, the cloud cleared just as the total eclipse was due to occur over Northern Ireland, and over our heads. With just seconds to go, I heard the clatter of Lindy's high heels approaching the rickety turnstile security gate where visitors came out.

She was hurrying. She got out and made straight for us. I asked if anything was wrong – had anything untoward been said or happened to her inside? (There were other loyalist inmates who, of course, had threatened me and my family before – and since.)

'Don't be daft,' she laughed. 'I was timing the total eclipse in there. And if it really is going to be the end of the world this time, I don't want to be going up to meet St Peter at the Pearly Gates with Michael Stone standing beside me!'

She didn't add that if it was indeed the end of the world, it could have been worse. It would have been *me* standing beside her.

Stone was to get through another set of gates, though – the huge, ornate gates of Stormont, the former seat of the Parliament of Northern Ireland, but now the home of the power-sharing Northern Ireland Assembly and ruling Executive.

Once again, he was alone.

Stone really was one of the first of the 'lone wolf' terrorists wreaking death and revenge, just like the evil and crazed killers spawned by ISIS. He'd been released from prison under the terms of the Good Friday Agreement's 'early release' deal, which saw scores of terrorist prisoners walk free. On a dark, foreboding day in November 2006, he set out to storm the Assembly Building at Stormont. He was again carrying weapons: an imitation Beretta gun, a knife – for 'close-quarter' killing – and a number of home-made explosive devices.

But this time he was stopped before he could commit more blood-curdling crime.

Courageous civilian security guards stopped and half-trapped him in the big revolving doors, after Stone had been spotted daubing graffiti on the outside of the white building. This is important, as Stone was later to claim that by doing that, and trying to storm Stormont single-handedly, he was simply putting on a work of performance art.

He was immediately arrested, and subsequently faced over a dozen charges, including the attempted murder of Gerry Adams and Martin McGuinness, who were inside Stormont at the time. He was later sentenced to sixteen years. He also had his Good Friday Agreement licence revoked, and had his original mammoth sentence for the Milltown and other murders reinstated.

That's where Lindy comes in, again. For Stone had written a long letter to her, in his own handwriting, which was posted on the morning of his sole storming of Stormont. And in it, there was no mention of 'performance art'. In this letter, he stated his intention was to break through the security at the building and murder Sinn Féin chiefs Gerry Adams and Martin McGuinness.

Lindy got the letter through the post three days later: she had left the *Belfast Telegraph* as a journalist by then, Stone had sent the letter addressed to her at the newspaper, and it took three days for it to be processed through their mail room and forwarded on. Lindy, of course, wrote the story of the letter for her former employer, for whom she was still a columnist.

And, rightly, the paper splashed the front page with the story, which amounted to Stone's own, handwritten confession as to what he really intended to do at Stormont. Which was indeed to kill Adams and McGuinness: both of whom, significantly, he'd missed on his mass murder mission at Milltown cemetery.

It painted a vastly different picture from Stone's claim that what he had planned was an act of 'performance art'. It was used, obviously, by the prosecution as a cornerstone of their case in getting Stone sent back to the clink.

Like many other terrorists – particularly within the ranks of loyalists – Michael Stone appeared to enjoy media attention, and seeing his name in print. Doubtless it fed his ego. But maybe it was more than that.

Stone had been born in England, the child of a liaison between a Protestant man from Belfast and a southern Irish Catholic woman. They hadn't been married. In the cruel lexicon of the era, Stone was illegitimate. His father brought him back to Belfast, where he was raised by an uncle and aunt. He was by all accounts a bit of a loner. A boy who didn't fit in, or who found it difficult to fit in. It cannot have been an easy childhood.

Who knows how much his later murderous actions, securing as he surely knew they would, the adulation of other loyalists, were about the desire to belong, to be part of something. To be accepted.

This man, whose mother abandoned him as a child, was perhaps clutching out for something: not love (Jesus, he had a string of relationships with women, which produced *nine* kids!), but some kind of genuine 'fellow feeling', perhaps even dating back to a forlorn and personally forsaken childhood. Maybe he thought there might be a thread of, let's call it 'communication', whereby he might be portrayed in the press as something more than a maniacal monster and mass sectarian murderer.

In that respect, he phoned me one Saturday morning when he was originally out of jail on parole. He had set himself up as an artist, hoping to sell his paintings, which he'd started putting on to canvas while in Maghaberry prison. Stone had set up his studio in an abandoned shop deep in the heart of the loyalist Ballybeen estate in east Belfast: a UDA stronghold.

That's where he wanted to see me.

It was close to the Twelfth of July. Our *Sunday World* photographer, Conor McCaughley, had no hesitation coming with me.

When we arrived, there was a huge pile of wood in the middle of the big square in Ballybeen being readied for the traditional Eleventh Night bonfire, on the eve of the Orange Twelfth. A few UDA 'heavies' had been designated to 'look after' Stone while he was working in his makeshift studio. When the photographer and I drew up in the car, we got out, and one of the minders said to me: 'McDowell, only you're here to meet your man [Stone], we'd love nothing better than to put you on top of that bonfire ... and light it.'

Stone came out of the studio and shut them up.

We went inside. He remembered where I had last met him, and that I had asked him the most pressing and prescient question the day he first got out of jail as part of the controversial prisoner early release scheme that was a condition of the Good Friday Agreement.

Is your war over?

That's what I had I asked him then. He'd assured me that it was. It was an answer that hit the headlines on news bulletins for the rest of that day.

So why were we here on this day? He now wanted the *Sunday World* to publish a story to show that he really was back on the straight and narrow, and working as an artist. That he was using his talent to paint pictures, rather than to pull the trigger of a gun to put people in their graves.

The photographer took the pictures. Stone did the talking. I took the notes.

We were about to leave. Conor was putting his cameras and equipment into the boot of the car outside. The UDA growlers were still muttering and murmuring outside, but Stone had come out with us to ensure safe passage.

He had strange eyes. Eyes that seemed to be spinning like the wheels of a Formula 1 Grand Prix car squirting out of the pits.

'Hold on, McDowell, I've something for you,' he said.

He went back into his studio. He came out with one of his paintings. He goes to hand the painting to me. I'm standing with my hands in my pockets.

The gorillas were watching and waiting for my reaction, with ill-disguised menace.

Stone, with a faint smile, looks me straight in the eye and says: 'I know what you want me to do with this. You want to tell me to stick it up my arse.'

Unlike many of the other loyalist egos, he had at least a degree of self-awareness.

He turned the picture over to show his signature on the back. Alongside, he'd added his thumbprint in black ink: the indelible proof of who painted it.

I still say nothing.

Stone turns to the photographer by my side. 'Here, you take this and give it to Lindy.'

My colleague takes the picture, puts it in the boot, gets into the driving seat of the car, and sinks the boot on the accelerator.

War over … this time.

It was at the press conference he staged when he got out of jail on licence, after the signing of the Good Friday Agreement, that Stone told me his war was over. Again, UDA heavies were loath to let me in that day. But one of their mob's consiglieri went in and told Stone I was outside. Journalists from around the world were packed inside. After all, Stone was a loyalist paramilitary icon. What he said at this press conference would, undoubtedly, count.

Stone sent out word that I was to be let in. I waited until the avalanche of questions were almost at an end.

It was then I'd asked: 'Is your war over?'

Even though he was flanked by some of the hardest men in this, his terror gang, he didn't flinch. He said: 'My war is over. I hope that all groups give the Good Friday Agreement a chance. I am going to do all I can to make a constructive contribution to the agreement and my community.'

However, as the abortive storming of Stormont was later to prove, Stone's war was far from over. And one of the prime reasons, I suspect, driving Stone back to violence and attempted murder at Stormont was some form of self-protection.

It goes back to Milltown cemetery, and Stone being caught by the mob of furious mourners who'd chased him down onto the M1. Stone told me later that not only had he got a bad beating – 'doing my back in', as he put it – a gun he'd used had also been taken from him.

He told me: 'The Provos are going to wait. That gun, my gun, will be used to murder me. It won't be one of their proven killers who'll pull the trigger, either. It'll probably be some young buck wanting to make a name for himself. But I firmly believe it will be a bullet from that gun that will eventually kill me.'

So why did he go after Adams and McGuinness, again, at Stormont?

It may, indeed, have been a case of him 'getting his retaliation in first' … because he was haunted by the spectre of that same gun he had used at the cemetery eventually being turned on himself.

28
DORIS DAY

Jim 'Doris Day' Gray was, they tell me, a good golfer. The ex-wife of the UDA gangster, who became the first 'Brigadier of Bling', told me that too. She said that when she married Gray, he was playing off a handicap of two. So he was good, as the Yanks cry out, at 'putting it in the hole'.

Anne Tedford began talking to me after Gray, the one-time brigadier of the East Belfast Battalion of the UDA, was murdered by the son of another UDA gangster. And Gray undoubtedly went to his grave knowing that his former wife had never forgiven him – because of what he did to their son.

Ms Tedford – she changed back to her maiden name – was married to Gray for just four years. But in that time, she bore their only child: a son, Jonathan. At the time, Gray was working in Short's Aircraft Factory, later to be taken over by the Canadian plane and missile manufacturing conglomerate Bombardier. He had a good job, with a good wage. And while other young men from east Belfast aspired to play soccer for the east Belfast team, Glentoran – known colloquially as the Cock'n'Hens – Jim Gray played golf.

According to his ex-wife, he had no paramilitary links then. She called him 'big, soft Jim'. Part of that, she now says, was because he was a 'soft touch': he could be easily led. And he was easily led, just days after the birth of their son, straight into the ranks of the UDA.

Anne Tedford told me that had happened as she lay in the maternity ward of the Ulster Hospital at Dundonald, nursing her newborn baby. Another new mother was in the same ward. Her husband was a senior figure in the UDA. Jim Gray, she says, 'half-knew' him. But Gray got talking to this other new father – they were later to end up partners in crime – and, as Anne tells it, 'big, soft Jim' fancied himself becoming a hard man, and joined the illegal organisation.

It was the first step to him becoming the terror gang's first Brigadier of Bling. With a leg-up from the hospital acquaintance, Gray quickly rocketed up the ranks of the UDA in the east of the city. And this was despite his ultra-colourful style of dressing and deporting himself.

We dubbed him Doris Day because of his blonde, floppy, carefully coiffured hair, pink or lemon cashmere sweaters, Miami-style shorts, sported even in winter, and his mahogany perma-tan, the product of a love affair with first-class Caribbean cruises with his drug-dealing, drug-abusing UDA cronies. Those cruises to far-flung places and foreign holidays were paid for by the illicit income from a spiralling drugs empire: set up, spearheaded, and steered by Doris Day himself. He ran the whole operation from the two bars he and his co-criminals ran, in the heart of the loyalist district known as Ballymcarrett in east Belfast.

Both pubs were also used for another purpose: as UDA 'romper rooms'. That name was gruesomely taken from an old children's television show. These romper rooms were where those who fell out of favour with the UDA hierarchy, or who were accused of, in the UDA'S warped view, anti-social behaviour, were taken to be beaten with baseball bats, kneecapped – or, in the case of Geordie Legge, a one-time big buddy of Gray's, battered and butchered to death.

It was from these two 'drugs central' HQs that Gray ran his dealing network. He even had a 'team' of his own runners, also always geared up in copycat bling clothes, whom he called his Spice Boys. Gray was given to wearing big round earrings. Now, in the old days, anyone who dressed and behaved as flashily as Gray – flash clothes, flash cars, flash women, flashing money around – would have been ridiculed and spurned in working-class areas of Belfast. But Gray had a whole battalion of the UDA in his grip: and in turn, the UDA had a whole community in theirs. Ordinary folk laughed at or defied Gray and his mob at their peril. While exposing his gangsterism, the press pilloried him for what he was: a poisonous paramilitary poseur. In a way, it was the thing the paramilitaries hated most: that we didn't just expose them, but held them up to ridicule. The apt nicknames and the lurid accounts of their debauched lifestyles showed them for the evil clowns that they were. (One murdering loyalist even acquired the name Coco.)

They hated it. They wanted to be seen as hard men protecting their community. We showed them up for the villainous goons they really were. With loyalists, especially, you really could not have made them up.

At one time in the early 2000s, the UDA's leading lights included Sammy Duddy, best known as the former drag act 'Samantha'. Duddy was devastated when his pet Chihuahua, Bambi, was shot dead during a failed gun attack on his own life. There was the Bookie's Brigadier, who'd replaced the Bacardi Brigadier. The Bookie's Brigadier, Andre Shoukri, was also called the Egyptian. Then there was the Mexican (Billy McFarland), so called for his Zapata moustache, plus Mad Dog Adair and Doris himself.

But even among that lot, Doris was the one who always stood out for his flamboyance. He once attended a meeting with then Secretary of State John Reid wearing his trademark open-necked flowery shirt and pink jumper combo. Johnny Adair, who chose an expensive Hugo Boss suit for the meeting, later complained, without any apparent trace of irony: 'That's some image for our organisation.'

Michael Stone also had his doubts about Doris's dress sense. He once said: 'There was always something strange about Jim, wearing slacks and shoes with no socks, even in winter.'

Although never a gunman himself – he gave the orders to others to do his dirty work – Gray was a vicious, brutal bully. The soft pastels he chose to wear belied his violent and increasingly volatile side. Often off his head and paranoid on cocaine, he'd a reputation for randomly attacking anyone he thought had looked at him the wrong way, or had 'disrespected' him. An example was the night he'd strutted into a local restaurant with a gang of his goons, sat down and slung his feet onto a table. A couple were seated nearby and the man looked up in surprise.

'What the fuck are you looking at?' snarled Gray, before launching himself at the man and hammering him in the face with his fists, breaking his nose.

A policeman friend told me he'd once seen Gray stagger along the Newtownards Road so out of his brains that he was stopping to talk to trees.

In his own bar headquarters he had a reputation for urinating in customers' drinks.

Nobody dared cross Doris.

And it was his position, his power, and not least his wealth, which was eventually to lead to his son Jonathan – or JJ as he was known – poisoning himself, dying in a hotel room in Thailand from a lethal cocktail of drugs, surrounded by prostitutes. And then being abandoned and left there by his own father – who flew home rather than face the music from the Thai police and legal authorities.

It was a cowardly act, which Jonathan's mother, Anne, still recalls bitterly, and reviles. And which the *Sunday World* told the truth about at the time.

Jim Gray tried to pretend he was back home in Belfast at the time of his son's death. But we'd found out that he and others in his gang had in fact been with Jonathan on a drink and drugs junket to Thailand. Gray had been in a bar when young friends of Jonathan's had phoned to tell him the boy had collapsed after snorting heroin. Gray tried the ultimate cover-up – and the ultimate betrayal of a son – by doing a runner from the hotel in which Jonathan's body was discovered, and jetting straight back home, putting on a false and shameless show of shock and sorrow back in Belfast.

But we found out – even after being warned not to print the story by a UDA inner council honcho, John 'Coco' White – and published the truth.

The word used to sum up the whole sorry charade and attempted cover-up – Jonathan was still a teenager, just nineteen years old at the time – was indeed 'betrayal'. And that was the word that tripped from Anne Tedford's lips when she talked to me.

She explained how Jonathan had been a smart kid. Passed Northern Ireland's Eleven Plus – the selection exam which transfers pupils from primary school to grammar school level in the province – with a high grade. High enough, indeed, to get him into one of Belfast's best schools, the Royal Belfast Academical Institution.

But the lure of his criminal godfather Da's lifestyle proved too much for Jonathan. In spite of what his mother describes as 'good, if not great' exam results, Jonathan quit school at sixteen – much to his mother's chagrin. He went to live with his father, who by this time was addicted to drugs himself. The white powder of cocaine was his poison.

Gray's first act when Jonathan left school and became a full-time member of his drugs gang was to buy him a flash suit.

'I'll never forget the first time my son came to see me wearing that suit,' Anne Tedford recalled. 'I said to him: "Where did you get that? Get it off your back! You are not going to turn out like your father".'

Tragically for both of them, Jim Gray and his son Jonathan, they did indeed turn out like each other: dead before their time.

Jonathan when he was found lethally overdosed in that hotel room in Thailand in 2002.

And Jim 'Doris Day' Gray when he was assassinated – by the son of a top UDA man he once called a friend – on an autumn evening in 2005.

Gray, who was facing money-laundering charges at the time, had been moving weightlifting equipment into his car outside his father's home. The gunman shot him at point-blank range.

I only met Doris Day once face to face. That was outside a courtroom in Belfast. One of his then COs in East Belfast, Geordie Legge, was in the dock, charged with knifing a man no less than eleven times. His attempted murder victim survived. Gray and his mob were in the court to show 'solidarity' with and support for Legge.

As Gray left the courtroom, I asked him did he want to comment on the case. He mumbled something about not talking to 'an asshole like you'.

I took that as a compliment.

As Michael Stone once told me, Jim Gray didn't do things himself. Or, as Stone put it: 'He didn't have the balls. He got somebody else to do it for him.'

He didn't need anyone else to 'do for' Geordie Legge, after the stabbing case. Years later, Gray accused Legge of trying to stab him in the back and organising a coup against him.

The next time I saw Geordie Legge was when a police officer showed me a close-up picture of his corpse, high up in the Castlereagh Hills, on the Clontanakilty Road hovering over east Belfast and the twin yellow cranes of the shipyard.

It was a Saturday afternoon. The first edition of the paper was almost wrapped up. My colleague Hugh Jordan and I wanted, for just one Saturday afternoon, to go and see a big rugby match at a club, Malone RFC, we were both partial to. We'd just watched the first half when a police officer we both knew, who was also at the game, came over and tipped us off that a body had been found on the Clontanakilty Road and police were now at the scene.

We drove there. The press pack were arriving, as word had spread.

The cops at the scene couldn't immediately identify the, as it turned out, badly mutilated body. The corpse had been found wrapped up in a partly scorched carpet. The only press pictures that could be taken were of a tent that had been erected over the body and the surrounding crime scene by the PSNI's forensic team, sifting for evidence, any evidence.

There was little information. Hacks like us would just have to start digging for details: there was very little for us except the 'colour' at the scene.

But then, as the rest of the press began dispersing, a detective approached Hugh and me. We knew who he was, but we didn't really know him personally. He asked could we stay behind for a few moments, as we might be able to help the police. We had no problem with that.

A few minutes later, the same officer asked us if we would mind having a look at a picture of the deceased taken by a police photographer at the scene. He warned us it was 'gruesome'. He told us that because of the murder victim's bulky build, one of the very early lines of inquiry was that it might be the big-time drug-dealer Liam 'Fat Boy' Mooney.

The picture was, indeed, gruesome. But even through the blood and the gore, we could tell it wasn't Mooney.

Later, through working our contacts in east Belfast – not least the late David Ervine of the PUP – we found out it was Geordie Legge. We drove to where he lived, off Island Street in the shadow of Queen's Island and the Belfast shipyard. We stopped the car. We could hear the crying of relatives coming from the house. That confirmed who it was. Two plainclothes detectives came out of the house as we waited in the car: it was too dangerous for us to be seen out in that area. They said nothing. But their presence clinched it.

We drove back to the office and splashed with the Geordie Legge story – brutally mutilated and murdered by his own – the next morning.

As it turned out, Legge had been 'court-martialled' for 'treason' – plotting to shoot Gray – and fiddling the East Belfast Battalion out of £30,000 in drugs and racketeering money. He had faced a UDA kangaroo court. Then he'd been taken by Gray and his mob to the romper room in the back of one of his bars.

He'd been hammered and hacked to death in an almost ritualistic torture killing. They'd then wrapped his body in a lump of carpet. They put it in the boot of a car or van and took it to the alleyway off Gray's other pub, less than half-a-mile away. They'd dumped the body, still wrapped in carpet, into a big metal wheelie bin at the back of the bar. They then tried to burn the lot: body, carpet and all.

That failed. So they carted the corpse to the verge of the Clontanakilty Road, and, still inthe dead of night, dumped the bundled-up body in the scorched carpet, the blood drying on what remained of it, by the hedgerow.

So, as Anne Tedford said, Jim 'Doris Day' Gray had not only the capacity, without compunction, to betray his own son, he also had the capacity to betray, in the most brutal and bloody fashion, those he believed were plotting against him. In this case it was his former close confidante and CO – the multiple knifeman Geordie Legge.

As we continued to expose Gray in the *Sunday World*, his rage against the paper, and me in particular, exploded. At one point police came to my home to tell me that they had information that Gray was standing in his pub 'with more snow up his nose than the Alps in January', giving orders that two of his men were to shoot me. The police officers were adamant that the threat was serious. At that point his men would have been afraid to defy Doris. The officers advised that my family and I get out of the country immediately. We did as advised.

By the time of his own downfall, Gray had made many, many enemies within the UDA, particularly among its hierarchy. As he became increasing volatile and unpredictable, spiralling out of control on drugs, even they began to view him as an embarrassment – and, more pertinently, as a threat to themselves.

Gray had been arrested as he tried to do a runner from the country with a substantial sum of money. The UDA hierarchy feared he might do a deal over the subsequent money-laundering charges and give police information that would put other bosses behind bars.

When Gray was released on bail, their suspicions seemed to be confirmed. And Doris didn't have the brains – or maybe just had too much blind arrogance – to realise that.

In the end, it was someone Gray still trusted who assassinated him.

He was unloading gym weights from the back of a car at his father's house, where he'd been staying. The last words the one time powerful paramilitary boss ever heard were: 'Sorry about this, pal.' The assassin was the son of the man doing the talking. No one has ever been convicted of this point-blank killing.

Gray's funeral was a modest affair for a man who was once the godfather of a UDA criminal empire in east Belfast. Fourteen men, including his elderly father, walked behind his coffin. A few others, presumably unwilling to be seen as mourners, gathered at the grave. Press and onlookers had been warned to stay away.

Elsewhere in east Belfast, a piece of hastily scrawled graffiti sneeringly marked his passing: 'Jim Gray. RIP. Rest in Pink.'

The showy Brigadier of Bling, the man they called Doris Day, was buried with little pomp and ceremony. He is buried alongside his son, JJ. The son whose life he ruined. The son he betrayed.

29
MAD DOG

Not many men would give the order to shoot their own son. Johnny 'Mad Dog' Adair, the CO of the infamous C Coy of the UDA/UFF on Belfast's Lower Shankill Road, did exactly that.

Adair was the man the IRA said they were trying to murder with the Shankill fish shop bombing. And it was Adair who ordered the execution of the Belfast City Council binmen on the city's Kennedy Way in brutal and bloody revenge. Adair was also one of the first loyalist paramilitary godfathers who became full-blown drugs barons, flooding their fiefdoms with, first, E-tabs, blow and cannabis, then cocaine, then graduating to prostituting their own communities, and the young people of those communities, with the hell of heroin addiction.

And although he was once convicted of being a director of terrorism – the only terrorist in Northern Ireland ever to face, and indeed confess to, such a charge

– he was seldom a hit-man himself. He ordered others – like his notorious henchman, Stephen 'Top Gun' McKeag, and another gunman, still alive, known as the Big Evil – to carry out the killings instead.

So the 'Mad Dog' moniker was merited. His wife, Gina, was, inevitably, known as Mad Bitch. And their son, Jonathan, had the nickname Mad Pup.

It was Jonathan, running beyond the control of even his own crime czar father's circle, whom Mad Dog decided he had to tame – by turning a gun on his own son and giving orders for him to be shot in the legs in one of the most bizarre paramilitary punishment shootings in the history of the Troubles.

It happened in the summer of 2002, when Jonathan was just seventeen years of age. Despite his youth, Jonathan had developed a reputation as a trouble-maker. Earlier that year he'd been beaten up – by a gang of his father's henchmen wielding baseball bats and iron bars – after he'd broken into the home of an eighty-four-year-old pensioner and stolen her purse.

Adair himself was reported to have also given his son a beating after he took his car without asking. But the incident that finally provoked his father to take even more extreme action involved an assault by Jonathan on a female shop assistant in a filling station on Belfast's Crumlin Road.

Mad Dog ordered one of his top C Coy henchmen to shoot his own son in both legs. The punishment shooting was carried out using a 9mm pistol. Of course, Adair didn't give orders for Jonathan to be kneecapped. That could have crippled him for life. Instead, the shooter only inflicted flesh wounds. Enough to cause pain. But also enough, in the eyes of his criminal UFF cohorts, to show that Adair would not tolerate *anyone* operating outside the boundaries he set. Even, when it came to it, if that person was of Mad Dog's own blood and brood.

It was while in jail – Adair, like Stone, had been allowed out on licence after the Good Friday Agreement, only to be hauled back in again later for breaching the terms of his parole – that Mad Dog lost that nomenclature.

If only while he was behind bars …

Drugs were, and still are, rife in jails in Northern Ireland, as they are in prisons throughout Ireland and the UK and other countries. While inside, the diminutive Adair (he's not much over five feet tall) became, like many other loyalist paramilitaries, a gym monkey. They put in the hard yards and hours pumping iron, building their macho men bodies. But like some body-builders outside prison, they also turned to drugs to bulk up. And one of their favourite drugs smuggled into Maghaberry was Clenbuterol.

Also known as Angel Dust, Clenbuterol is used, illegally, by some farmers for bulking up, or helping to put beef on, cattle. It is banned in Britain and Ireland because it can do damage to human beings if it gets into the food chain. Mad Dog and his gym monkeys didn't give a cow's lug about that. They weren't concerned about any food chain syndrome. They were putting it into their bodies direct.

And Adair became addicted to it. So much so that behind bars, he lost his Mad Dog tag: and became known as Mad Cow.

Adair had first been imprisoned in 1995 on a charge of directing terrorism. Tapes of him boasting about his role had been recorded by brave undercover police officers, including my old friend Jonty Brown. In 1998 he was visited in prison by then Secretary of State Mo Mowlam, who was hoping to persuade him and other loyalist leaders to come aboard the peace process.

Adair, whose slogan had always been 'Shove Your Dove', was among those released from the Maze in 1999 under the terms of the Belfast Agreement's early release scheme. Back out on the streets, he was soon back to his old ways, strutting around the Lower Shankill, provoking feuds with other loyalist groups.

The most serious of these was a bloodletting between C Company and the UVF in August 2000. Adair's mob launched attacks on the homes of several prominent UVF men, including the veteran leader Gusty Spence, the man who announced the Combined Loyalist ceasefire in October 1994. Another feud caught fire. Two top paramilitaries, one from the UDA, the other from the UVF, Jackie Coulter and Bobby Mahood, were gunned down.

Adair was rearrested and the new Secretary of State, Peter Mandelson, signed orders to revoke his licence and return him to prison.

In May 2002, however, he was released again, ironically on the same day the Queen visited Northern Ireland. Her Majesty may have been touched by the sight of welcome fireworks exploding in the sky as she visited St Anne's Cathedral in Belfast that day. The display had not been laid on for her benefit, however, but to salute the return of

Mad Dog to the Lower Shankill area where he still reigned supreme.

When Adair was first let out of jail he was still in favour with the UDA, so a huge party was arranged for his Lower Shankill homecoming. Fireworks had been bought in and crates of 'champagne' were ordered. The man tasked with getting this dubious plonk was Jimmy 'Nick-Nick' McCullough, a Del Boy-style wheeler and dealer.

Jimmy did as he was told. The champagne wasn't vintage, but it had been personalised, with labels carrying a picture of Mad Dog posing at his most muscular. The label also bore the name *Johnny 'Mad Dog' Adair*. I managed to get a bottle: no questions asked, and definitely none answered.

It did look impressive. But the label was to get Jimmy into a bit of bother.

Mad Dog snarled when he saw it. He summoned Jimmy 'Nick-Nick' and growled: 'I no longer want to be known as Mad Dog. 'I'm now a f*****g community worker!'

Still, the corks were popped, and the bubbly duly downed … by both the 'new' Mr Adair, and his mob of 'new', well, community-spirited colleagues in C Coy.

It wasn't long after his release that Adair asked to see me up in the UDA ex-prisoners' aid centre on the Shankill Road. We'd had head-to-heads before, of course. Quite a few times. And each time it was about what we were saying, or not saying, about him in the paper.

Ditto this time.

We were still, accurately, labelling Mad Dog the top dog in the UDA/UFF mob on the Lower Shankill. He wanted to talk to me about that. As it turned out, he'd also just been sent a bullet, a big one, in the post.

Myself and *Sunday World* photographer Alwyn James went up to the ex-prisoners' centre. It was around lunchtime. Johnny was dressed almost completely in black: black Hugo Boss suit (his theme song wasn't only 'Simply the Best': he dressed in the best, it was Hugo Boss everything, from underpants out), black Boss shoes, socks, tie, white Boss shirt. Maybe trying to send a message there?

With him was his consigliere, his main fixer, John 'Coco' White. (Clown by name and evil clown by nature – White had been convicted of one of the most gruesome double murders of the Troubles. He been imprisoned for the savage murder and torture of a Catholic politician and a young Protestant woman.)

We went into a room at the back of the centre.

I said to Adair: 'You've been to a funeral.'

'Aye,' he said, 'and the next one could be yours.'

Nice start.

Anyway, he took off the jacket, loosened his tie, pulled up three chairs, and talked – no barking or bristling this time – about how he was now trying to be, and wanted to be known as, a community worker, not a gangland boss.

I humoured him. There was no chance of me or the paper complying, of course. But he still fancied himself as the dog's balls. We were in Mad Dog's lair, after all. And we wanted to leave with our balls, and everything else, intact, if possible.

Then, as the 'discussion' was about to end, he came to the other point he wanted to talk to me about. He'd got a bullet – a big son-of-a-gun bullet – in the post that morning. He wanted me to print that story in the next day's paper.

Sure. Good yarn. No problem.

Alwyn reaches into his camera bag to take the appropriate pic: Adair with the big bullet. And then Alwyn perches his glasses on his forehead, and says to your man: 'I was in the army cadet force at school. I think I recognise the calibre of that bullet. Let me see it.'

He reached out to take it. I gave him the l-o-n-g-e-s-t look in history. He pulled his hand back.

He knew instantly.

If he took the bullet, his fingerprints would be on it – and God knows where it might go next … or end up.

So we got the pic. We got the story. And we got out.

Community worker or not, Adair was now making overtures to the LVF, commanded by Mark 'Swinger' Fulton, who'd taken over after the killing of King Rat Billy Wright. Fulton and Adair had become friendly in prison. UDA bosses were alarmed by the liaison, which they saw as a move by Adair to seize overall power.

Meanwhile, he'd again crossed the UVF. In the inevitable feud that followed, there was another spate of killing and driving rival supporters from their homes.

In September of that year there was a gun attack on Jim 'Doris Day' Gray as he left the wake of another loyalist – LVF man Stephen Warnock, who'd been shot dead. Adair is believed to have issued specific orders. The notoriously vain Gray was shot in the face. He survived.

The UDA now had to act.

Adair was summoned to a showdown meeting in September 2002, and a few days later he was expelled from the UDA for what they pompously described as 'treason'. He declared it was business as usual. But old allies, including the Shoukri brothers, who were running the UDA in North Belfast, now sided with the mainstream grouping.

By January 2003 he was back in prison. Yet another Secretary of State, this time Paul Murphy, had signed the order to revoke his licence. A few weeks later, C Company hit back at the mainstream UDA with an audacious attack on senior member John 'Grug' Gregg, who was shot dead along with another UDA man as they arrived back in Belfast from the ferry that had taken them to a Glasgow Rangers game.

The UDA now descended on the Lower Shankill, forcing Adair's UDA/UFF clan to flee. His wife, Gina, and children headed to England on the night ferry to Liverpool from Belfast. Only Adair's once prized Alsatian, Rebel, was left behind, abandoned in the panic to get out.

When police stopped the mob as they were about to get on the boat, they searched their belongings. Gina was carrying a shoe box in her luggage. When cops looked inside, there was seventy grand in hard cash, plus the Mad Bitch's not insubstantial collection of jewellery. For that reason, the expulsion of Adair's C Coy UFF mob from the Lower Shankill became known, in tongue-in-cheek Belfast parlance, as the Flight of the Pearls.

And as a nod to the name of the high-speed ferry that then operated between Belfast and Scotland, the once-feared C Company was also sneeringly dubbed the Seacat Company.

Adair, meanwhile, remained in prison. Two days before he was due to be released from jail again, I got a tip-off.

When the time came round for Adair's release, the authorities were not going to allow him back onto the streets of Belfast, in case he tried to return to his old turf of the Lower Shankill and stage a counter-coup, which could spark another bloody internecine loyalist feud.

Secretly, a source told me, Adair was going to be airlifted out of HMP Maghaberry and flown by helicopter to the British mainland three days later, on the Monday.

That information suited *Sunday World* fine. We, of course, were publishing on the Sunday. And now we had a scoop.

I wrote up the story on the Saturday afternoon. It went front page the next morning.

And Adair was indeed airlifted by chopper out of Maghaberry jail, amid heavy security. He was whisked across the water to join his brood, and the rest of his exiled gangster clan, in, of all places, the town of Bolton, earning the now exiled rump of C Company the nickname the Bolton Wanderers.

It was there that Adair set up another drugs mini-empire, implicating both Gina and his son Jonathan as well. Both mother and son had their collars felt by the English cops. Gina was charged with dealing heroin and crack around Christmas 2003, but the charges were dropped. Later, Jonathan and two of his mates from Belfast were convicted of drug dealing and banged up for five years each.

Gina and Adair split up following a domestic incident when he attacked her. She was having treatment for cancer at the time. The relationship still appears to be amicable, though, and they've been pictured together since.

When he and Gina split up, Adair moved to another innocuous location, the town of Troon in Ayrshire, Scotland. He has remained there since. Although the one-time 'gaffer' of one of the most ruthless drugs and killer gangs of the Ulster Troubles has yet, I understand, to take up golf, in what is reputed to be one of the birthplaces of the Royal and Ancient game.

Jonathan Adair was never a 'frontline' terrorist like his father. But when he was back in Belfast, he was reputed to be no stranger to wielding a gun himself.

While behind bars, his father had fallen out – big time – with another criminal, also, coincidentally, dubbed Mad Dog. (The nickname, not surprisingly, was common among underworld criminals.) On release, that con man – he once got hold of a credit card stolen from Ian Paisley Jr and was caught trying to use it in a supermarket in, of all places, Ballymena – was known as a regular customer in a Belfast downtown bar.

At one stage, a gunman walked into that pub in broad daylight, when it was packed with customers. The masked man pointed a gun at the other Mad Dog, with whom Adair was still feuding. The gun jammed. The shooter, who was wearing a baseball cap, fled.

The wannabe assassin was reputed to be Jonathan Adair.

In spite of CCTV images being recovered by police from the pub, he was never identified, and never charged.

Some would say that, growing up in the shadow of his Mad Dog father, Jonathan never stood a chance. A politician I know told me about going to meet Johnny Adair at his Big Brother House HQ (as it was called) on the Shankill. Mad Dog was one of the UDA's first Brigadiers of Bling – gold necklaces, gold rings, gold earrings. As they used to say in Belfast, 'the bigger the earrings, the smaller the brain'.

The politician recalled that Jonathan would have been only about three years old at the time. He said: 'Johnny came up riding a quad. He had the wee lad perched up in front of him. The wee child was wearing a thick gold chain round his neck and, even then, earrings.'

Like father, like son, indeed.

After he had moved to join his father in Troon, Jonathan had been in and out of the courts a number of times, mostly on drugs-related charges. At one point he was imprisoned for attacking a woman who'd refused to sell him drugs.

In September 2016 he was released from prison following a sentence for motoring offences. But he was still facing charges of possessing drugs in prison. Once out, he celebrated with the inevitable drugs binge – in this instance, heroin. The thirty-two-year-old son of Mad Dog Adair was found dead at a house in Troon on Saturday 10 September 2016.

His father was informed, and then had the task of making what he called 'the hardest phone call of my life' to inform Gina and Jonathan's other siblings that their son and brother was dead.

The similarities between the fates of the sons of Jim Gray and Johnny Adair are striking. Indulged and influenced by the terror chiefs, what hope did either really have of a normal life?

The sins of the godfathers visited upon the children.

The once-feared Johnny 'Mad Dog' Adair, the man who had inflicted so much pain and grief and suffering on others, was later to tell the *Sunday World*: 'You don't expect to bury your son. It's hard.'

All too many fathers, and mothers, who had to bury their sons because of Mad Dog and his infamous UDA/UFF C Coy would agree.

30

THE BOOKIE'S BRIGADIER

Andre Shoukri was the UDA big-timer we dubbed 'the Bookie's Brigadier', because he embezzled almost a million quid of the terror gang's money – betting it, and losing all of it, on the horses. Other UDA men have been shot dead for less. Much less. How this particular ex-brigadier is still alive is a mystery to me: and to many other people, both inside and outside the terror gang.

Shoukri took over as brigadier of the UDA in north Belfast after his predecessor in the post, Jim 'Jimbo' Simpson, was stood down – not because he had lost his bottle, but because he became too fond of it. Simpson was known as 'the Bacardi Brigadier' because of his penchant for white rum.

Shoukri took over from him. His brother, Ihab – later to die of a drugs overdose while staying up one night to watch a televised Ricky Hatton world title fight being beamed from America – was Andre's second-in-command, and he took over the main role at one stage when his elder brother was banged up with his gangster sidekick, John 'Bonzer' Boreland, on racketeering and arms raps. (Bonzer Boreland was to fall victim to another internal UDA vendetta. He was gunned down at point-blank range as he walked home from the pub on the night of 7 August 2016.)

I wrote a book about the Shoukris. They and their other brother, Yuk, were of Egyptian extraction – that's why the book was called *The Mummy's Boys*. Their father, a Coptic Christian, is said to have fled from Egypt because the sect was being persecuted there. He married an Ulster woman, the Shoukris' mother, who came from Belfast, where the family settled.

The mother was a Christian, and she just couldn't bring herself to admit that both her sons, Andre and Ihab, had become godfathers in a gangster mob – even after an inquest found Ihab's body to be riddled with drugs, including cocaine and heroin, which, significantly, he and his brother and their UDA pariahs had been peddling to young people on the streets of Belfast.

However, the trio of sons all loved their mother. Which is how Andre Shoukri was almost assassinated by the IRA at one stage.

Only I saved his life ...

I'd often said to our staff, and anyone else who wanted to listen, that no story was worth a life. Yes, we would expose, and continue to hound in print, killers and criminals of all kinds. But if we found out, through our network of contacts, that there was going to be a murder bid on them our first obligation was to save lives, not become in any way caught up in, or even silently complicit in, the taking of lives. Even if the lives concerned were bad, evil people, some of whom had threatened, abused or, in Martin O'Hagan's case, killed one of us.

So it was that the Shoukris' mother, who was, as already pointed out, a good Christian woman, was a volunteer helper at the Northern Ireland Hospice on the Somerton Road in north Belfast. The hospice was situated only about three-quarters of a mile from the IRA stronghold of the New Lodge Road, also in the north of the city. Andre Shoukri went to the hospice a few days a week to collect his mother.

The Provos gleaned intelligence about that. They planned to send a 'hit team' from the New Lodge on a certain day to assassinate Shoukri when he drew up in one of the flash cars he was accustomed to driving. Anybody with him – his brother Ihab, his main mate and minder Bonzer Boreland, any other buddies or bodyguards – were to be wiped out, too.

We got wind of the plan from contacts on the republican side. I alerted someone close to Shoukri – Sammy Duddy, an old UDA hand and founder member who tried to keep back channels open to us in the *Sunday World* – to warn Andre Shoukri that the Provo gunmen would be lying in wait. He tipped off Shoukri. Andre didn't go to collect his mother that day. The Provos realised he wasn't coming, and aborted their shoot-to-kill operation.

I never got any thanks from Andre Shoukri. All I ever got was abuse, mostly over the phone.

But although he was, at one time, a UDA brigadier, Mr Shoukri would never have won a *Mastermind* heat ... never mind get to the final.

I was standing in the Morning Star bar one day, having a pint. My mobile rang. No number came up. Withheld number.

Shoukri, who had been behind a previous unsuccessful attempt to stop people buying the *Sunday World*, had operated unilaterally and imposed yet another boycott on us – but this time with the backing only of his own brigade. He was on the other end of the line, in foul – and foul language – form. He ranted and raved at me, accused me of 'telling lies about me and my family and this organisation [the UDA]'.

I wasn't taking it. I'd already attended a meeting with the UDA leader Jackie McDonald, with Sammy Duddy and others present, in an upstairs room of a Belfast hotel, where 'representations' – to put it diplomatically – were made about what we were writing about the north Belfast mob, and about Andre Shoukri in particular. Shoukri himself didn't turn up at that meeting, for whatever reason.

In the meantime, nothing had changed in how we were reporting his activities and those of his criminal crew. So he was livid: albeit at long distance, on the end of a phone, not having turned up to take me on face to face. He was phoning me from a landline. I found out afterwards he didn't want me to know his mobile phone number. Some chance, given what happened next.

'How do you know what we're saying about you in the paper, anyway, if you're boycotting it?' I asked him.

I wasn't taking any shit from him, and the head on my pint was dying. I cut him off.

My mobile pinged again. It was a text this time. From Shoukri. In a badly spelled message he accused me of being *'ignerrent'* (sic) in an obviously furious two-line tirade. *Do not disrespect me*, he warned self-importantly.

I phoned him straight back. He seemed genuinely surprised, if not shocked.

'Where the f**k did you get my mobile number, McDowell?' he demanded.

'From you,' I told him. 'You just sent me a text with your number on it.'

Did I say *Mastermind* contender?

Anyway, that conversation went nowhere, too. And I took great delight in splashing the Bookie's Brigadier on the front page of the paper the next Sunday. After all, he had forced his brigade to put a boycott on buying, or talking to, the *Sunday World*. And here he was, the main man himself, breaking it by talking to me! Gold dust. Or in his case, own-goal dust.

Mr Shoukri had shot himself not only in one foot, but in both. And that no-brainer, breaching his own boycott, played no small part in the Bookies' Brigadier being stood down and booted out of the UDA. Allied with another, rather more significant blot on his copybook: the nearly a million quid of the organisation's ill-gotten gains he'd blown at the bookie's.

Big Andy McMorran is a good friend of mine, and a great teacher and now retired headmaster. He at one time taught at the Boys' Model School in north Belfast, under another great school principal, E.W. Davis, or Ernie as he was known to his friends. Andy himself went on to become headmaster of Ashfield Boys' School in east Belfast, a school not unlike the Model, which did a brilliant job in educating boys from disadvantaged Belfast Protestant districts.

Headmaster McMorran didn't only turn the school around: he turned it on its head, academically speaking, in terms of the community – welcoming input from pupils and teachers from Catholic schools, and even having Gaelic football and hurling interchanges between soccer-playing Ashfield and GAA-playing schools.

Andy, before his retirement, was to go to Buckingham Palace, to receive a gong, courtesy of the Honours List, for his outstanding work as an educationalist, and as someone who practised his passion for bringing kids together, rather than leaving them stuck in the educational apartheid that still, lamentably, exists in Northern Ireland.

A couple of days before Christmas one year, I was having a pint with Andy in the Duke of York bar. He told me a story about how he had taught Andre Shoukri and 'Bonzer' Boreland, when they were both classmates at the Boys' Model. As Andy tells it, he was driving along Belfast's York Road one Saturday lunchtime, on his way to an Irish League soccer game – he was a handy footballer himself, and an even better coach, who at one stage was recruited to take his considerable coaching talents to the USA – when he fancied a bet. So he stopped at a bookmaker's, and went inside to have a look at the lists of horses running that afternoon.

'The betting shop,' he said, 'was full of ordinary blokes and oul' punters in their duncher caps doing their usual Saturday business, having a few bets on the horses. And I was just noting down a few knackers' yard candidates to have a couple of shillings on when all I hear from behind me is: "Hello, sir! How are you doing, sir? It's good to see you again, sir."'

Andy says he swivelled round. And there, standing before his very eyes, were two of his former pupils, the now Bookie's Brigadier Mr Shoukri himself and the bold Bonzer.

'You should have seen the looks on the faces of the rest of the customers in the bookies,' recalls Andy. 'They must have assumed that with this pair addressing me as *Sir*, I was even further up the ranks of the UDA than both of them!'

Andy says they appeared 'as if by magic'. And he says it only took him a couple of seconds to do a disappearing act of his own. To this day, he says, he remembers the name of the horse he was going to back. But he never got the chance. And it won!

But back to that meeting about Shoukri, and the *Sunday World*'s coverage of the Bookie's Brigadier and his gangster mob. It had taken place in the upstairs meeting room of a Belfast hotel with the UDA boss, Jackie McDonald, present.

Well, when it was over I went down to the public bar below with McDonald. This wasn't the first time we had gone head to head. Sometimes, it was in the Taughmonagh social club in south Belfast – effectively his HQ. But I never backed down from meeting any of the paramilitary bosses. After all, I, our staff and the *Sunday World* had nothing to hide. We weren't the killers and drug dealers and racketeers. We were merely exposing them, in the public interest, in order to protect the communities we all came from and, more important, were raising our families in. So Jackie and his minder and I went down to the bar. McDonald has been off the drink for a long time now. He wasn't then. He and I had a pint.

We are from similar backgrounds: both Protestant working-class, and both from the lower end of the scale, as well. As we supped our beer – the minder constantly watching the pub door, and at the same time making sure I knew of his close (very close) presence – Jackie said to me: 'You know, McDowell, I could like you as a man if it wasn't for that paper you run.'

'Jackie,' I replied, 'I could like you as a man if it wasn't for that organisation you run.'

Judging by the look on the minder's face, if he had been having a pint with us, he wouldn't only have choked on the beer … he'd have swallowed the glass and shit it out the other end at the same time.

I don't think anybody ever talked to Jackie McDonald like that. But I think he had a sneaking respect that I did. And still does.

31
TOUTS

The story of the IRA's 'bog bodies' – those people deemed to be informers, or, in street parlance, touts – is one long, grim tale of woe.

On the republican side, there were the revelations about Freddie 'Stakeknife' Scappaticci, the one-time head of the Provos' so-called 'nutting squad' in Belfast – the special interrogation unit that kidnapped and tortured suspected touts, and then executed them summarily, often after brutal kangaroo courts. The top Provo, codenamed Stakeknife, turned out to be himself a tout for British intelligence. He scarpered – some say to the homeland of his forefathers, Sicily – before the IRA could catch up with and, to use his own crude terminology, 'nut' him.

Speaking of crude terminology …

In brutal Belfast terms, both in republican and loyalist circles, when that kind of summary execution was meted out, it was also referred to in street slang that mockingly invoked the British honours system. When someone was shot in the head, it was said they'd received a 'Belfast OBE'. That stood for 'One Behind (the) Ear'.

Denis Donaldson, a top Shinner and IRA veteran from East Belfast, wasn't as lucky as Scappaticci. Just before Christmas 2005, at a press conference in Dublin, he publicly confessed to being an informer. The implications for the republican movement were profound. The diminutive Donaldson had been a 'made man', a major player in the ranks.

A long-term IRA volunteer, he had been imprisoned for paramilitary crimes. An old photograph from 1980 shows him with his arm slung around the neck of his friend and fellow prisoner, the hunger striker Bobby Sands. He was also a close personal friend of Sinn Féin leader Gerry Adams.

Down the years his name had been associated with a number of IRA atrocities, including, most damningly, the La Mon bombing, when twelve innocent people enjoying a dinner in the restaurant were murdered by an inferno of carefully placed IRA firebombs on 17 February 1978.

His outing came after an investigation by the PSNI into a suspected spy-ring at Stormont, where Donaldson was working in the Sinn Féin office. The result of the police raids on the office was to 'out' Donaldson as an MI5 tout.

After the press conference, and his very public confession, he fled to a cottage hideaway in County Donegal. The Provos caught up with him.

There was only one sentence in the little green book of rules, which every volunteer had to sign up to on being sworn into the IRA, that applied specifically to informers. And that was the death sentence. Donaldson thought he was safe in this secluded, if primitive, hideaway among the hills of Donegal.

He wasn't.

A nutting squad – still believed to be from Thomas 'Slab' Murphy's South Armagh Brigade, although that's never been proved – knocked on the door of his bunkered-down billet. And shot him dead, full in the face, with a shotgun.

The Provos still maintain they had nothing to do with the brutal killing of their former friend. Few believe them.

Of course, the most infamous of the 'disappeared' at the hands of the Provos was mother of ten Jean McConville, who was kidnapped in the winter of 1972. A Protestant who married a Catholic, and who lived in the heart of republican west Belfast, she offended local republicans by attending to a young British soldier lying wounded during a terror attack close to her front door in the Divis Flats complex. Her husband had died just a few months before and poor Jean, left to rear her family of young children, was wrongly and maliciously accused of being a tout.

On one occasion she was savagely beaten by a gang. She still hadn't recovered from her wounds from that assault on the winter's night she was dragged away at gunpoint from her screaming young sons and daughters.

She was never seen again, until her body was dug up, from where it had been buried on Shelling Hill Beach, over the border in County Louth, in August 2003. She had been shot in the head: summarily executed.

Gerry Adams, no less, made headlines in the international press when, at one stage after her body was discovered, he was arrested by police and questioned about Mrs McConville's murder. The Sinn Féin President was held at the anti-terror interrogation centre at the PSNI barracks in Antrim, where he was questioned, in the presence of his solicitor, before being released without charge.

Afterwards, Mr Adams vehemently denied that he had anything to do with Jean McConville's kidnap and killing. For years, he has also vehemently denied being a member of the IRA.

Touts, or 'informants', as their RUC/PSNI Special Branch or British undercover force handlers called them, also peppered the ranks of the loyalist paramilitaries.

A former top cop and close acquaintance of mine, Jonty Brown – he was significantly instrumental in putting away Johnny 'Mad Dog' Adair on Adair's eventually self-confessed rap of being a director of terrorism – wrote in his acclaimed book *Into the Dark* that three out of ten members of one illegal loyalist gang alone, the UVF, were informants.

I have met, and interviewed, on a number of occasions the man who says he was the only Catholic ever to join the ranks of that loyalist killer gang. His name is Terry Fairfield. I flew to interview him in a lounge at Stansted airport in England shortly after Jonty Brown's book was published. I wasn't there to interview him about the book. I was there to ask him how he, born a Catholic, had become a member of a loyalist killer gang hell-bent on murdering Catholics.

The tale is too long to repeat here: suffice to say he had a best friend, a Protestant, who was singled out and slaughtered by the Provos, and he swore revenge on the IRA for that. But during the interview, when I gave him a copy of Jonty's book, he came out with the startling confession that he, too, was a tout. He'd also been recruited by the then RUC Special Branch.

And when I put it to him that Jonty had said in his book that three out of ten members of the UVF – Fairfield's own mob – in particular, were touts, he threw his head back and started laughing heartily.

When he'd 'gathered himself', as we say in Ulster, I asked him what was so funny.

'McDowell,' he says, 'catch yourself on. There's no way *three* in every ten UVF members are touts. *Seven* out of every ten UVF members are touts.'

Significantly, as a string of UVF so-called 'supergrass' trials have proved over recent years, Terry Fairfield's reckoning may be right, but I'll stick with Jonty's assessment – it's startling enough as it stands!

Unfortunately, all of those trials collapsed, because of the unreliability of the touts involved: when they had given their recollections of killings and other crimes, their evidence could not be corroborated. Often the reason for that was that they themselves were either on drink or on drugs at the time the crimes were committed.

I found this out to my own cost when, having pursued our reporter Martin O'Hagan's killers for years, we thought we had turned the corner when one of the LVF killer gang from Lurgan decided to become what is now called an 'assisting offender'. In legal terms, in former days he would have been said to have 'turned Queen's evidence'.

His name is Neil Hyde. He pleaded guilty to a long list of LVF-related terrorism charges. The prosecution papers showed that he was actually in the room where the gun was produced on the afternoon before Martin's murder. Although, conveniently enough, he put himself at arm's length from the murder itself. The old 'I wasn't there, guv' line.

For a time we in the *Sunday World* thought, or at least hoped, that we were going to get Martin's killers nailed, at last. But at the last minute, the Public Prosecution Service (PPS) said it wasn't going ahead with what would have been another supergrass trial: a case that could have put the whole of the LVF terror gang in Lurgan in County Armagh, and, more specifically, Martin's murderers, behind bars.

Hyde had already confessed to a litany of crimes in open court. I went to every one of the hearings. I reported all of them, and gave interviews outside afterwards, stressing the hope that we were going to see justice for Martin after all those years. Hyde had even been handed down a 'patsy' sentence. As a reward for becoming an assisting offender, he would be jailed for just three and a half years. He'd already been in police custody, giving all his detailed evidence to top anti-terror cops, for a long time. Because of time already spent in custody, he'd have walked free almost immediately after the supergrass trial – albeit with a new identity and in a different place and under armed police protection, for a time, anyway.

But the trial was called off. And just minutes before an open press conference to announce the cancellation, I was invited round to the PPS HQ, in the shadow of the Ulster High Court, for a preliminary, one-to-one briefing with the head of the PPS in Northern Ireland, Barra McGrory.

To be fair, he and all his staff appreciated the intense sensitivity surrounding Martin's murder among the *Sunday World* staff and, more important, Martin's family. But I was told the Hyde case was being guillotined. His evidence could not be corroborated.

And although there were millions of words and thousands of files of his testimony to police, the official reckoning was that it would be destroyed by expert – and well-paid, out of the public purse under legal aid – defence barristers.

Why?

Because it was judged – if I can use that word – that the ultra-hedonistic Mr Hyde had been under the influence of either alcohol or drugs before, or during, many of the crimes he had committed. His evidence was ruled unreliable on that score.

I used the word 'guillotined' a little earlier. There's another clichéd word that didn't even go near how I felt in that PPS executive office: gutted.

And then I had to go outside and phone the office and tell our people that all our hopes and expectations on the Hyde case had been hammered: right into the ground. And with that went what we believed was the biggest chance to bring Martin's killers to book.

And here's the incredible criminal corollary to all this.

Even though the PPS collapsed the Hyde supergrass follow-up trial, the trivial sentence of three and a half years he got for confessing to no fewer than forty-six terrorist crimes still stood. He's now walking the streets again, somewhere, as a free man. Is it any wonder that I, a law-abiding citizen, who has always supported the police and what they stand for, am still left using a word with which I started this chapter?

That word is 'tout'.

I still believe – and I'm not on my own – that two of the men who have questions to answer over Martin O'Hagan's murder, the brothers Drew 'the Piper' King and Robin 'Billy' King, were indeed touts. For which agency, I cannot pinpoint. But whether it was the RUC Special Branch of old, or an arm of the British undercover intelligence network of MI5, or the hugely discredited military wing, the Force Reconnaissance Unit (FRU), responsible for colluding in so many killings in Ulster – the shameful fact remains that Martin's killers are still running free.

And no one – and I mean *no one* – has yet given me, or the *Sunday World*, or his family, a credible reason why.

32

THE DIRTY WAR

Freddie 'Stakeknife' Scappaticci and Denis Donaldson may have been the two most notorious touts on the republican side. That same shady status can be applied to two of their counterparts in loyalist terror gang ranks.

Stakeknife, who is still on the run from the Provos to this day, has been accredited in various sectors of the press with, in collusion with his British 'spook' handlers – whether MI5 or the FRU military outfit – setting up or murdering more than forty people.

But the most prolific – if that is the right word – informant/double agent on the loyalist side was Brian Nelson. A former soldier, he rose to become the intelligence officer for the whole of the UDA. And it was in April of 2016, after months of hard digging, that I eventually got my hands on the proof of how many victims he had helped send to their graves.

The documents I had slogged so long for were worth it: 125 pages, in Nelson's own handwriting, of what amounted to him confessing to either setting up, or being involved in, the murder of some *fifty-six* people. And not only did the self-penned dossier of death show that Nelson, again, an ex-soldier himself, was actively stalked and recruited by the FRU, but that he was out of Northern Ireland and working in Germany when he was approached.

It proved, once and for all, that British military intelligence had foreknowledge of a litany of murders being planned and/or carried out by the UDA. He lists the names of his squad of handlers down the right-hand column of his 'confession', detailing his intelligence gathering for his UDA bosses. He also says that all information he supplied to his handlers went upstairs to 'the Box': the shadowy central army intelligence HQ responsible for running undercover operations in Ulster, but not covering the SAS.

Perhaps most remarkable of all, he reveals in the neatly handwritten and concise papers that at one stage he was ordered by the UDA command to travel to South Africa, to set up an arms deal and gun-running operation from there. He says he told his handlers this. They came back and gave him the go-ahead. And he records that one of them told him the illegal arms-smuggling attempt on behalf of the UDA had been OK'd 'right at the top', by 'Maggie' herself.

Margaret Thatcher was the Prime Minister in Downing Street at the time. Nelson was in no doubt that she was the 'Maggie' mentioned.

What we headlined as 'The Nelson Files' in the *Sunday World* were dynamite. It had taken delicate, time-absorbing negotiations – taking months, rather than weeks – always in another country, to eventually obtain the handwritten, and wholly damning, dossier. And when I eventually got it, I was advised by our legal people not to bring it back into the jurisdiction of Northern Ireland, or the UK for that matter.

I had to fly with it to Dublin, which is, of course, under the jurisdiction of the Republic of Ireland – and therefore outside the ambit of anyone trying to get their hands on the documents, legally or otherwise (the FRU weren't known as the masters of dirty tricks operations for nothing), or the British government trying to gag publication of them by hitting us with a D notice, which bans a newspaper from publishing a story in (allegedly) the interests of national security.

So the amazing story was written from down there.

We ran with it for three weeks in a row in the northern edition, where, of course, it was most potent. The first week we ran eight pages, from the front in, the second week six, and the third week four. We revealed that, among other factors that sparked considerable fall-out, Nelson himself had acted as a scout to set up assassination bids for UDA hit squads.

Among the targets were Sinn Féin chiefs Gerry Adams and Martin McGuinness. Adams, indeed, was scouted out twice by Nelson, who dressed up in builder's hard hat and other gear and climbed scaffolding opposite a housing office where Adams was known to attend regularly once a week. The plan was to wait until Adams and his minders, or bodyguards, drove out of the one-way street in which the office was situated. As the car moved out of the cul-de-sac and into usually slow-moving traffic close to Belfast City Hall, a motorbike would pull parallel with Adams's car. A bomb, a crude limpet mine made with a special magnet smuggled out of the Belfast shipyard, would be placed on the roof of the car by the pillion passenger. It would blow up, killing, or decapitating, everyone inside the car.

This plot was aborted at the last minute. However, in his files Nelson names the terrorist who was the pillion passenger and who was detailed to prime and plant the bomb. He is still a well-known UDA commander in the Woodvale area of west Belfast. He has never been charged or convicted on the Adams attempted murder rap: for legal reasons, therefore, we were not able to name him in the paper, and can't here, either. In spite of Nelson naming him, clearly and unequivocally, in his files.

Nelson also scouted out – and even went into – the converted Conway Street mill in the heart of the republican Falls Road in West Belfast. His mission there was to find out when the late Martin McGuinness was travelling from Derry to attend Sinn Féin or IRA meetings in the old mill – McGuinness was a self-confessed former 2OC (second in command) of the Derry Brigade of the IRA. Nelson even found a house on the loyalist side of the Peace Wall, which split the Shankill and the Falls district, from where, through an upstairs window, a UDA sniper could have a clear shot at McGuinness.

That plot, too, was foiled.

But it showed the devil in the detail that Nelson was able to supply, as designated overall intelligence officer, to his UDA superiors. And also to his handlers in the FRU, who he clearly and consistently claims in the Nelson Files were kept fully informed of what he was doing, every time he was doing it.

The whole of the Nelson Files are now locked up in a safe somewhere in Dublin – I don't know where, and don't want to know: job done. Nelson is dead, having died of cancer in Cardiff in 2003, aged 55. He too, just like his files, was locked up for a spell when the truth about his murderous activities eventually surfaced. But like double agents, or touts, before him and since, he confessed to a litany of crimes and was handed down a much lighter sentence – just ten years, believe it or not – for what was his leading and very lethal part in Ulster's 'dirty war'.

The other top tout on the loyalist side is still languishing in an English jail – after being charged and convicted of the attempted murder of ... yet another tout!

He is Mark Haddock. He ran a brigade of the UVF's 3rd Battalion, based in the ultra-loyalist Mount Vernon housing estate on the Shore Road in north Belfast. Except the cops didn't call the UVF thugs who lived in the enclave – where, again, many decent people live – the Mount Vernon brigade. Because of the sectarian murder machine – and the drugs rackets – run from this very tight ghetto (only one road in, and one road out), anti-terror cops dubbed them the 'Mount Vermin' brigade.

It should be stressed, again, that the vast majority of residents of that area are, and always have been, decent people who want no truck with the UVF lowlife.

During the worst years of the Troubles, the RUC's Special Branch ran informers. And it has been established indisputably that they ran Mark Haddock as one of their main touts – even though he and his UVF team were committing the most horrendous sectarian murders and other heinous crimes.

But the record shows that three men, in particular, stood up bravely against this reckless regime. They are two former RUC CID detectives, Jonty Brown and his professional police partner, Trevor McIlwrath.

Both 'good cops' repeatedly tried to point up what certain Special Branch cops were at, but the police anti-terror culture of the time saw them pilloried and mocked. They both ended up paying a heavy price for trying to lay bare the iniquity in Special Branch tout tactics.

The third brave man is Raymond McCord, who I am proud to call a friend. Haddock's mob savagely murdered his son, Raymond Jr – a former member of the Royal Air Force – in 1997. Raymond, a welder by trade, has since relentlessly pursued justice for his son, at a huge cost to his own personal safety and wellbeing. He has had many death threats from the UVF. But that has not stopped him. Even to the extent of confronting John 'Bunter' Graham, the overall godfather of the UVF, when he happened upon him in a Belfast downtown bar, and taking on this Don Corleone of Ulster's most ruthless loyalist Paramafia face to face.

Raymond also asked for a face-to-face meeting with the then Police Ombudsman for Northern Ireland, Nuala O'Loan, now Dame Nuala O'Loan. What he told her about his son's murder, about Haddock, about the

'Mount Vermin' mob, and about the whole UVF led to her team producing a lid-lifting report that was volcanic in both political and policing terms.

The report lacerated Special Branch and its 'handling', literally, of Haddock and his bunch of murdering 3rd. Company UVF hoods and drug-dealing gangsters. It openly accused the UVF gang of committing up to fifteen killings, most of them sectarian.

I was at the O'Loan press conference in the Stormont Hotel in Belfast in January 2007 when she launched her blockbuster report. She referred to Haddock as 'Informant 1'. And also as 'a serial killer'.

During the period 1991–2003, she said, he had been implicated directly in ten murders, and potentially in five more. He had been paid, during that same period, over £79,000.

In countries around the world, the police and other state agencies – Britain's MI5 and MI6, and the FBI and CIA in America, for instance – pay informers. It's routine practice, 'to protect the public'.

But the difference with Haddock, as exposed by Police Ombudsman O'Loan, was that he was a paid police informer while he, and his UVF terror gang, were still killing people: and his handlers knew that. In other words, instead of protecting the public, Haddock was being paid out of the public purse ... as he continued to kill members of the public.

The O'Loan report sparked revulsion and outrage. And the *big* question then arose – and still remains: how many more like him were, or still are, out there?

After the press conference, I shook Raymond McCord's hand.

We in the *Sunday World* had relentlessly backed his campaign for justice, not just for his own son Raymond Jr but, as it later turned out, other families of victims of all terror gangs – republican and loyalist – who had turned to Raymond Sr for support and to spearhead their quest for justice. We had been with Raymond from the start. We gave him many headlines and many column inches, reporting his very just cause.

But still, but still … Haddock escaped jail when a major UVF supergrass trial collapsed, and he remained on the streets. True, his own former mob – accepting at last that he was indeed a tout (and, as it turned out, there were even more in the UVF's Mount Vernon ranks) – tried to shoot him dead. But Haddock survived: again.

And then he moved to England. To be beside another self-confessed UVF tout: Terry Fairfield.

Fairfield was mentioned earlier as the only Catholic to join the UVF. He told me that he had felt sorry for Haddock, wanted to help give him a fresh start, and even gave him a job in the pub Fairfield now owns close to Luton. Haddock repaid him by trying to slit his throat.

A few days after that incident, I flew to England to interview, once again, Terry Fairfield, and to get pictures, with a photographer, of the fresh scar running from just under his ear to his throat.

'I'm lucky to be alive,' said Fairfield.

And in time he gave live evidence from the witness box which saw Haddock found guilty of attempted murder. As a result, Haddock is now banged up in an English jail, serving a twelve-year sentence.

Haddock's barbarity didn't come as news to us in the *Sunday World*. We'd already dubbed him 'Hannibal' Haddock in the paper. He'd tried to snatch a camera from one of our photographers who was snapping a picture of him in the street. The brave photographer resisted. And Haddock bit a lump out of his eyebrow.

So it was goodbye Hannibal Lecter of Hollywood movie fame. And, hello Hannibal Haddock.

33
PULLING A STROKE

The Nobel Prize-winning Irish poet Seamus Heaney co-compiled an anthology of verse called *The Rattle Bag*.

I am that rattle bag.

Because every time I step down off the pavement, I rattle. It's not the sixty-eight-year-old bones. Although after thirty-six years in a rugby scrum, training for and running eleven marathons, and doing a bout of boxing (both inside and outside the ring!), they do grind and groan a bit too.

No, it's the pills.

A legacy of the stroke that snuck up on me on 20 December 2015, the Sunday before Christmas. It's not that I'm on a tower block of tablets daily to bully my blood, chisel my cholesterol and keep a bin lid on my blood pressure. But I am on enough pills to make me sound like a percussion-playing refugee from Tin Pan Alley in public.

And in the pub after a few pints. Well, let's just say I could pass an audition for the wind section of the Ulster Orchestra without playing a note on a musical instrument.

The medics and dieticians also advised me to watch what I eat. Fatty Ulster fries are out. As are plate-loads of spuds and butter. And fish and chips. And, in the main, red meat is a red-light culinary cul-de-sac as well. Fish and chicken now get the green light in the grub stakes. Plus, they're easy to swallow, as long as you watch out for the bones.

And that's how I knew something was badly awry around 8.00 p.m. on that December Sunday night, when the stroke so silently stole up on me.

The swallowing part. It was the first smoke signal that something was badly wrong.

We were at a Christmas party thrown by our friend Carolyn Stewart, from U105, the sister radio station of Ulster Television, for which Lindy worked as a co-presenter on the radio breakfast show and as producer for Frank Mitchell's phone-in show later in the day. I should have known something was amiss earlier in the day, when I was out running. I'd left my car in the company car park in downtown Belfast the night before, after we'd been out for a meal and a couple of jars with a few friends. I was up, as usual, around five the next morning, and thought I'd jog the four miles into town from our house to get the car early. We'd a lot of driving to do that day, delivering presents to Lindy's relatives in South Derry, and then to my own family around Belfast.

On the jog into town, which was normally non-stop, I had to pull up to a hobble or a halt about half a dozen times, and then finally I just walked the last half-mile to the car. There was this dull pain, deeper even than a thigh muscle cramp, which repeatedly slammed the brakes on my right leg.

It hit. I stopped. It went. I jogged. It kept biting again.

I got the car. Got home. Showered and dressed. I shrugged off the pains in the right leg, thinking, even at my age, that I'd maybe tweaked or stretched a hamstring.

Then, after breakfast, I was driving for about seven hours, intermittently going into the families' homes to leave and receive presents. Looking back, it was almost a replica of a longish-haul flight, with the attendant risk of deep vein thrombosis. Reflecting afterwards, I think that's what it was.

Also, Lindy had remarked a few times during the day that I looked a bit drained and fatigued. We'd planned to take a taxi to Carolyn's Christmas 'do' down at her home in Bangor, County Down, later that evening. But at the last minute I said I'd drive, as I simply didn't fancy drinking that night. Maybe it was an instinctive premonition. Journalists, after all, intuitively rely as much on instinct when chasing and filing stories as they do on judgement. That's the sort of 'take-a-gamble' game it is.

So I was the designated driver, and would therefore be able to ferry ourselves, and a few friends, back to Belfast later that night … or, more likely, early the next morning.

I'd just had a wrap with some meat in it to eat. And I was drinking a bottle of still water. If anyone had taken a picture of that and put it up on YouTube or Facebook, my reputation was totally out the window: kaput.

I was standing having a yarn with the good lad who cooked the food. And then I found I couldn't talk. My words were coming out slowly, and it was as if they were shifting gear, by themselves, as I struggled to control the flow. The fella with whom I was talking asked me if I was OK.

I mumbled: 'Aye …' But then it was as if my throat was contracting: I felt that I was beginning to suffocate.

I managed to hirple, rather than walk, out to the outside terrace. Fresh air will clear my head, I thought. I walked over to the patio edge and grabbed the railing, peering over a clear black night sky framing Belfast Lough, with the Copeland Island lighthouse blinking back at me over Ballyholme bay. I breathed deeply. Tried to 'gather myself', as we say in Ulster.

Then I tried to turn to go back to the chairs on the patio. I tried to lift my right hand off the cold metal rail. It wouldn't move: seemed like it was stuck with superglue. My left hand was still working. I used that to prise the other free. I half-turned. Tried to walk. My right leg was dead. Inflexible. Immobile. Like getting a 'dead leg' in rugby when another player's knee catches you right on the meat of the thigh muscle. But there was no pain with this.

You're in soapy bubble here, McDowell, I thought.

But I managed to half-drag the side of my body that, I now realised, was paralysed over to one of the seats. It was beside a big window into the kitchen where people were gathering to eat and drink. I tried to swivel and wave in with my good hand, the left. Lindy, amid a throng of chatting people, saw that. But she thought I was just outside yarning to someone, and was waving to call her out. Usually she ignores me. Or at least takes her time. Fortunately, this time she came out right away. And right away she saw I was in real trouble. I told her I couldn't move my arm or my leg.

Lindy's mother had had a stroke, so she recognised it. 'I think you've had a stroke,' she said.

My first reaction was no, that couldn't be happening to me. But Carolyn and our other friends, Joanne and Jacqui, had come out and they confirmed Lindy's fear. They ran through the FAST checklist – that absolutely vital, accurate and life-saving advice from Northern Ireland's Chest, Heart and Stroke organisation which featured on TV ads.

They checked for F – face drooping. Negative. Then A – arms drooping or immobile. Positive. S – speech affected? Positive also. T– time to dial 999 and get an ambulance.

So they did.

Lindy, meanwhile, had reached for her handbag. I thought she was digging to find the insurance policy: *my* life insurance policy. She wasn't. She was hoking for an Ibuprofen pill. She also thought about giving me a glass of water to take with it.

She thought the pill might have the same effect as aspirin in thinning the blood. For the record, you should not give someone you believe is having a stroke *anything* to swallow. Not even water.

The paramedic, a good lad whose name I learned later was Ian, arrived first to answer the emergency call. He almost broke his leg stumbling over a low wall to get round to the back of the house where I was in the

December dark. But he wrapped a blood pressure band round my arm, saw that the pressure would lift a barrage balloon, and quickly confirmed it could be a stroke.

He summoned an equally professional ambulance and crew. And they got me into the Ulster Hospital A&E at Dundonald, on the eastern outskirts of Belfast, within about forty minutes from when I first knew something was up (or down): well within the three- to four-hour window that the medics need to treat a stroke victim if there's to be a decent chance of full recovery.

Or of sidestepping death.

Dr Gerry Sloan, whose ID I later made it my business to find out too, was on duty in A&E. He had me stretchered into the big scanner. He told me there was a clot on my brain. There was an injection that might fix it: it's called a 'clotbuster' by ordinary punters like us. It's called thrombolysis by the clinicians.

It can cure you. It can have little or no effect, and can leave you permanently disabled by the stroke. Or, in some cases, it can kill you.

The odds were explained to me. They were daunting enough. But it was a 'no-choice' response. I signed the consent form. Albeit with a squiggle with my left hand while lying on my back; I'm right-handed, and was still paralysed down that side.

The clotbuster worked. By 5.00 a.m. the next morning I was groggily half-sitting up in bed, and able to shake the doc's hand – with my right hand – when he came round to see how I was. And to thank him, and the nursing staff, profusely for the modern-day miracle they had performed on me.

Two days later, I was out of 'the Ulster'. Three months later, the consultant, another smashing medic, Michael Power, closed the file.

Writing this now, almost two years later, I feel like I've placed a bet with Dr Power's namesake, Paddy Power the bookmaker, and hit the jackpot. Yes, I shrug it off – kind of – when people kindly ask how I'm doing and I reply: 'Ach, sure it was only another traffic bump on the road of life.'

It wasn't, folks.

I've come close to shaking hands with the Oul' Fella with the straggly beard brandishing the big scythe a few times. Not least when, almost twenty years before the stroke, that helicopter I was in failed, feathered and flopped into a field from 1,500 feet up over County Fermanagh, when a few of us got away with broken backs. Or when I got that kicking from the UVF terrorists almost on the steps of the City Hall, and wrote the front-page headline:

THEY TRIED TO KICK ME TO DEATH

Or during the cascade of other crises I've come face to face with while facing down and exposing, with my *Sunday World* colleagues, for a quarter of a century, the terrorists, gunmen and gangsters living on our own doorsteps.

But, as a footnote to all of it, I'm also in debt to Dr Gerry Sloan for one other not inconsiderable act of kindness he showed me. When he pulled me out of that big scanner in the Ulster Hospital, he confirmed that I had, indeed, a clot on the brain. In doing so, he confirmed that I do, indeed, have a brain.

For that, I am eternally grateful.

Because having lived, and survived, almost all of my Old Testament allotment of three score years and ten on this earth, it surprised me.

And, truth be told, it surprised a helluva lot of other people, too.

34
FAMILY FIRST

Too many people in my family died far too young. My father, my mother Cherry from breast cancer on 3 September 1979 and my only sister, Anne.

My Da collapsed and died of a heart attack when I was twenty-one years old. I'd heard about it as I was crossing Shaftesbury Square in Belfast, about a quarter of a mile from our family home in Donegall Pass. Ironically, it was in 'the Square', as it was known, that my father started his first job, as an apprentice in a butcher's shop.

I sprinted, heart pumping, the whole way home. It was no good. I couldn't do anything for him. Neither could anyone else. My father had died before I got home.

That was 29 September 1970. I've lived over two-thirds of my life without him. And I still miss him.

I got married six weeks later. To Linda. I was a Protestant. Linda was a Catholic. Some people, even members of my family, didn't like it. Others, less close acquaintances, loathed it. And let it be known that they did. Though seldom to my face.

Still, I loved Linda back then. We were married for thirteen years. Like any marriage, it wasn't all bliss. We had to scrimp and save for the deposit for our first house: number 12 Jerusalem Street, in the heart of what is known in Belfast as the Holy Land, where all of the streets are named after biblical locations. It was a humble wee house, which cost just 12,000 quid. But we had good neighbours in what was then a close-knit community. These days, the Holy Land is a horror story, with most of the terraced houses, big and small, converted into student bedsits by an army of make-a-quick-buck landlords. The campus of Queen's University is a mortar-board's throw away. The landlords saw the opportunity, and seized it. But the smattering of residents still living in the Holy Land now pay the real price: being tormented by rowdy revellers, and having to endure drink-addled riots before, during and after St Patrick's Day every year.

However, having thrown all we had at the deposit, and getting a mortgage for the biblically named abode, that was our honeymoon destination: the very night of our wedding. And there was no plush reception, either. Just beer and sandwiches *EastEnders*-style at one of the pubs at the end of our street.

My mother, Cherry, in spite of her still fresh grief after the sudden death of her cherished husband Jimmy, came to the wedding. She was a brave woman. And she embraced Linda fully into the family: in spite of the mixed reception to our 'mixed' marriage among some of our more distant family relatives. My Ma also embraced, fondly and fully, our lovely daughter, Faye, who was gifted to us in that marriage.

I should reveal Faye's age here. But I can't. For security reasons. My own security, that is. She'd kneecap me. With her teeth.

But in turn, Faye has gifted Linda and me, and all of us in our now extended family, with two smashing grandchildren. Well, they're no longer children. They are sporting, surfing, smiling, charming and disarming teenagers: Niamh, aged eighteen, and now driving a car rather than fairground dodgems, and soccer and rugby player Ewan, who is sixteen.

I don't see enough of them.

Faye moved to be with Linda, who was living and working in Devon, in her late teens, having lived with us and her two brothers – no 'half' brothers or sister between Faye, Jamie and Micah – back in Belfast. And for a spell, she also shared 'the Big House' in Newton Park with Estella, a Romanian kid.

Lindy had gone out to interview Eric and Elizabeth Carson, who were doing tremendous work with Romanian orphanages at the time, and she came home with Estella, a sixteen-year-old who had been working with the Carsons in her home country. Lindy had been so touched by Estella's story that she decided we would offer the girl a home. She didn't even have to ask me. She knew I'd agree. Micah was just six months old at the time. We now had four kids in the house with, between them, three mothers and two fathers.

We eventually got Estella into one of Belfast's top schools, Methodist College, and she eventually went on to Cambridge University.

By that stage, too, Faye was moving on, aged just eighteen. Like many of her generation, she'd had enough of the chokingly constricted lifestyles inflicted on them by the so-called Troubles. The inevitable cascade of questions and advice from parents before the youngsters even put a foot out the door. 'Where are you going tonight?' 'Watch yourself.' 'If there's the first sign of trouble, run, get away from it.' 'Wherever you are, phone us. Let us know where you are.'

And, the one unending query that young people of all ages liked least, but which had a different meaning in the context of the carnage and violence racking Northern Ireland, and Belfast in particular: 'What time will you be in at?'

No one could have blamed them for jumping on a plane or a boat. And getting out for a while. Or for good. And in many cases, that's exactly what happened. Young people headed for universities across the water in England and Scotland. And never came back. The so-called Ulster brain drain. And that's exactly what it was.

Faye was part of that teen exodus. Emotionally, for Lindy and myself, that was tough. Lindy loved her as much as myself and our boys. Still does. And Niamh and Ewan too.

Faye's partner is Jarrod, she having gone through a divorce, too. Just like I did from her mother, when Faye was just eight. Then, as now, it is difficult for children, especially at such a young age, to understand their parents splitting up. That was my fault. I could trundle out excuses. I won't. I had an affair. With Lindy. We were both working in the same newspaper at the time. It happened. I put my hands up to that in the High Court.

I was waiting in the Great Hall of the Ulster High Court for my divorce proceedings to be called. A certain lawyer who I knew came up to me. He asked what I was doing there that day, if I wasn't down to report a case. I told him my divorce was going through that morning. He pushed back his wig, stared me straight in the eyes, said 'Lucky bastard', turned on his well-polished heel and strode off, leaving me puzzled.

The following week he did a runner with his mistress, leaving the missus and kids in his wake. That solved the puzzle.

But I still didn't, on the day he talked to me, feel particularly 'lucky', or a 'bastard' either. In fact, after the case Linda and I went for a drink. I signed over the car, the house, and everything in it to Linda. And, hopefully, looked after both Faye and her as best I could financially.

It was a rocky road to travel at first: whatever claims are made to the contrary, breaking up, as the Righteous Brothers say, is so very hard to do. Still, for many years now, Linda and her partner, Paul, have always been made welcome in our home by both Lindy and myself, and the four of us have shared celebrations and other candle-lighting occasions with Faye and her family.

That's the way it is.

That's the way it should be.

It's all a part of my life, which I cherish.

There are some folk who live by the mantra, 'Never step back, never look back.' That's all right on the rugby paddock. But I am neither afraid nor ashamed to look back. And I would never step back from the life I've lived. Especially the loved ones, all of them. My family and my friends.

They have all – like my dear sister Anne, who died so young at the age of only forty-four, like my beautiful and always supportive sister-in-law, Marlene, who we lost so recently, and like my brother-in-law, William McIlvenna, also now passed on, but who I played shoulder to shoulder with in many a rugby scrum – they have all given me so much I can never repay.

And, knowing them as I do, I also know, in my heart, they would never ask.

Like myself, their lynchpin in life was always 'family first'.

Again, that's how it should be.

And that's how, for me, it always will be.

35

THE PEOPLE'S PAPER

They say that politics and sport don't mix.

Rubbish.

Just recall the huge rows over cricket and rugby tours to South Africa during the appalling era of apartheid. Or, closer to home in Ireland, the now thankfully redacted GAA ban on hurlers and footballers playing so-called 'foreign' sports, like soccer and rugby. Or, both in Glasgow and Belfast – and elsewhere – the politics and, even worse, sectarianism that can be associated with wearing a Rangers or Celtic shirt.

In newspapers, too, there was an old adage of 'never work with friends or family' when doing a story. Some of the best stories I've ever scribed sprang from source material from family or friends. And some of the best human interest yarns were picked up while having a pint with people in a pub.

Recently, however, another rule should have been written concerning the gathering of news, and its publication in a newspaper. And that is that no politician – especially a serving politician – should be appointed editor of a newspaper.

So it was with utter disgust, and dismay, that I – and many others in the newspaper industry (and, to be fair, in politics, too) – greeted the appointment of a just sacked Chancellor of the British Exchequer, and still sitting MP at Westminster, one George Osborne, as editor of the *London Evening Standard*. I went on record then – in March 2017 – saying that appointing the former Conservative government minister, who Prime Minister Theresa May promptly sacked from the Tory parliamentary front bench – was akin to appointing Attila the Hun as editor of the *Christian Herald*.

Both notions are bizarre almost beyond belief. The main difference being, of course, that Attila the Hun was a winner. Big time. And George Osborne was a loser. Bigger time.

During the referendum on whether the UK should stay in the EU or get out – the Brexiteers won by a small margin – Osborne backed the Remain campaign to the hilt. And lost. Ignominiously.

And then he was sacked by the new PM, Mrs May. Also ignominiously.

Then, most ominously, he was quoted in the Sunday papers as saying he had gone for the *Evening Standard* editor's job because he thought it might be 'fun'.

Well, as the former editor of two newspapers published in Belfast – the old *Sunday News* and the northern edition of the *Sunday World* – had I had a chance to have a word with Mr Osborne in private, and while his private parts hadn't even started to drop in terms of running a newspaper, I'd have told him: 'Have I got news for you.'

I certainly have had some fun in the jobs. But there is a string of other 'f' words – apart from the obvious – which fit the job description pertaining to any editor's chair. Just some of them are frustrating, feisty, fraught, frenetic, fierce, and having to stand up and fight your corner.

And that's only with some members of staff in your own newsroom at times!

Mr Osborne would have quickly discovered that even the most combustible parliamentary debates are like a kindergarten compared to a newsroom on a hot news-breaking night.

Plus, there's another 'f' word: fatigue. It's a 24/7 job editing any newspaper: you sleep, eat – and, yes – drink it at times. And sometimes you don't do any of those three, because of threats to yourself or members of your staff, or a court case looming, or the spectre of a crunch meeting with the bean counters, the accountants, over budgets the next day.

Moreover, there is a moral and professional requisite in a real journalist's code of conduct that requires her or him to remain impartial and objective at all times. I know there are exceptions in wartime: like during the dirty little sectarian war we endured here for almost forty years, when journalists were morally bound to take the side of the common, decent, peace-loving people, for the common good, and expose the gangsters and paramilitaries and terrorists for what they were. And still are.

But how a working politician who is deeply partisan to one party, the Conservatives, could be impartial or objective in running a newspaper is beyond me. It's like saying Donald Trump should be editor of the *Washington Post*. (Although, hold on a minute: a stranger thing has happened – he *was* elected to the White House, after all.)

Plus, there is the not inconsiderable matter of professional pedigree allied to newspaper nous, and a nose for news. Most newspaper editors come up through the ranks: from cub reporter to senior journalist to departmental head to, eventually, editor. In that way, they will have gained the respect and loyalty of their colleagues: a totally necessary alliance for any editor's role.

A newspaper is, after all, a living organism: it reflects all of human life. It is of the people, and by the people. It tells their stories – of tragedy, triumph, sorrow, and tear-tugging romance. It is, in essence, the pulsebeat of the people.

That's why the *Sunday World* carries a proud proclamation just underneath its masthead on the front page. It simply states: 'The People's Paper'.

A newspaper lives, or dies, on the pavement: that's where the stories emanate from. And that's where the stories end up: being sold on the street, by news vendors – in the old days, newsboys – newsagents, and in high street supermarket chains. Or today, read on smartphones as people wait in bus queues, or on tablets as they grab a coffee in the café.

Believe me, as an editor I've been put on my back on that pavement, both physically and metaphorically, more than a couple of times. Because the job triggers moments of pride and joy. And hours of panic, trepidation and painstaking, meticulous decision-making. None more so than when deadline looms, there's a big, but perhaps legally dicey, story ready to run, and the staff gathered in your office look you straight in the eye and tell you: 'It's your call, boss ...'

Joy when the paper breaks a big story: like getting exclusive pictures of the then press officer of Ian Paisley's DUP, Belfast councillor and former Lord Mayor Sammy Wilson, running about without clothes on in the Cotswolds. And then splashing them from page one over another eight pages inside. We sold some papers that Sunday.

Something for which Sammy, to his credit, has forgiven me. I think. At least, he still talks to me. And it didn't hurt his political progress.

Back then, as I've pointed out, he was a mere Belfast councillor and DUP press officer. Now, he's a Westminster MP and elder statesman of the party the late Reverend Paisley founded. Though rue the day that Sammy ever 'does an Osborne' and becomes editor of a newspaper. He'll have a JCB digger-load of old scores to settle. Starting with me ...

Aye, there's pride. Like when the paper is picking up gongs at the Press Awards. Gongs and good stories spark the good times. There was a six-year spell when the northern edition of the *Sunday World* won either Sunday Newspaper of the Year or Newspaper of the Year at the Northern Ireland Press Awards.

Mind you, it was during that gold medal-winning streak that a certain judge pinged us for a £50,000 fine – and hit me, as the editor, with a £10,000 quid slap – after finding us guilty of contempt of court. Delivering his verdict, he also accused us of 'shoddy journalism'.

Those half-dozen NI Press Awards first places delivered a rather different opinion of us than 'shoddy journalists'.

That contempt of court judgment epitomises the hours of pitfalls, and potential pitfalls. When a story goes wrong. When a source can't be stood up. Or when hurt or distress is caused, however unintentionally or unwittingly.

One of the worst for me was when we, in the *Sunday World*, published a front-page picture of a man hanging from a bridge. First reports from the scene indicated, as it proved wrongly, that he had been the victim of a gruesome revenge attack by paramilitaries. As it turned out, he had taken his own life.

I spent a week apologising, both in public – on TV, in newspapers, and on the radio – and in private, to almost thirty families who had also lost loved ones through suicide, for a crass misjudgement and a spur-of-the-moment deadline-busting mistake that will never be repeated.

I went and conveyed my apology, sincerely, to the man's mother in her home, too.

It was an emotionally wringing week, which left me with bubbles of sweat on my bald head and emotional barbed wire being pulled through my very being.

My last meeting was with that beautiful group of benevolent and caring folk, the Samaritans. At the end of it, a very kind lady asked me into her office for a cup of tea. She could see I was wrecked, physically and emotionally. And as we supped from our cups, she compassionately queried: 'Jim, do you think you could do with some counselling yourself?'

The front-page story we ran did have the picture of the man hanging from the bridge, with his face pixelated, or obscured. The eventual thrust of the lead story, after any paramilitary involvement was checked, and discounted, was that the body had been left dangling for a number of hours in full view of families, with children, driving to a superstore just yards from the bridge. The photograph showed a car with children inside being driven past.

There had been a flurry of phone calls to the paper about the incident. They were blaming the police for not covering the body up, and demanding to know why it hadn't been cut down for such a long period of time. Our story asked the same question of the PSNI.

Sir Matt Baggott, the chief constable at the time, tried to take the heat off himself and his force by publicly chastising us. But we weren't copping to that. And that was made clear to him.

However, it was wrong. I admitted it. Hands up. And it was a sorry lesson, well learned and at tremendous emotional cost, especially to those families who had been affected by suicide. Circumstances like that counter the vaunted and vain notion that being an editor, of any newspaper, is all about 'fun'.

Yes, sometimes sitting in an editor's chair can be a dream job. At other times, it can be a nightmare.

As when Martin O'Hagan was murdered. The impact on our entire staff was profound and harrowing. We were quite literally grief-stricken. In the immediate aftermath, I think we were all just numb with shock. And raging with anger.

Our response – the only response there could be – was to put out a paper on the Sunday that paid tribute to Martin's courage and also said to the LVF lowlife: we are not going to be intimidated by you.

On the Saturday morning, just hours after his murder, we came into our office, past his empty desk, and did our jobs. The whole *esprit de corps* of our newspaper, and other newspapers, and broadcasters, and other journalists, kicked in then.

And nowhere more strongly than among the folk in our own paper's HQ, in Dublin.

The roll of honour there is too long to recite here, but the way editor Colm MacGinty, then MD Michael Brophy, and Gavin O'Reilly, son of the then proprietor, the rugby legend and business mogul Sir Anthony O'Reilly, acted so bravely in the run-up to Martin's danger-fraught funeral, and so kindly and generously looked after his widow, Marie, and her three daughters afterwards was way above and beyond the call of duty.

Except they made it their duty to do so ... and continued long after that, too.

In the weeks and months that followed, we continued to grieve for Martin. His desk sat just as he'd left it.

I had always been aware that the threat against the lives of *Sunday World* staff was real and deadly. As editor, I had to juggle the paper's role of exposing the gangsters with responsibility for safeguarding reporters' wellbeing and, indeed, their lives.

I have always argued that no story is worth a life.

That responsibility weighed upon me very, very heavily. When threats came into the office, my first thoughts were for the wider families involved, because they too would have to bear the brunt of it. There were reporters with young children. We, all of us, lived in the community menaced by the godfathers. We weren't like the visiting hacks who came and went, dropping in, doing their stories and then moving on to the next conflict zone.

We were part of the community we reported on and were committed to it. This was our children's future.

So yes, there were many times when I lay awake worrying about the wisdom of certain stories, wondering about the possible retribution it would bring down upon our heads.

But knowing, too, that it had to be done. That it was our job as news reporters to tell the truth about the evil lowlife who wanted to shut us up. To be on the side of the people. Against the ogres committing bloody savagery on the streets. This was the right fight.

The good fight.

And there were other times, too, when there was little sleep before 4.00 a.m. on a Sunday morning as the paper was going to press. And there was even less afterwards as I lay with bubbles of sweat on the baldy head, and more bubbles right the way down to – dare I say it? – my buttocks, trying to anticipate the reaction to the next day's main story: or any of the main stories in the paper.

Positive or negative? Pleasure or panic? Congratulations, or a High Court writ? Delight, or perhaps causing distress: the moral compass. Or at times, when I spiked (stopped) a story, the moral imperative.

And then, especially in Northern Ireland, when we pinpointed the godfathers of crime, the terrorists, the gangsters, the gunmen, there was that peculiarly historic accusation of 'felon setting'. I've had to face down that charge more than a few times: and face it coming from some very unexpected places.

In the same genre, there were also what we called the 'slabbers' in the street, hurling abuse at us in public, accusing us of setting up their co-criminals for the police, for paramilitary so-called punishment beatings and shootings, or for worse.

A case in point is the drugs baron Brendan 'Speedy' Fegan, who survived the first assassination bid on him, but, as described earlier, then confronted me in public, pulled up his top, pointed to where two slugs were still in his chest, and accused me of getting him shot.

For the record, I have never taken pleasure in the news of any man's wounding or of his death – no matter who he was, no matter what he did. I am opposed to violence, full stop. And when I, or our reporters, gleaned advance word of an impending attack on someone, we did our best to try to thwart it.

There were other confrontations I certainly enjoyed despite the quicksand hours of such puerile and misplaced vitriol, though. Like when hoods or lowlifes passed me in the street and hollered: 'Your paper's full of shite, McDowell!'

It gave me the greatest pleasure to instantly and equally loudly retort: 'That's because you're in it every week.'

Then there was the constant carping from some doyens of the politically correct class about us adorning what we called the paraMafia bosses and other mobsters with – ahem – *noms de guerre*. Those complaining would say we were either romanticising the shysters or giving them nicknames that might cause annoyance or distress to their families.

On the 'romance' charge: how in hell can dubbing someone 'Ugly Doris' or 'King Rat' or 'Doctor Death' romanticise them?

And as for the latter charge, causing annoyance or distress to families: well, the families live with the mobsters, so they know who and, more important, what they are. Take, for example, Anne Tedford, an honourable woman whom I've come to know and a person of impeccable integrity. This was proved when she took the decision to leave UDA east Belfast boss Jim 'Doris Day' Gray as his wife of only four years, when she realised what he had become.

Many of the nicknames actually came from the street: some had more unusual origins.

Take Nuella 'Luella' Fitchie. The 'Luella' came from her days as the queen of live, on-stage porn sex shows, smack dab in the heart of Ulster's Bible Belt. But then she did the double, and added peddling drugs to Luella's lewd porn act.

In fact, her drug-running racket became so big, she herself became Ulster's first drugs godmother. But she eventually died in police custody in England. She stabbed a guy in a row over drugs in Blackpool, and had a stash of drugs on her when arrested and put in a cell. She tried to swallow all of them in a plastic bag while behind bars. But they passed through her system. She tried a second time. The bag burst. The cops discovered her dead in her cell.

Finally, the jibe is often made at newspapers – and 'red-top' tabloids, like the *Sunday World* in particular – that we pay for stories.

The counter to that is that newspapers are a business. You go to the tailor for a suit, he has to pay for the cloth to make it.

Same with a story. Sometimes, just sometimes, a reporter may have to pay for information that makes the fabric of a story. Just like the tailor. And an editor has to sanction that. At times, I did. And there were times when I needed to do the same myself when chasing a story.

There were also times when my heart was in my mouth as editor, times when my heart soared, and times when my heart was breaking. But when I look back down the half-century I've been a hack, at that kaleidoscope of colourful characters I've encountered, both on and off the job, and the cascade of killers and mobs of gangsters, the madmen and the monsters I met face to face, the mayhem and the murder I witnessed and reported on, and I'm asked: would you do it all again?

My answer to that – and my colleagues, family and friends know this so well – is simply: 'I'm not bate yet … and never will be.'

Best job in the World.

AFTERWORD

We were having a drink in the Duke of York pub. I'd used that famous hacks' bar in Belfast since I started as a cub reporter. Big Willie Jack is the owner.

He said to Lindy and me: 'I'm going to name an upstairs lounge after McDowell.'

Lindy asked him what he was going to call it. He replied: 'the Jim McDowell Lounge.'

'No, you're not,' Lindy said. 'He'd be mortified. That sounds too pompous.'

And sipping from (another) glass of vodka and slimline tonic, she told Mr Jack: 'So just call it McDowell's Hole.'

And that's what the big lad did. There's even a neon sign at the top of the stairs to the McDowell's Hole lounge in the Duke's that says just that.

And most of the people I'm going to mention here, by way of thanks for all they've done for me, and meant to me, throughout my now almost half-century as a hack, have, at one time or another, been up my Hole for a pint.

As for those who maybe haven't – I'll make that up at this book launch which will, I hope, be taking place – where else? – up in that very same McDowell's Hole ... or in the same great pub, at any rate.

So family first, as always. Most of them are already mentioned in these pages, but a very special thanks to all of them, for standing by me through the rough and tough times, and especially to Lindy, who kicked the aforesaid McDowell's Hole often enough to make sure I saw this book through, and who did such a smashing job of bringing structure to the myriad stories. And a special thanks too, to my other first-class family: my in-laws, the late Robert and Florence 'Ma' McIlvenna, Heather and Robert Taylor, Roberta and Noel Ferson, their families and all the McIlvenna clan, including, of course, June and Oscar Maginnis.

The staff of the *Sunday World* Belfast bureau through my twenty-five years as northern editor: Richard Sullivan; Paula Mackin; Roisin Gorman; Conor McCaughley; Steven Moore; at times his father, Chris Moore; Steven Looney; Ivan Martin; Graeme Smyth; Gerry Millar; Phillip Mackintosh from way back; the irrepressible reporter Hugh Jordan and the irascible photographer Alwyn James the same; and now my son Jamie, who came in just before I left (although he now says that may indeed be the reason for me vamoosing). And the PA who kept us all glued together, the lovely Grainne Campbell.

They all stood up and fought – not least, at times, with me!

And one other *Sunday World* Belfast bureau hero in particular: Martin O'Hagan, of course.

He stood up for the truth and was gunned down for doing so on that black Friday night of 28 September, 2001, aged just 51. That was over *sixteen years ago*, folks, and the absolute shame of it is that only we in the *Sunday World* seem to be left fighting for justice for Martin.

But it won't stop us. We'll keep fighting to bring Martin's evil Loyalist Volunteer Force assassins to where they rightfully belong – behind bars, for a long, long time.

The debt we owe to our *Sunday World* colleagues in the paper's Dublin HQ, also heroes in bringing to account the criminal underworld, is immeasurable. The editor, Colm MacGinty, and the MD, Gerry Lennon, in particular stood shoulder to shoulder with us to win many a fight, not least when the godfathers of terror tried to gag us in court.

The same can be said of our two outstanding frontline lawyers and libel readers, Kieran Kelly in Dublin and Olivia O'Kane in Belfast. That redoubtable legal pair – along with another star man, the barrister Brett Lockhart – were, and still are, irrepressible and irreplaceable in defending the freedom of the press.

And for keeping less legally minded editors – like me, and other hacks I could name – out of jail.

They are all friends, among a host who, as we say in Ulster, 'gave me a han' out' in my life. So here are a few I'd like to put on record as acknowledging, and not in any particular order, just the usual old-fashioned hack's top-of-the-head way.

I don't have room to pay individual tribute to every one of them, but they themselves will know why they're on McDowell's both personal and professional roll of honour.

I have many people to thank for their friendship and support over the years, but prime among them are Paul Gibson and Janice (and Victoria); Alan Moneypenny and Georgie; Colm MacGinty and Philippa; and Gerry Lennon and Noirin.

I also want to salute here the wives, husbands and partners of all the *Sunday World* Belfast team for putting up with us through thick and thin.

All the drivers and staff at Dick Hughes' old WNS outfit, and not least the late Mr Hughes himself, who delivered the papers through the thick and threats of the Troubles.

I want to thank too all the policemen and women, who can't be named here for obvious reasons, who looked after both my family and the *Sunday World* staff during the rough and tough times; another peeler, and friend from the old rugby days, Sir Ronnie Flanagan, for other, and the best of, reasons; the aforementioned Willie Jack, another friend, for all that he and his staff, especially Karen and Paul at the Duke's, and all at his other Harp and Dark Horse establishments, have done for us down all the years.

Ruth Dudley Edwards and Sean, Billy Swail, John 'Mo' Shaw, 'Big Harry' Doherty and Phyllis, Gerry Storey, John Bittles for sticking me down all the years, Peter Lavery, Gerry 'Snowy' Vernon, Gail Walker, the editor over at the *Belfast Telegraph*, and, of course, Jim Fitzpatrick at the *Irish News*, whose dear wife Alice took so much pleasure out of me poking fun at politicians in my 'Dome of Delight' column published in that famous family-owned paper.

And then, just another two of my newspaper heroes, Walter McAuley of the Belfast 'Tele' and Ciaran Barnes of the *Sunday Life* – both also born with ink in their blood.

Finally, a very sincere word of thanks to the team at Gill Books for their ultra-professional advice and guidance in shepherding and seeing this project through: Conor Nagle for taking it on, Sheila Armstrong and Rachel Pierce for their editing expertise, and Teresa Daly for the cover, frightening as it is – and I'm just talking about my mugshot! – and the team's input into the title.

As for anybody else I have failed to mention above, I'll make it up to you by buying you a pint back where we started.

Up McDowell's Hole…